EARLY
AMERICAN
LITERATURE

EARLY
AMERICAN
LITERATURE

A
COMPARATIST
APPROACH

A. Owen Aldridge

PRINCETON UNIVERSITY PRESS
PRINCETON, NEW JERSEY

Copyright © 1982 by Princeton University Press
Published by Princeton University Press, 41 William Street, Princeton,
New Jersey
In the United Kingdom: Princeton University Press, Guildford, Surrey

All Rights Reserved
Library of Congress Cataloging in Publication Data will be
found on the last printed page of this book

This book has been composed in Linotron Trump
Designed by Barbara Werden

Clothbound editions of Princeton University Press books
are printed on acid-free paper, and binding materials are
chosen for strength and durability

Printed in the United States of America by Princeton
University Press, Princeton, New Jersey

1-30-92

To

J. A. Leo Lemay
George Panichas
Kenneth Silverman

CONTENTS

PREFACE

AMERICAN LITERATURE as a separate entity in the university curriculum does not have a long history. Indeed, in a realistic sense, it can be said to have come of age as an academic discipline between the two World Wars almost concomitantly with comparative literature. The journal *Revue de littérature comparée* was founded in 1924; *American Literature*, in 1929. The consideration of the seventeenth and eighteenth centuries as a major segment or independent dimension of American letters represents an even later development.

Until very recently comparative literature as practiced both in Europe and the United States has been strongly oriented toward Europe. In the formative years of this discipline, comparatists paid scant attention to either Anglo-American or Ibero-American authors, and European literary historians made no effort to distinguish between the two groups. Even now this bias toward the European continent is revealed in a project of the International Comparative Literature Association for a series of volumes to represent a comparative history of literatures in European languages. It is not surprising that in projects of this kind the literatures of the Americas should be treated as mere appendages to European letters. History, however, indicates recurring relationships on a triangular basis; that is, the presence of various waves of influence and resemblance joining serious writing in Anglo-America, Ibero-America, and Europe. Even in the period before 1800, each of the Americas made substantial contributions to universal literature.

While comparatists, on one hand, have tended to overlook the Western Hemisphere, scholars of Anglo-American literature have exercised a related selectivity by concentrating upon American authors to the neglect of relationships with the rest of the world. Paradoxically, they have shown least interest in Latin America, particularly in regard to the period before 1800. My purpose in this book is twofold: to draw the attention of comparatists to the vitality of literary activity in the Western Hemisphere during the seventeenth and eighteenth centuries, an activity which in part borrowed from European sources and came to be reflected in subsequent European productions; and to suggest to specialists in early American literature that their subject matter does not represent an isolated, provincial phenomenon, but one that responded to the same influences, concerns, and idiosyncrasies affecting or accompanying other literatures of the period.

ACKNOWLEDGMENTS

OF THE ESSAYS in this book, three have never before been published in any form. The five others are based in varying degrees upon one or more of the following previously published articles: "Polly Baker and Boccaccio" in *Annali dell'Istituto Universitario Orientale*, Sezione Romanza, 14 (1971): 5-18; "Paine and Dickinson" in *Early American Literature* 11 (1976): 125-38; "Thomas Paine in Latin-America" in *Early American Literature* 3 (1969): 139-47; "The Vogue of Thomas Paine in Argentina," *Actes du VIème Congrès Internationale de Littérature Comparée* (Stuttgart, 1975), pp. 281-85; "The Concept of Ancients and Moderns in the Federal Period" in *Classical Traditions in Early America*, ed. John W. Eadie, pp. 99-118 (Ann Arbor, 1976); "The Enlightenment in the Americas" in *Proceedings of the 7th Congress of the International Comparative Literature Association*, 2 vols. (Stuttgart, 1979), 1: 59-67.

EARLY
AMERICAN
LITERATURE

ONE

INTRODUCTION

THE THEME of national consciousness, a concept that came into being immediately after the American Revolution, has been widely discussed in the literary history of North America. This patriotic spirit, as it flourished in the early years of the republic, may be interpreted as either the expression of a cultural identity distinct from that of England and, consequently, a salutary development, or, conversely, as an induced insensitivity to the rest of the world and, therefore, a deplorable example of intellectual insularity. Even before the period of 1776, the American people existed, according to Thomas Paine, "at a distance from, and unacquainted with the world." A staunch patriot at the turn of the eighteenth century, Jedidiah Morse, held the same opinion. "Before the Revolution," he maintained in the preface to his *American Universal Geography* (1793), "Americans seldom pretended to write or to think for themselves. We humbly received from Great Britain our laws, our manners, our books, and our modes of thinking; and our youth were educated as the subjects of the British king, rather than as the citizens of a free and independent republic." The accusations of insularity made during the colonial and federal periods have never been adequately investigated to determine whether they are true or false. The political part of Morse's statement must stand without contradiction, but the notions of complete literary dependence upon England cannot be supported. Ideas and styles of writing entered America from continental Europe as well as from Great Britain. Most historians of American literature, however, seem to be unaware that there is a problem to be clarified and are quite content indiscriminately to accept all works written in English in the Northern Hemisphere prior to Washington Irving as being products of Anglo-Saxon culture exclusively.

Two complementary, but, nevertheless, contrary explanations have been offered for the long-standing acceptance of this notion of British intellectual domination. First of all, both Europeans and Americans, during the seventeenth and eighteenth centuries, took for granted that any belletristic work produced in the American colonies (in either the English, Spanish or Portuguese languages) was an inherent part of the literature of the mother country. Although the colonial literatures were obviously outgrowths or transplants from the original stock, they were moreover regarded as integral parts of the culture of the nation from which they derived. A work produced, for example, in the English hegemony of America—that is, in the English literary zone, to borrow a term from Soviet literary criticism—would automatically be considered a part of English literature. Its nationality would be conferred by the same process as the birthright of its author.

From the perspective of colonial times, both nationality and birthright were indeed English, but the practice of classifying American writers as part of English literature continued in England and Europe after the American Revolution and throughout the nineteenth century. Major authors in the United States such as Whitman, Twain, and James, for example, were customarily classified under the rubric of English letters. It has been only since World War II that European universities have carved separate niches in their curricula for North American and Latin American literatures. Logically, geographical or political difference should not constitute a sufficient reason for separating the literature of the United States from that of England.

Only fundamental differences in language and culture warrant distinct categories. Swiss language and culture, for example, are so close to French on one side and German on the other that the Swiss authors Rousseau and Dürrenmatt are customarily treated as belonging to French literature and German literature respectively. Cultural differences between the United States and England justify the present method of setting apart the literatures of the two nations, but cultural differences have always been present and were perhaps even more pronounced in the seventeenth and eighteenth centuries than in our day. There is no question that political independence led Americans to proclaim their literary production as separate from English early in the nineteenth century, but the rest of the world had an insufficient knowledge of American writing to observe the distinction. At the present time when early American literature is being studied more seriously and more extensively than ever before, evidence is constantly being adduced to erode the opinion that the writing of the eastern seaboard in seventeenth- and eighteenth-century America was a product of British culture alone.

A second explanation, other than the colonial heritage, of why the relations between early American writers and Europe have been neglected may be found in a theory of ethnic roots. This is the view, based ultimately on a biological theory of the influence of climate upon human character, that the soil and other physical features of the American continent established the national identity or autonomy of its literature. The concept is exemplified in a passage from Paine's *Rights of Man* rhapsodically affirming his belief that the grandeur of the landscape inspires sublime concepts and promotes artistic creation. Other aspects of the landscape are presumed to impart specifically "American" characteristics to literature. The concept of topographical influence exists also in Europe, but it has not been taken seriously since the Romantic period. In Latin America, literary criticism is still dominated by notions of what is termed the telluric foundations of its literature, that is, effects of soil, climate, scenery, and, to some extent, racial strains.

Earth, blood and birthright are undoubtedly significant elements in the development of every national literature, but these elements are supplemented by the historical contribution of major writers from other literatures. However remote they may seem, Dante, Erasmus, Rabelais, and Cervantes as well as Chaucer, Shakespeare, and Milton constitute the heritage of the colonial and later literature of North America. Thomas Paine's comment in *Common Sense* about racial strains could be applied to literary production as well: "Europe and not England is the parent country." Obviously from the linguistic perspective, American and English literature are essentially a unit, but from the point of view of culture they are distinct. The circumstance that American and English literatures share the same language is no justification for failing to recognize, or for not investigating, similarities of a different kind between American and continental literatures. If English writers of the seventeenth and eighteenth centuries have been studied comparatively, that is, in relation to their counterparts on the continent, the same method might profitably be applied to American authors of the same chronological period. One may believe that the literature of the English colonies derived its basic materials from the mother country or that it acquired some of its distinct characteristics from the New World environment and still accept the premise that many American writings resemble those of other countries and that many American and European authors have come into contact with each other's works.

As early as 1830, pioneer literary critic William Ellery Channing advocated study of relationships of this kind.

In an essay "On National Literature" in the *Christian Examiner*, Channing earnestly recommended "a more extensive acquaintance with the intellectual labors of continental Europe." The reading of his countrymen, Channing felt, was "confined too much to English books, and especially to the more recent publications of Great Britain." Channing urged, moreover, that "we ought to know the different modes of viewing and discussing great subjects in different nations" and we "should be able to compare the writings of the highest minds in a great variety of circumstances." This awareness of European letters he specifically proposed as a means of fostering "our own intellectual independence and activity." In other words, Channing actually prescribed what is now known as the comparative method of literary study as a means of promoting American letters. At the same time he considered that it "would be better to admit no books from abroad than to make them substitutes for our own intellectual activity." The America of his time, he felt, needed a literature of its own both to counteract and to appreciate imported ones. The reverse is just as applicable in the twentieth century—that students of American literature need a knowledge of relevant foreign works as an aid for the understanding of domestic ones.

The major omission from Channing's prescription for literary study is any reference to parallel developments in Latin America. This deficiency is excusable in Channing's essay since at the time he was writing, technology had not sufficiently advanced to permit general awareness in either Anglo-America or Latin America of literary activity in the other hemisphere. Today, however, readers of book reviews in any major newspaper of the United States are regularly apprised of literary activities in Mexico, Brazil, and Argentina. Unfortunately the process has not worked retrospectively. Even though the literature of the United States in many ways has more in common with the lit-

eratures of other American nations than with those in
Europe, few scholars have taken the trouble to investigate
parallels, influences, and other relationships. Linguistic
and cultural resemblances cause the literatures of Latin
America ordinarily to be associated with those of Spain
and Portugal, and the literature of the United States to be
associated with that of England. Belletristic connections
among the various American nations, however, are just
as close as those between any American and any European
literature. The periods of conquest, colonization, revolution, expansion, and national consciousness draw the
writings of the American nations together in a historical
framework just as movements of greater esthetic intensity
such as neoclassicism, Romanticism, and realism provide
them with links of another kind with each other and with
their European forebears.

One of the major topics treated by comparatists has
been the problem of tracing and defining the various literary movements and periods, five of which touched both
North and South America between 1635 and 1810: The
Renaissance, the baroque, neoclassicism, the Enlightenment, and Romanticism. Students of national literatures
have relatively little difficulty in assigning chronological
limits to these movements or periods, merely placing them
in consecutive order and allowing for overlapping on either
side. When several literatures are considered together,
however, the chronological limits of a movement in one
literature do not necessarily coincide with those in another. The Renaissance, for example, began in Italy in the
thirteenth century, but did not have a major influence in
England until the sixteenth. Neoclassicism also had its
origins in Italy (in the sixteenth century), reached its ze-
nith in France in the seventeenth century, but did not
dominate in England until the eighteenth. Until very recently, scholars have paid scant attention to the effect of
any of these movements on American literature except

for Romanticism. Even then the emphasis has been on the quest for American nationality, which neoclassicism is "supposed to have hindered" and Romanticism "to have promoted."[1] The conscious efforts in America at the turn of the eighteenth century to promote independence from European literary traditions parallel those of Herder and other Europeans to glorify folklore and ethnic writing. The great difference is that in Europe critics looked almost reverently to the past; in America they looked rhapsodically toward the future.

Paradoxically, scholars of American literature have given more attention to the European antecedents of New World Romanticism and to parallels between European and American manifestations of Romanticism, a movement that presumably encouraged independence and individualism, than to the origins and manifestations of the Renaissance, the baroque, and neoclassicism, movements that placed a premium upon convention and imitation. In actuality, all of these European movements had repercussions in America. The effects of some critical theories that originated in Italy and Spain may be discernible in poetry written in colonial Virginia or Massachusetts, and certain elements of colonial neoclassicism have as much in common with French as with English traditions. Eighteenth-century American literature represents much more than the infiltration of the rhetorical art of Pope and Johnson into the milieu of New England Puritanism. Neoclassicism and the Enlightenment were not exclusively Anglo-Saxon, and they embraced much of European culture before being felt in America. Neoclassicism, moreover, did not reach its apex in the New World until after the creation of the United States, when it had been completely superseded by Romanticism in England, France,

[1] William L. Hedges, "Toward a Theory of American Literature, 1765-1800," *Early American Literature* 4 (1969): 5.

and Germany. Indeed, neoclassicism flourished so late in the United States that it coexisted with many elements of Romanticism, sometimes in the work of a single author.

The theory that Colonial American literature was an outgrowth of English, or even of English and continental together, suggests not only an intellectual dependence of the colony upon the metropole but also a colonial cultural lag. A major critic of early American poetry, Harold Jantz, accepts these assumptions for the eighteenth century, but not the seventeenth. He argues that "American literature was to an unusual degree independent during its first hundred years" and that "only after the 1720's or '30's does it become a more fully dependent, a genuinely colonial literature, imitating the approved homeland models."[2] Jantz establishes this hypothesis upon the purely political grounds that the early settlers of Massachusetts and Connecticut created model societies based on Puritan ideals and that many of their leaders were later recalled to England to serve in the Cromwellian government. Because of their political experience, the colonies could be considered temporarily ahead of the mother country instead of lagging behind. A weakness of this theory is that it applies only to the New England colonies. An even greater weakness is that it fails to account for the disparity in literary production between the English colonies and those of Spain. The latter in the first half of the seventeenth century boasted a brilliant concentration of poets, chroniclers, and diarists far exceeding the modest talents of those to the north. It is hard to see, moreover, why there should have been a greater degree of literary independence in the early years of the North American colonies than a century later when they had accumulated a larger and more diverse

[2] "American Baroque," in *Discoveries & Considerations*, ed. Calvin Israel (Albany, 1976), p. 8.

population, established newspapers, created educational institutions, and developed native traditions. Some literary historians have accepted the notion of an "Anglo-American cultural lag,"[3] that is, the notion of late American awareness and imitation of English literary fashion, but one never hears even the suggestion that America may have trailed behind the continent.

One way of avoiding the question of cultural lag—with its connotations of superiority in the originating or emitting body and inferiority in the receiving one—is to think in terms of an universal literature rather than a national one. In the broadest sense, universal literature represents the sum total of all texts or works throughout the world. The concept assumes that all writing in all geographical areas and in all chronological periods has equal historical validity—and that any particular work may profitably be considered in relation to any other that is relevant through subject matter, style, or historical circumstances. The perspective of universal literature has been adopted primarily by critics in small or emerging countries in order to promote international attention to minor literatures. Otherwise world attention would be monopolized by the great writers of Europe, the United States, China, and Japan. Since there is a real conflict between concentration on world masterpieces and concentration on national literatures, those nations without a claim to recognized masterpieces naturally support the universal perspective. This method of study brings minor literatures and minor writings into contact with major movements and even with world masterpieces. It enables specialists in minor literatures to deal with matters of universal rather than merely local concern or significance. America before 1800 was, in regard to literary production, in much the same position

---

[3] Robert D. Arner, "The Connecticut Wits," in *American Literature, 1764-1789*, ed. Everett Emerson (Madison, Wis., 1977), p. 242.

as that of the emerging nations in the second half of the twentieth century. In the words of Samuel Miller's *Brief Retrospect of the Eighteenth Century*, published in 1803, America belonged at that time among the "nations lately become literary." It would seem, therefore, that the universal perspective would be ideally suited for the modern study of early American literature.

The adoption of this perspective does not by any means invalidate or rule out studies of local or provincial literatures. Serious investigation of the literary output of each of the colonies in North America will obviously add to the store of knowledge concerning the continent as a whole. Each of the British colonies had its own population center, produced its own intellectually dominant individuals, and fostered its own literary circles.[4] It is just as important to know how each writer reflects the particular conditions of his local environment as it is to perceive how he fits into the international literary mosaic of his own and earlier times. As Henry F. May has said of the eighteenth century, "The American Enlightenment, like American Romanticism or for that matter American Christianity can be at once American, Anglo-American, and European."[5]

The universal perspective shares with the local perspective the assumption that all literary works have equal historical validity, but this assumption does not by any means imply that all works are equal in esthetic or intellectual importance. In other words, all works may be legitimately considered as documents in the history of culture or the history of ideas, but the literary merits of individual texts differ widely, and it is the obligation of scholarship to notice and to comment upon these varia-

---

[4] J. A. Leo Lemay, *Men of Letters in Colonial Maryland* (Knoxville, Tenn., 1972), p. x.

[5] "The Problem of the American Enlightenment," *New Literary History* 1 (1969): 204.

tions. Notions of who and what are important, moreover, change with the times. An outstanding example is the tremendous interest in the black poetess Phillis Wheatley that developed after World War II.

Literary merit does not necessarily coincide with the esthetic criteria that happen to be in vogue at a given period of time. The critical standards of neoclassicism and of Romanticism, for example, are quite at variance with each other. Much of the scholarship devoted to early American literature during the past twenty years consists of elaborate formalistic analysis, despite the fact that nearly all of the significant writing of the seventeenth and eighteenth centuries was pragmatic rather than belletristic. World critical opinion undoubtedly considers Franklin's autobiography to be the major literary work of the entire period, but Verner W. Crane (a professional historian, but, nevertheless, the outstanding authority on Franklin's style) is quite correct in affirming that Franklin was "not a literary artist of the first order." Paine, Edwards, and Jefferson were even less gifted as stylists. Of the four, Franklin is the only one to have made a substantial contribution to imaginative literature. He successfully used genres in which the manner of expression shared importance with the ideas or information being conveyed or in which the subject matter was personal rather than utilitarian. *The Way to Wealth*, a compendium of proverbs taken from several cultural traditions, and "The Speech of Polly Baker," a satirical hoax, belong to the first of these categories, and his *Memoirs* belongs to the second. The major literary genres in vogue throughout America before 1800, however, were singularly uncomplicated—the sermon, the essay, the treatise, the didactic poem—and their subject matter was primarily political and theological. It can hardly be questioned that both the most extensive and the most readable part of this literature is a literature of ideas. As such, it would seem to lend itself particularly well not only to intellectual analysis, but also to the type of literary history that is international in outlook. It is a paradox that most scholars have slighted the technique best adapted for colonial and Federal literature—that of the history of ideas—and have concentrated instead upon formalistic analysis, which requires almost no reference to the mainstreams of thought and expression.

A second paradox has been noticed by Henry F. May, that much of the eighteenth century in North America as well as in Europe was the Age of Enlightenment, but scholars have neglected American writings of the period that stress the Enlightenment themes of reason, scientific progress, toleration, and the dissemination of knowledge in order to concentrate on the milieu of Puritan religion and anti-Enlightenment figures such as Cotton Mather, Jonathan Edwards, and Edward Taylor.[6] One reason for this emphasis on Puritanism may be the same that, according to Leo Lemay, accounts for the predominance of New England writers as subjects of scholarly study, that is, that the earliest compilers of histories of American literature were natives of the New England states. To restore the balance, new attention needs to be given to the Enlightenment as a literary movement in North America. The attitude of progressive eighteenth-century writers that they belonged to a republic of letters transcending political boundaries is based on essentially the same suppositions as the modern concept of international literature.

A third paradox is that the writers regarded most highly in American universities are, with the exception of Franklin, not those who have acquired an international reputation. This is probably in large measure a result of the emphasis of esthetic criteria over ideas and historical relationships. The only true objective measure of a writer's

[6] Ibid., pp. 201-2.

importance is the number of editions of his works published at home and of translations done in other parts of the world. This measure indicates that only Franklin, Paine, and Jefferson among Americans before 1800 have achieved a noticeable degree of international recognition. This objective evidence is confirmed by Rudolph Haus, a professor from the University of Hamburg, who delivered a lecture commemorating the American Bicentennial at three American institutions in which he attempted to assess the American contribution to world literature. He summarized the colonial period as furnishing "interesting and significant impulses to the field of religious poetry, of homiletics, books of edification and diaries," but the only writers before Cooper whom he named were Franklin, Paine, and Jefferson. It is possible that a visiting professor from France speaking on the same subject would have added Crèvecoeur.[7] The American editor of a recent collection of essays on the period 1764-1789, however, confidently affirms that Edward Taylor, Benjamin Franklin, and Jonathan Edwards are "the three greatest writers of early America."[8] Yet Taylor is recognized only by a narrow clique even in the United States. Edwards, except for the Anglo-American world and a small number of Dutch Puritans, was completely unknown in his own time, and even today his works are published only in the United States. Actually the Quakers William Penn and John Woolman have had more European translations than Edwards or any other American Puritan. It is not Edwards's philosophical works which have been translated, moreover, but merely two or three minor pietistic ones.

At the end of the eighteenth century three of the greatest works of the American post-Revolutionary period were printed for the first time in Paris in the French language:

[7] "Some American Contributions to World Literature," *Yearbook of Comparative and General Literature* 26 (1977): 17-23.
[8] Everett Emerson, ed., *American Literature, 1764-1789*, p. 15.

Franklin's *Memoirs*, Paine's *Age of Reason*, and Jefferson's *Notes on Virginia*. All three, moreover, were published in part to influence French public opinion. Franklin sent a manuscript copy of his autobiography to his Paris friends Le Veillard and La Rochefoucauld, and as a result the story of his life became known and appreciated in France before being printed anywhere else. The first collected edition of Franklin's works was printed in 1773 in Paris in French translation. Paine published his *Age of Reason* partly to dissuade the French people from adopting atheism as an official belief, and Jefferson wrote his description of Virginia to counteract fallacious notions concerning his native country that had been spread by various French *philosophes*.

The problem of how authors should be ranked hierarchically is almost unsolvable. Should they be placed according to their reputation in their own culture or according to their reception in the world at large? The problem is, of course, not limited to early American literature, but is endemic. Writers in eighteenth-century England such as Shaftesbury and Young can be adduced whose reputation in other major literatures is far greater than in their own. From the opposite perspective, other British writers such as Johnson and Boswell are considered of major importance in the Anglo-Saxon milieu, but remain unknown elsewhere in the world. The best solution may be to reserve the designation of masterpiece for works that show bibliographical strength in both the culture of origin and abroad. No serious scholar would advocate as criteria for excellence his personal feelings, inclinations, or prejudices—even though cliques or vogues based on little else than shared prejudices sometimes dominate academic criticism. There is much to be said for the attitude of sociologists of literature: that the test of a great book is its being widely read with approval and pleasure by a public different from that for which it was originally intended.

If the principle of public acceptance is taken as the dominant standard for evaluating early American writers, they may be classified according to at least four categories or degrees of recognition.

1) There are those who attained a fair amount of celebrity in their own times in the Anglo-Saxon world, but are now forgotten. An example is Richard Lewis, the author of "A Journey from Patapsco to Annapolis," the first poem by an American author to be widely reprinted in England and considered by Leo Lemay to be "the best neoclassical poem of colonial America."

2) There are writers who were completely unknown in their time, but have been brought into prominence by modern American scholarship. The obvious example is Edward Taylor.

3) There are writers who were known in the Anglo-Saxon world in their own time, are equally recognized at present in England and America, but are unknown elsewhere. An example is Jonathan Edwards.

4) There are writers who attained international recognition in their own time and who have maintained an international reputation until the present. Franklin, of course, is a prime example.

Purely esthetic criteria would not justify Franklin's high reputation as a literary figure, based as it is on the reflection of his ideas and personality, even though his prose style compares favorably with Addison's. Critics who accept the doctrines of the New Criticism of the 1940s and 1950s would consider it appropriate to rank Edward Taylor as a major author. These criteria might also confirm Lemay's judgment concerning "A Journey from Patapsco to Annapolis." The doctrines of New Criticism, however, have absolutely no relevance to the works of Edwards and

Paine and very little to those of Franklin. If taken as the standard of judgment, these criteria would effectively reduce these literary giants to dwarves.

A viable compromise might be to classify writers in both the first and second of the above categories as minor and those in both the third and fourth as major. The perspective of universal literature offers a further escape from the dilemma. From this vantage, all authors may be valued for their ideas, historical significance, ability to reflect personality or social milieu, or even for antiquarian charm.

The purpose of comparative literature is not, however, to erect a universal hierarchy of literary merit or to place authors of one culture in competition with those of another, even though it provides an important service by portraying various national literatures in a proper perspective. The comparative method seeks to increase the understanding and enjoyment of the works of two or more cultures by bringing them into contact with each other. Also it discriminates between the elements of each culture that are truly unique and those that are shared with one or more similar cultures.

The chapters that follow represent an effort to show that the study of American literature before 1800 need not (and perhaps should not) be confined exclusively to the American continent. They illustrate the principles that some aspects of movements, trends, and themes in early American literature parallel previous developments in Europe; that some well-known American texts have sources or analogues in other literatures; and that some American works have had a significant influence upon writers in other traditions. Even though in these introductory remarks I have maintained that the scholarly method of the history of ideas has in general more relevance to early American literature than the method of esthetic analysis, I do not wish to suggest that the latter should be abandoned. The chapters on Anne Bradstreet and Edward Taylor that come first in this collection treat matters of style and structure primarily. The others stress themes and ideas. I am treating Bradstreet because of her undeniable historic importance as the first American poet, and Taylor because much criticism has decreed him to be preeminent among American poets before 1800.

PART I

STYLE
AND
STRUCTURE

WHEN SETTLERS go from one country to another they naturally carry with them their cultural traditions, including the predominant literary style of their period. This is true whether they are emigrating to a new world, which has never before been settled, or to an area with well-established communities. When Spanish colonization occurred early in the sixteenth century and English colonization followed over a century later, both Spain and England were in the midst of the Renaissance. This literary movement had traveled to Spain from Italy early in the fifteenth century and to England in the sixteenth. The English colonies at first suffered little or no cultural lag since their settlers continued to write in the manner to which they had been accustomed in England. By the turn of the eighteenth century, however, distinct differences may be noted in the poetry of the colonies from that of the homeland, although in prose the straightforward approach of Addison almost instantaneously found imitators in America, of whom the most illustrious was Franklin. The Spanish colonies experienced almost no intellectual retardation in either the sixteenth or seventeenth centuries, during which literary centers flourished in Mexico and Peru that rivaled those of Spain itself. No reason has been advanced to explain this literary fecundity, but it may have been due to the frequent movement back and forth from the New World and Spain, at least among the higher levels of society. A cultural lag does not become evident in Latin America until the period of the Enlightenment, and even then the disparity was not between the colonies and Spain, but between Spain and her colonies as a unit and the enlightened parts of Europe and North America.

The two chapters that follow concern two products of the seventeenth century, Anne Bradstreet, a representative of the Renaissance, and Edward Taylor, a practitioner of the style known as the baroque. I compare Bradstreet to Sor Juana Inés de la Cruz, a Spanish-American contemporary poetess. Although one was a wife and mother in rural New England and the other a nun, a symbolic bride of Christ, in a rich and thriving Mexican city, they both reflected the literary standards of the times in which they lived. Sor Juana is considered to be one of the major poets of all Spanish literature, but Bradstreet is minor even in the limited scope of the British colonies. Yet Bradstreet conforms to the literary conventions of her time equally as well as Sor Juana, even though she may not have adorned them with the same brilliance.

Edward Taylor, however, was an anomaly in the period in which he lived, and he remains a puzzle today. Although he was born about 1642 and died in 1729, his poetry was not published until the third decade of the twentieth century. He has been regarded by one admirer as "the initiator of a great tradition"[1] and by another as one of the three greatest writers of early America.[2] On the other extreme, he has been considered "at best a mediocre poet."[3] A critic who has devoted to Taylor a book of over 300 pages nevertheless admits that "on the conventional scale of canonization, Taylor is a second-string poet, perhaps even a poor poet."[4] Whatever his merits, the three elements upon which he must be judged are his subject matter, his personality as reflected in his work, and his style. Taylor's subject matter is for the most part Calvinistic doctrine, material that not even a genius could successfully render poetical. Milton is no exception, for *Paradise Lost* stands out because of its epic, not its didactic features, and it is neither Calvinistic nor doctrinal. Wordsworth's *Ecclesiastical Sonnets* is a good example of what may be expected of doctrinal verse, and on comparison Taylor appears to advantage. Some of his human characteristics do indeed shine out in his poetry. Even though consisting primarily of a wry delight in the perplexities of religion, his personality grants to his verse a certain individual charm. Taylor's style is the single element critics have admired, and it is true that his linguistic tricks and intricacies set him apart from fellow Puritan versifiers. He is individual, however, only within the New England frame of reference. When placed in contact with his predecessors in the European baroque, his uniqueness

[1] H. H. Waggoner, *American Poets: From the Puritans to the Present* (Boston, 1968), p. 22.

[2] Everett Emerson, "The Cultural Context of the American Revolution," introduction to volume edited by Emerson, *American Literature, 1764-1789* (Madison, Wis., 1977), p. 15.

[3] Sidney E. Lind, "Edward Taylor: A Reevaluation," *New England Quarterly* 21 (1948): 519-30.

[4] Karl Keller, *The Example of Edward Taylor* (Amherst, Mass., 1975), p. 3.

completely disappears. Instead he becomes an example of the cultural lag from which Bradstreet had escaped.

The baroque style flourished in Italy, Spain, France, and England during the first half of the seventeenth century, after which it was replaced nearly everywhere by neoclassicism. Apart from the inevitable overlapping on both sides, the change was about as abrupt as any in major styles that has ever been recorded. The duration of the baroque in England was so short that with the exception of Taylor it does not seem to have crossed to the English colonies of America. Anagrams and acrostics in which Puritan verse abounds are not touchstones of the baroque.

Taylor was presumably introduced to the baroque while he was a student at Cambridge University. At least he acquired no books by baroque authors for his personal library in America. He came to the New World in 1668, and by the time that he began writing poetry, apparently around 1671, not only metaphysical style but also devotional subject matter had given way in England to John Dryden's neoclassical innovations. In the colonies, late Renaissance style still prevailed and would continue to do so until the introduction of neoclassicism early in the eighteenth century.

The following pages will demonstrate how Bradstreet is related to the Renaissance in other countries and how Taylor is related to the baroque. The process will not make either American poet seem less important, but, if anything, elevate their stature by bringing them into contact with poets in other cultures of international significance.

TWO

ANNE BRADSTREET: SOME THOUGHTS ON THE TENTH MUSE

THE PHILOSOPHER PLATO, according to legend, bestowed the flattering appelation "the Tenth Muse" upon Sappho, the female poet of Lesbos in ancient Greece. The phrase was subsequently applied in the seventeenth century to two poets of North America, one writing in English, the other in Spanish. In 1650, there appeared in London a book of over 200 pages with the title, *The Tenth Muse Lately Sprung up in AMERICA, or Severall Poems, Compiled with great Variety of Wit and Learning, full of Delight.* The author, according to the title page was "a Gentlewoman in those parts," but she was several times identified in the book itself as Anne Bradstreet, a married lady of New England. Thirty-nine years later (1689) a similar title introduced a collection of Spanish poems published in another European capital, Madrid. In English translation, the title page proclaimed *The Muses' Inundation of the Unique Poetess, Tenth Muse, Sister Juana Inés of the Cross, Professed Nun of the Monastery of Saint Jerome of the Imperial City of Mexico. Who in Various Metres, Idioms, and Styles, Fertilizes Various Subjects, with Elegant, Subtle, Clear, Witty, Useful Verses.*[1]

[1] The original Spanish reads: *Inundación Castálida de la única poetisa, musa décima, soror Juana Inés de la Cruz, religiosa profesa en el monasterio de San-Jerónimo de la Imperial ciudad de México. Que en varios metros, idiomas, y estilos, fertiliza varios asuntos, con elegantes, sutiles, claros, ingeniosos, útiles versos.* In the remainder of this chapter,

Titles of the second editions of both collections were rendered less flamboyant; that of Anne Bradstreet deleted the appellation *Tenth Muse* and that of Sor Juana discarded *The Muses' Inundation*. The latter metaphor implies that the Castalian springs in Greek mythology had descended upon the author in a flood of poetic inspiration. The Peninsular poet Quevedo had previously said of himself, "Inundación será la de mi canto," and in both contexts "inundación" suggests a torrent or an extraordinary force, a hyperbole typical of the baroque style. The word "wit" in Anne Bradstreet's title also has strong overtones of the baroque even though in her work itself there are few of the verbal eccentricities her contemporaries would have recognized as wit.

Bradstreet is the founder of the literature of English America, and one of its most respectable early poets. Sor Juana ranks with Cervantes, Calderón, Lope de Vega, and Quevedo as a luminary of the Golden Age of Spanish literature.

Although the exact birth date of neither Tenth Muse is known, it would appear that each poet was thirty-eight years old at the time of the publication of the first edition of her book. Both of the collections of poems, moreover, were taken in manuscript from the New World to a metropolis of the Old, there to be published, and each author wrote a verse prologue for her volume.

Apart from these bibliographical and biographical coincidences, it is possible to trace several intellectual and literary parallels between these representatives of separate American literatures. Both Anne Bradstreet and Sor Juana were acutely aware of their double identities as writers and women; both revealed a compulsion to compose serious verse; both were deeply religious, but developed sec-

---

it will be understood that quotations from Sor Juana translated by me into English were originally composed in Spanish.

ular as well as pious themes; both experienced a period
of skepticism before crystallizing their religious seeking
into firm faith; both echoed major linguistic conventions
of their times, and both incorporated metaphors and subject matter from the world of science. Perhaps most significant of all, both introduced a catalog of the nine muses
into a poem, naming each of the Greek allegorical sisters
and indicating the genre personified by each.[2]

Naturally there exist many differences, both biographical and literary, separating these representatives of two
opposing cultures, and the major ones should be noted
before a detailed exposition of parallels or similarities.
The private life of Anne Bradstreet was essentially conventional, despite the rigors of the frontier community in
which she passed her adult years. The second of several
children born to a solid English family with connections
to the Puritan aristocracy, she was married before emigrating at the age of seventeen with the first contingent
of settlers to Massachusetts Bay in 1630. There she lived
for the rest of a long life as a devoted wife and mother of
eight children. During her English girlhood as a member
of the household of the Earl of Lincoln, she had enjoyed
the amenities of a well-stocked library, but in the pioneer
environment of Massachusetts she was able to draw upon
only a limited number of texts in history and theology.

Not only the actual birth date, but also the antecedents
of Bradstreet's Hispanic counterpart Sor Juana are obscure,
but it appears that she was one of six children born in the
extreme southern tip of Mexico to an unmarried mother.
Showing prodigious intellectual talents as a child, she
persuaded her mother to send her at the age of eight to
Mexico City, a thriving capital of 50,000 Spanish colonists
and twice that number of Indians. Here she avidly read

---

[2] Bradstreet: "Elegy upon . . . Sir Philip Sidney"; Sor Juana: "Romance"
no. XI. All titles and quotations from Sor Juana are taken from Sor Juana
Inés de la Cruz, *Obras escogidas*, ed. Juan Carlos Merlo (Barcelona, 1968).

the classic Spanish and Latin authors. Her physical beauty kept pace with her intellectual maturity, and in her early teens she attracted not only the glances of a number of young male admirers but also the notice of the wife of the Viceroy, who invited her to the court and made available rare books vital to her studies. The young girl's brilliance was so extraordinary that during her sixteenth year forty experts in theology and the humanities were summoned to the palace for the purpose of conducting a public oral examination, at which she astounded the audience by the extent and profundity of her knowledge. Her later poetry has given rise to the theory that she suffered disillusionment over a romantic attachment at this time, but this is only speculation. A few months after her intellectual triumph at court, she took religious vows and entered a convent for life—the same age at which Anne Bradstreet entered upon matrimony. Although subject to strict cloistral rules, Sor Juana still received visitors from the outside, had the services of a Negro slave, possessed a personal library as vast as any in the territory, and had ample free time for study and writing.

In brief, Anne Bradstreet, after a placid childhood in a conventional English family, dedicated her life to the domestic duties of wife and mother in a harsh pioneer environment, responding in all social and intellectual situations in the approved austere manner of Puritanism. Sor Juana, overcoming the stigma of illegitimacy, emerged as a child prodigy in the bustling capital of New Spain and spent her mature life as a cloistered nun, dominated intellectually by Roman Catholic religion and culture.

Fundamental as these differences may be, they are overshadowed by resemblances in the writings of the two women, one of the most important of which in the present climate of opinion is the repudiation of prejudices against women poets. Both insisted on the right of women to be taken seriously as literary artists, each using the arguments most appropriate to her own circumstances.

Bradstreet, for example, had to contend with the opinion of Thomas Hooker's *Ecclesiastical Polity*, widely accepted in her milieu, that the judgments of women are "commonly weakest by reason of their sex" [Preface, chap. III, sec. 13]. She characterized herself, therefore, in the "Prologue" to her poems as "obnoxious to each carping tongue" who "says my hand a needle better fits." Critics such as these she branded as so prejudiced against "female wits" that they would say of anything good in her work that it was either copied or the result of chance. On the contrary side she cited the ancient Greeks as proponents of women since they conceived of the nine muses as feminine and ranked poetry as the child of one of them, Calliope. Apparently she was not aware that Calliope was considered to be the muse of specifically epic or heroic poetry. After this relatively strong defense, however, Bradstreet retreated by admitting that "men have precedency" and "women know it well." In the end she asked merely that masculine fellow poets allow her humble efforts to exist as a foil to their superior achievements. It must be remembered, however, that in the seventeenth century the prologue to a collection of verse, like the prologue to a play, was intended to show the author in a favorable light, and male authors also conventionally displayed an attitude of respectful humility such as Bradstreet's. Her conclusion should, therefore, not be considered as a complete surrender to the claim of masculine superiority. Her only forthright concession to the preeminence of male poets appears in a line from another poem in which she apologizes for not having completed an encyclopedic project of versifying the history of the ancient world. "This task," she laments, "befits not women like to men." In various other references to the deficiencies or inadequacies of her poetry, however, she does not attribute them to her sex, but rather to lack of time, poor health, and other difficulties that beset men as well as women.

Bradstreet rises to militancy in defending the record of women as rulers of great nations in an elegy on Queen Elizabeth, who "hath wiped off the aspersion of her sex / That women wisdom lack to play the rex." She further remarks that the "personal perfections" of Elizabeth were so extraordinary that in order to record them one

> Must dip his pen in the Heliconian well,
> Which I may not; my pride doth but aspire
> To read what others write, and so admire.

These self-deprecatory lines are intentionally ironical since Bradstreet is obviously doing that which she says is forbidden to her—extolling the queen's perfections in verse.

Sor Juana also professed humility concerning her intellectual accomplishments. Indeed, after confounding her forty interlocutors, she claimed to have felt no more satisfaction than if she had demonstrated needlework in the schoolroom, almost the same metaphor previously used by Bradstreet, but turned in a contrary sense.[3] She displayed a similar indifference in the prologue to the second edition of her works, and later in the volume dispraised her own poems as idle pastimes or mere exercises in penmanship.[4]

In a completely different frame of mind, however, she defended herself in a sonnet against those who had objected to her poetic vocation. By means of a technically superb series of paradoxes, she inquired how her dedication to poetry could possibly give offense to anyone. She pointed out that her intention was to weigh beauty by her understanding, not understanding by beautiful things; that she esteemed neither wealth nor riches and was, therefore,

---

[3] *Obras escogidas*, p. 18.
[4] "Romance" no. XI, p. 53.

much happier to weigh riches by her understanding than her understanding by riches; and that she considered it preferable to spend time with the vanities of life than to spend her life in vain [Soneto II].

Sor Juana's most brilliant defense of the female sex in general appears in a lyric poem rejecting as stupid and irrational the common complaints of men against women. Primarily literary in inspiration and reflecting the atmosphere of the court rather than the convent, it still mirrors the battle of the sexes in common walks of life. Sor Juana charges men with inconsistency in expecting women to be virtuous while inciting them to vice; in attributing to feminine looseness the result of masculine persistence; in wanting their amorous conquests to be like Thais before possession and like Lucretia after; in complaining of those women who reject their addresses and ridiculing those who accept them; in blaming one for being cruel and another for being easy. Which has greater responsibility for a guilty passion, she asks, the one who succumbs to entreaties or the one who entreats to succumb; the one who sins for payment or the one who pays for sin?[5]

The sentiments of these poems, although sincere, are somewhat conventional and abstract. The work in which Sor Juana expresses an intensely personal defense of the rights of women to intellectual freedom and development and to literary creation is an extensive argument in prose entitled *Reply of the Poetess* [*Respuesta de la poetisa*], a vindication of some critical remarks she had previously published on a theological matter. As much intellectual autobiography as polemical theology, *Reply of the Poetess* combines an impassioned recital of the author's artistic career with a justification of the claims of women to education and culture. It ranks with Milton's *Areopagitica* as one of the major seventeenth-century documents in

[5] *Obras escogidas*, pp. 177-78.

the history of the assertion of human rights. Among the topics relevant to the work of Anne Bradstreet are the interconnection of all academic disciplines; the example of the metrical parts of the Scriptures as a justification for poetry itself; the vindication of secular rather than religious themes; a catalog of eminent women, including biblical characters, saints, rulers, and writers; and an interpretation of the various passages of St. Paul and the Church Fathers that seem to deny intellectual functions to women. Sor Juana admits that it is forbidden for women to read publicly in cathedrals or to preach in pulpits, but insists that it is by no means improper for women to study any and all subjects and to write, or to teach in private. She herself, she maintains, did not study to write or to teach, but in order to minimize her ignorance.

She asks whether the Church in any of its principles requires that she believe with closed eyes. She suggests that there is no harm in her being free to dissent from her antagonist, a Jesuit father, provided that everyone else have the same freedom to disagree with her. After giving an example of free speech which the ancient Romans derived from natural law, she argues that Catholics, who have been given a positive command to love their enemies, are equally obliged to tolerate them. To justify her secular studies, Sor Juana cites two nuns of her acquaintance. One had memorized her breviary so thoroughly that she could recall any part of it in perfect order at any time; the other had familiarized herself with the style of St. Jerome so that she could apply it to the exposition of scientific principles. Sor Juana concludes that the talent of one is as valuable as that of the other.

Sor Juana also devoted herself to the study of the sciences and used them as poetic material, one of the major parallels with Anne Bradstreet. Indeed she declared in her *Reply* that the only work she had written to satisfy her own taste without external considerations was a long poem,

Primero sueño, The First Dream, part imaginative, part descriptive, which combines scientific observation, mythology, and private fancy. As such, it has much in common with Bradstreet's cosmic poems, "The Four Elements," "The Four Humours," "The Four Ages," and "The Four Seasons." Sor Juana describes the physiological details of dreaming and sleeping, classifies the phenomena of the earth, both organic and inorganic, in a hierarchical grouping, and explains the circulatory and recuperative processes of the human body with appropriate attention to the four humors.

Some of the physiology in Anne Bradstreet's poems is directly paraphrased from Dr. Helkiah Crooke's treatise, *Microcosmographia, or a Description of the Body of Man* (1618).[6] Sor Juana for her vast scientific lore in physics, astronomy, and mathematics depended chiefly upon the famous German Jesuit Athanasius Kircher, whose works included *Magnes sive de arte magnetica* (1634), *Ars combinatoria* (1640), *Ars magna lucis et umbrae* (1646), and *Mundus subterraneus* (1664). Indeed Sor Juana drew so extensively from Kircher that she invented the verb *kirkerizo,* the present indicative of "to Kircherize."

Bradstreet's biographer, E. W. White, has indicated that the notion of the Great Chain of Being is implicit in her cosmological poetry.[7] In Sor Juana, the concept is explicit, expressed in her *Primero sueño* as a hierarchical ladder and in her *Respuesta* as a universal chain, which was imagined originally by the ancients and developed in modern times by scientific investigations of magnetism.[8] It is not clear from Sor Juana's citation whether she is referring to William Gilbert's *De magneto* (1600) or to Kircher's *Magnes sive de arte magnetica.*

[6] Helen McMahon, "Anne Bradstreet, Jean Bertault, and Dr. Crooke," *Early American Literature* 3 (1968): 118-23.

[7] *Anne Bradstreet, "The Tenth Muse,"* (New York, 1971), p. 183.

[8] *Obras escogidas,* p. 532.

Hispanic scholars have concluded from the *Primero sueño* that Sor Juana had read Harvey's *De motu cordis* (1628), and from a reference in another poem to the sun making the tour of the world that she was not aware of the heliocentric theories of Copernicus.[9] The method of comparative literature suggests that a similar inquiry be made concerning Anne Bradstreet. No evidence can be found to show whether she placed the sun or the earth at the center of her cosmic system, but it appears from the following passage from "The Four Humours" that she understood the circulation of the blood.

I am the fountain which thy cistern fills
Through warm blue conduits of my venial rills.
What hath the heart but what's sent from the liver?

The speaker in this passage, the personification of blood addressing choler, seems to give an accurate picture of the flow of blood through veins from the liver to the heart. The meaning of "thy cistern" is ambiguous, however, but it probably refers to the brain. In an earlier passage, choler affirms that she heats the blood in the liver.

What comes from thence my heart refines the same,
And through the arteries sends it o'er the frame;
The vital spirits they're called, . . .

This resembles a passage in which Sor Juana describes the heart as the human clock (*Reloj humano*) as well as the King of the parts of the body and center of the vital spirits. Sor Juana also incorporates the four humors in her *Primero sueño*. It may be that the notion of the four humors is incompatible with the theory of the circulation of the blood, but neither Sor Juana nor Bradstreet apparently saw any contradiction.

[9] *Obras escogidas*, pp. 199, 29.

Este, pues, miembro Rey y centro vivo de espíritu vi-
tales.

[ll. 210-11]

One may point to an individual poem by Bradstreet
which, taken as a whole, has an extraordinary resemblance in theme and feeling to one by her southern counterpart. In "Before the Birth of One of Her Children,"
Bradstreet describes her distress at the thought that she
might die and be separated from her husband. Sor Juana
similarly describes the anguished love that a woman feels
for her deceased husband in a poem that differs from Bradstreet's mainly by depicting an imaginary rather than a
real situation.[10] The wife depicted by Sor Juana is mourn-
ing a husband who is actually dead rather than anticipat-
ing the feelings that a husband might experience after her
own death. To be sure, the lamenting of a wife for her
dead partner is not a common theme for a cloistered nun,
but Sor Juana's techniques for expressing grief are as appropriate and convincing as those of the New England
mother—even though differences in culture and temper-
ament give their poems an individual tone. Bradstreet,
reflecting Christian fortitude and acceptance of the mor-
tality of existence, reveals greatest concern for her husband and children who will survive. Her tone is placid,
and the only conceit in the poem consists in the reflection
that by writing her verse she will belong to him even
though being taken away.

I may seem thine who in effect am none.

Sor Juana's persona, to the contrary, is passionate and
inconsolable, but conveys her emotion by means of in-

[10] *Obras escogidas*, "Que expresan el sentimiento que padece una
mujer amante de su marido muerto," p. 211. Sor Juana has another poem
on the same theme to which has been assigned an almost identical title,
"Expresa, aún con expresiones más vivas, el sentimiento que padece una
mujer amante de su marido muerto," p. 143.

tricate verse patterns and brilliant conceits. She argues
that it is justifiable for her to complain to heaven, which
has robbed her of her precious loved one, but at the same
time admits that heaven with deaf and righteous ears would
account her complaint as blasphemy. In another stanza
she affirms that she does not envy the happiness of others;
the eternal suffering she goes through is so great that all
she can envy is the misery of other people, which, no
matter how great, is less than hers. Bradstreet does not
use this kind of hyperbole in the poem written during her
pregnancy but something less extreme appears in "A Letter to Her Husband, Absent Upon Public Employment."
Here she maintains that only the person who numbers
the stars, the grains of sand, the leaves of grass or the
drops of rain may count her sighs or teardrops, certainly
not a startling or an original trope, but one of the few
passages in her work related to the general tradition of
baroque style to which Sor Juana belongs.

Sor Juana's complex hyperboles have little in common
with the simple and unpretentious style of the New England Puritan, but the feeling of deep sorrow is genuine in
both poems. Critics have not felt the need to certify Bradstreet's sincerity, which has been taken for granted since
her poems concern her actual husband and children. Sor
Juana, as a cloistered nun, however, had neither spouse
nor issue, and her poetic expressions of love and grief are,
therefore, subject to the charge of being imaginary and
contrived. Spanish critics, including one of the most distinguished, Menéndez y Pelayo, have consequently taken
pains to affirm that the profane poems of Sor Juana are
spontaneous and from the heart.[11] Other critics have even
suggested a strain of lesbianism and argued that her poems
about husbands or lovers may, like the sonnets of Shake-

[11] *Obras escogidas*, p. 66.

speare, be ostensibly devoted to a member of one sex, but in actuality refer to the other.

In fact, it is no more possible for a reader to determine the sincerity of any literary passage that an author intends to be taken as genuine than it is for him to know whether a person is lying or telling the truth. All that can be said about a literary passage is that it appears to be sincere or that its portrayal of emotion is effective—in other words, that it communicates sincerity. From this perspective of the communication of feeling and the parallelism of situation, Bradstreet's lines to her husband have much more in common with Sor Juana's portrayal of a grieving wife than with Bishop Henry King's *Exequy* to his dead wife, the English work to which these lines have several times been compared.

Some American scholars have complained that Bradstreet's poetry does very little to portray indigenous New England life, that all of her allusions, metaphors, and illustrations are taken from English sources, and that none of her descriptions reflects the American landscape. The culture and topography of the New World are equally absent from the work of Juana Inés de la Cruz, but Hispanic critics do not consider this a shortcoming. They realize that she was working in a recognized poetic tradition combining artificial style with ideological substance, allowing for a high degree of personal emotion, but not local color or topography. Essentially the same is true for Bradstreet.

In the scholarship that has grown up around these two New World representatives of established literary traditions, a controversy has developed over the indebtedness of each one to a European forerunner. Spanish scholars have debated the influence on Sor Juana of the greatest exponent of the baroque in Spanish poetry, Góngora, and Americanists have sought to estimate the influence on Anne Bradstreet of an outstanding Renaissance poet of France, Du Bartas. The link between Sor Juana and Góngora was first established by the editor of the second edition of her poems in 1692, who added to the title of her *First Dream* a phrase affirming that it was composed in imitation of Góngora. From then until modern times, both when Góngora was in critical favor and when he was not, it has been assumed that Sor Juana should be considered a faithful disciple of the Spanish stylist. In 1939, a member of the Modern Language Association published a study arguing that the supposed imitation of Góngora consisted in little more than reminiscences of some metaphors, allegories, and special constructions, but other scholars still adhere to the view that a close relationship exists between the two poets.[12]

Most Americans who know Du Bartas at all know him only by name and as the author of a biblically inspired epic about the Creation of the world, *La Semaine* (1578), which is supposed to have influenced Milton and perhaps Anne Bradstreet as well. The view that Bradstreet derives inspiration directly from Du Bartas is based upon a number of references to the French poet in *The Tenth Muse* and upon a line in a commendatory poem by Nathaniel Ward indicating that "The Authoress was a right Du Bartas girl," a parallel to Sor Juana's editor adding to her *First Dream* the phrase "imitating Góngora." Almost everyone who has written about Bradstreet has quoted Ward's line or some part of it. The anti-Bartas position did not come into prominence until 1941 when Austin Warren affirmed: "Save for their pentameter couplets and their panoramic scope, Anne Bradstreet's long poems have nothing in common with Du Bartas; she does not or cannot imitate his conceits. . . . The humbler ingenuities were what the New Englanders could reproduce."[13] The expression "Du Bartas girl" is an exact parallel to the appelation "Bartas

---

[12] *Obras escogidas*, p. 67.
[13] *Rage for Order. Essays in Criticism* (Chicago, 1948), p. 8.

Junior," which Edward Cooke used in 1631 as part of the title to a poem which, like that of his French predecessor, deals with the Creation. The full title of Cooke's work, which appeared in London the year after Bradford sailed for Massachusetts, is *Bartas Iunior: or, The World's Epitome. Man. Set Forth in his 1. Generation, 2. Degeneration, 3. Regeneration*. Bradstreet also treats man as an epitome of the universe by means of her parallel exposition of the four elements (earth, air, fire, and water), the four humors, the four ages of man, and the seasons.

A German scholar, Hans Galinsky, has superbly traced and analyzed all the external evidence that has so far come to light concerning Bradstreet's allegiance to Du Bartas and all of the substantive stylistic resemblances between the two poets.[14] His conclusion places him somewhat closer to Nathaniel Ward than to Austin Warren, but it does not really settle the question for future writers of literary history. According to the paraphrase that E. W. White has made available for Americans who do not read German, Galinsky has shown that Bradstreet followed various suggestions derived from the works of Du Bartas and Shakespeare, but that "there was a 'transformation,' as well as a 'transplatation,' of whatever they contributed to her work."[15] Galinsky has treated the subject so thoroughly that there is no need whatsoever of reexamining his evidence or that of previous scholars. His method is impeccable and his conclusion completely warranted.

It is still possible, however, to demonstrate remarkable similarities between the work of Bartas and Bradstreet in

[14] "Anne Bradstreet, Du Bartas und Shakespeare im Zusammenhang kolonialer Verpflanzung und Umformung europäischer Literatur," in *Festschrift für Walther Fischer* (Heidelberg, 1959), pp. 145-80. I am following Galinsky in my depiction of the history of Bradstreet scholarship. In future references to the French poet, I shall follow the seventeenth-century English form of Bartas rather than Du Bartas.

[15] *Anne Bradstreet*, p. 65.

areas other than those elements of literary style upon which previous scholars have concentrated, chiefly the use of conceits, metaphors, and the compound epithet. A good starting point is the title itself of Bradstreet's collection, *The Tenth Muse, Lately Sprung up in America*. There is reason to believe that contemporary readers of this title would associate it with the English translation of Bartas's major work, *Les Semaines*, by Joshua Sylvester and published in London in 1605 under the title *Bartas: His Devine Weekes and Workes*, with other editions appearing in 1608, 1620, and 1641, the last one, nine years before the publication of *The Tenth Muse*. Eleven pages of the introductory material to Sylvester's work are devoted exclusively to the muses—one complete page to each of the individual muses, one to their mother Mnemosyne, and one to "Sylvestres: nove musae," that is, Sylvester of the nine muses. All of this material as a unit is entitled "Corona Dedicatoria." This repeated association of Sylvester with the nine muses would seem to indicate that a subsequent title referring to an American poet as representing the Tenth Muse would immediately remind English readers of its predecessor. On the page in Sylvester devoted to Mnemosyne, the muses crown James I as laureate and present him their coat of arms,

Thrice Three Pennes Sun-like in a Cinthian field.
Sign'd by THEM-SELVES, and their High Treasurer
BARTAS, the great; In-gross'd by SYLVESTER.

A line by J. Rogers to one of the dedicatory pieces in the second edition of Bradstreet's poems seems to refer directly to the *Thrice Three Pennes* in the first line. Rogers declares,

I saw the Muses treble trine.

An even closer link between Bartas and Bradstreet may be seen in the general structure of their published volumes. Sylvester's translation comprises two works of Bartas, originally published as separate volumes, *The First Week* and *The Second Week*. The latter is divided into four days, each of which is subdivided into four internal divisions, and there are also two separate poems at the end, not directly related to the four days. Exactly the same arrangement exists in *The Tenth Muse*: that is, four main divisions internally compartmentalized into four sections, comprising "The Four Humours in Man's Constitution," "The Four Ages of Man," "The Four Seasons of the Year," and "The Four Monarchies." At the end there are added, as in Sylvester's volume, a group of miscellaneous poems. In the original work of Bartas, *The Second Week* does not limit itself to the literal events of the second seven days of creation, but treats the history of the world after the fall of man, even including the discovery of the Western Hemisphere. A later French poet, J. Gailhard, wrote an addition of 630 lines, calling it part of the fifth day, which he published in 1659.[16] The four divisions of Bradstreet's *Tenth Muse* would also qualify as additional days in the scheme of Bartas, even to their internal separation into four parts. Indeed the precise subject matter of three of Bradstreet's sections is set forth in outline form in Bartas's "Second Day." In the effects of the wind, he enumerates and describes

> . . . fower Tempraments,
> Foure Times, foure Ages, and foure Elements.[17]

These are, in other words, the four humors, the four seasons, the four ages of man, and the four elements (air, earth, fire, and water). The first three obviously corre-

[16] *The Works of Guillaume de Salluste, sieur Du Bartas, a Critical Edition*, ed. Urban Tigner Holmes, Jr. et al., 3 vols. (Chapel Hill, N.C., 1935-1940), 1: 96.

[17] *Bartas His Devine Weekes and Workes (1605)*. Translated by Joshua Sylvester. Facsimile edition (Gainesville, Fla., 1965), p. 52.

spond to Bradstreet's "The Four Humours of Man's Constitution," "The Four Seasons of the Year," and "The Four
Ages of Man"; the material of the fourth topic, the four
elements of the universe, moreover, is interspersed
throughout all three sections.

Bradstreet's second group of four major poems, "The
Four Monarchies" is suggested in Bartas's "Fourth Booke,
of the first Day, of the second Weeke," entitled "The
Handie-Crafts" in which the history of the world is divided into six ages between Adam and Christ. Bradstreet's
poem continues the record into later ages. Bartas himself
sketches the development of subsequent history in "The
Colonies," but indicates that he will not undertake the
topic in depth because of the obscurity of historical records. An actual parade of monarchs, something like Bradstreet's, appears, moreover, in "The Triumph of Faith," a
separate poem also present in the Sylvester edition.

Bartas even provides a metaphysical explanation for the
significance of the number four.

> The (Cubes-Base) Foure; a full and perfect summe,
> Whose added parts just unto Tenne doo come;
> Nomber of Gods great Name, Seasons, Complexions,
> Windes, Elements, and cardinall Perfections.[18]

To be sure, Bartas also gives the metaphysical significance
of the other primary numbers, but it is the number four
that is the basis of his own poetic structure. He describes
the Hebrew tongue, for example, as being figuratively upheld by four pillars, that is, by Moses, David, Solomon,
and Isaiah. He enumerates as well the four major writers
in each of the other major Western languages: Greek, Latin,
Italian, Arabic, German, Spanish, French, and English. In
Bartas's original, the French authors come last, immedi-

---

[18] Ibid., p. 473. The Hebrew name for God with the vowels eliminated,
as in Hebrew practice, is J-h-w-h. The number 4 when added to each of
its parts produces 10: $4 + 3 + 2 + 1 = 10$.

ately preceded by the English, but in Sylvester's translation the order is reversed. The same poets, however, are included in each roster.

Bradstreet seems to have been the first to apply the mathematical term quaternion to the poetic structure of "four times four." Her own four-part division has usually been attributed to the example of her father, Thomas Dudley, on the basis of a dedicatory poem in which she refers to his "four sisters, deckt in black & white," glossed by a marginal note, "T D on the four parts of the world." Further in her poem she says that in order that her lowly pen might wait upon those four,

> I bring my four; and four, now meanly clad.

No other trace of Dudley's work on the four parts of the world has ever come to light, however, but if it were indeed a work written in verse, it could very well have been, like his daughter's, after the manner of Bartas-Sylvester. No matter what the form or substance of Dudley's work may have been, it cannot detract from the obvious structural similarity between Bartas and Bradstreet.

There is another passage in the dedication to Bradstreet's father that has been interpreted as a declaration of freedom from the influence of Bartas.

> Something of all (though mean) I did intend,
> But fear'd you'ld judge, one *Bartas* was my friend,
> I honour him, but dare not wear his wealth,
> My goods are true (though poor) I love no stealth,
> But if I did, I durst not send them you;
> Who must reward a theife, but with his due.

Here Bradstreet is unequivocally repudiating the charge of plagarism, but she is certainly not disclaiming strong resemblance to Bartas or denying that she has taken him as her model. The mere fact that she recognizes that her father, or any one else, would conclude Bartas to be her friend indicates that the similarities between her work and his are apparent. The passage quoted above is preceded by a summary of her method of dealing with the four elements, air, water, earth, and fire. In its context, therefore, Bradstreet's declaration means that she is using material already handled by Bartas, but treating it in an original manner.

In recent years, two students of *The Tenth Muse* have discussed its internal organization. One of these, E. W. White, affirms that "there is both chronological and textual confusion" in the order in which its constituent poems were printed. She adds that "if Anne Bradstreet had been in a position to supervise their publication she would undoubtedly have arranged them differently."[19] This scholar then rearranges the various poems in a chronological order, according to date of composing, as "their most logical form of presentation."

More recently an article on "The Structure of Anne Bradstreet's *Tenth Muse*" has maintained that the published arrangement was that which Bradstreet herself preferred and that her book "is far more impressive, finally, when it is considered as a unit than when we isolate individual poems for analysis."[20] After arguing for a considerable degree of thematic unity and structural complexity in *The Tenth Muse*, this article suggests that Anne Bradstreet herself was aware of the principles upon which it is organized and published. It makes the valid point that the fact that the poems were supposedly printed without her knowledge is no argument against their incorporating a deliberate structural design, for "she had evidently given her father a complete manuscript" and there are no signs of editorial work by anyone else. The article, therefore,

[19] *Anne Bradstreet*, p. 253.
[20] By Robert D. Arner in *Discoveries & Considerations*, ed. Calvin Israel (Albany, 1976), p. 47.

comes to the conclusion that "the careful attention Bradstreet paid to the structure of her book ought to be immediately evident to anyone who considers" its "pat-
terned arrangement."[21] Anyone who goes a step further
by comparing the thematic and structural unity of *The
Tenth Muse* in its original format with the same features
of Sylvester's *Devine Weekes* would realize almost at a
glance that Bradstreet's volume contains a conscious pattern of organization deriving from its forerunner.

The Sylvester-Bartas edition provides an explanation of
why Bradstreet selected three of the four subjects included
among her elegies and epitaphs. One of these consists of
a paraphrase of King David's lamentation for Saul. The
other three are dedicated to near-contemporary figures,
Bartas himself, Sir Philip Sidney, and Queen Elizabeth.
There is no mystery over why Bradstreet should conse-
crate an elegy to her model, Bartas, but one may wonder,
perhaps, at the choice of such unlikely heroes as Sidney
and Elizabeth in the climate of opinion of Puritan Massachusetts in 1650. E. W. White reports, for example, that
so far as she has been able to discover, the elegy to Sidney
is the only seventeenth-century New England tribute to
him ever written.[22]

Bradstreet may have decided to honor Sidney because
he was one of her family ancestors,[23] but she may also,
or otherwise, have been impelled to write in his praise by
a page in Sylvester's translation of Bartas addressed to the
reader, "Lectoribus," following the table of contents, a
page entirely devoted to Sidney and thus serving as a kind
of secondary dedication, the primary one having been offered to James I. In keeping with one aspect of the English
baroque style, shaped verse, Sylvester's verses to Sidney
are printed in the form of a pencil, and Sidney is described

[21] Ibid., p. ·63.
[22] *Anne Bradstreet*, p. 141.
[23] Ibid., p. 11.

as England's Apelles and the world's wonder. Bradstreet
specifically refers to these verses in her lines

> How to persist, my muse is more in doubt,
> Which makes me now with Sylvester confess
> But Sidney's muse can sing his worthiness.

Bartas himself in the second day of *La Seconde Semaine*
or "Babylone" treats Sidney as one of the four major writers of England, a passage to which Bradstreet alludes in
her own verses on Sidney:

> Noble Bartas, this to thy praise adds more,
> In sad, sweet verse, thou didst his death deplore.

This is a reference to the Sylvester translation, not to the
original French text, as E. W. White observes, since Sidney's death had not yet taken place when Bartas himself
was writing.

Bartas also provided a precedent for saluting Queen Elizabeth, for he devotes twenty-three lines to her immediately following his lines on Sidney. Sylvester, moreover,
interpolates a two-page tribute to Elizabeth in "The Third
Day of the First Weeke," in which she is compared to a
lotus flower, to the daughter of the sun, and to a phoenix.
The latter metaphor was, of course, one of the most common in the Renaissance, used by almost every poet in
every language. Anne Bradstreet also applied it to Queen
Elizabeth, and Sor Juana Inés de la Cruz was called the
Phoenix of Mexico in the title of a posthumous edition
of her works. In her elegy of Bartas, Bradstreet suggests
that she had wished at one time to imitate the French
poet, but had given up in despair of achieving her ambition. She further reveals that more recently she had achieved
her purpose in a modest way. According to her metaphoric
terms, while she was rereading his lines, the rays that
they emitted enabled her to produce a homely daisy in
her "later spring." If she should produce a richer harvest

in her summer and autumn years, she promises, this mature production will be dedicated to Bartas.

The tone of all of Bradstreet's poetic references to Bartas is that of deep humility. She speaks of herself disparagingly, for example, "Thus weake brain'd I, reading thy lofty stile." This artistic self-abasement is not necessarily representative of Puritanical mortification or of feminine submission, however; it may just as well be the reflection of a purely literary device that can be traced back to Sylvester and Bartas himself. The latter in the fourth day of the first week repudiated the notion that poets attain everlasting glory through their efforts. In other terms, he rejected a common topos in Renaissance verse, the "proud conceit" or the poet's boast that his own lines will last through future ages or eternity. Bartas, in direct contrast to this poetic convention, after admitting that his verses had caused him great pains, declared that he expected no glory from them, but hoped merely that they would inspire more gifted poets to undertake his theme in the future. Sylvester paraphrased these lines in such a way as to apply them to himself. Repudiating the practice of the "best English wits," whose verses revealed flattery, courtship, sycophancy, and affectation, he dedicated his works to God's glory, not his own, until posterity may find more dextrous poets to record the same events

> And foot by foot with far more life and grace,
> follow Great BARTAS admirable pace.

Rather convincing evidence that Sylvester's modesty was merely a literary reflection of Bartas's delineation of the humble conceit may be found in his dedication of another translation, "The Triumph of Faith," to his deceased uncle. His "Toombe of Words," he affirms,

> . . . shall out-last
> The proud cloud-threatning Battlements,

> Th' aspiring Spires by NILUS plac't,
> And Hell-deepe-founded Monuments.

Bradstreet, however, was following Sylvester in his modest rather than his proud attitude. It is probably not through mere coincidence that she addresses her model as "Great, deare, sweet *Bartas*" or that she concludes with a reference to those who will excel her efforts in the future:

> Ile leave thy praise, to those shall doe thee right,
> Good will, not skill, did cause me bring my mite.

If it is true that Bradstreet followed the Bartas-Sylvester model closely and consecutively rather than casually and sporadically, it would follow that she possessed more than elementary acquaintance with French culture and history. It would also follow that her poems should not necessarily be interpreted exclusively in the light of an Anglo-American background. With these conclusions in mind, I should like to suggest alternate interpretations of two passages from the quaternions.

In the first of these, "Old Age" is reporting historical and political events that he has witnessed.

> I've seen one stabbed, and some to lose their heads,
> And others flee, struck both with guilt and dread.
> I've seen, and so have you, for 'tis but late,
> The desolation of a goodly state
> Plotted and acted so that none can tell
> Who gave the counsel but the prince of hell—
> Three hundred thousand slaughtered innocents
> By bloody popish, hellish miscreants.

The "one stabbed" would seem to be Henry IV of France, who was assassinated by Ravaillac in 1610, and the "three hundred thousand slaughtered innocents" the victims of the St. Bartholomew's Day massacre in Paris. Whether or

not Bradstreet could read French, it is almost certain that
she knew of these events. Sylvester, for example, inter-
polated in his translation a reference to St. Bartholomew's
Day "when SEIN did swell with blood."[24] White assumes
that two English noblemen, Buckingham and Strafford,
were alluded to as the victims of stabbing and beheading,
which is also plausible, but her explanation that "three
hundred thousand slaughtered innocents" were victims
of the Irish Rebellion of 1641 is most unlikely.[25] Even if
that many English soldiers had died in Ireland, they could
hardly be considered "slaughtered innocents" as were the
Huguenot citizens of Paris and other parts of France. The
number "three hundred thousand" is, of course, a gross
exaggeration in regard also to the St. Bartholomew's massacre.

Bradstreet had many anti-Catholic prejudices, as was
natural for one in her environment, but she sometimes
had misgivings about her biased conceptions and once
even wondered, as she confided to her children, "why may
not the Popish religion be the right?"[26] Caution should
be used, therefore, in reading anti-Catholic sentiments
into her poetry. The following lines of the "Apology" appended to "The Four Monarchies" in her second edition,
for example, have been misinterpreted.

> Although my Monarchies their legs do lack:
> No matter is it this last, the world now sees,
> Hath many ages been upon his knees.

According to White, the final line represents "a pleasant
example of Anne Bradstreet's individual turn of humor,
that deftly twists a punning dig at popery out of her own

[24] *Bartas*, trans. Sylvester, p. 95.
[25] *Anne Bradstreet*, p. 214.
[26] *The Works of Anne Bradstreet*, ed. Jeannine Hensley (Cambridge,
Mass., 1967), p. 244.

misfortune."[27] Bradstreet's humor is there well enough, but the reference is not to the Catholic religion, but to the commonplace Renaissance doctrine that the world was degenerating or running down and, so to speak, in its dotage. Bradstreet could have acquired this notion from many sources. The most obvious is Sir Walter Raleigh, who wrote in his *History of the World*, "We have neither giants such as the elder world had; nor mighty men such as the elder world had; but all things in general are reputed of less virtue, which from the heavens receive virtue."[28]

White's criticism suffers at another point from under-estimating the influence of the European literary milieu. After labelling the subject matter of "The Four Monarchies" as "grim and unfeminine," she observes that there is not in Bradford's poem "a sin of the flesh or the spirit that is not described, often with revolting detail, in her account of the ambitions, conquests, cruelties, and licentious self-indulgences of the monarchs of antiquity."[29] Whether or not Bradstreet's historical poetry reveals a masculine cast to her mind and personality, there are few of her alleged grisly or ferocious elements that cannot be

[27] *Anne Bradstreet*, p. 235.

[28] (Edinburgh, 1820), p. 1. Not only did Bradstreet know this work, but she paraphrased large sections of it in "The Four Monarchies." Ann Stanford, *Anne Bradstreet: The Worldly Puritan* (New York, 1974), p. 137. Critics have been willing to acknowledge the humor in Bradstreet, but have ignored it in Du Bartas, which to me seems an injustice. He compares, for example, the sheets of water in the seas to the floods of words in his poem [*Première Semaine. Troisième Jour*, 1. 217]. And as an illustration of the effects of lightning, he describes having often seen in his youth a flash sear off in an instant the pubic hair from a woman and do no other harm whatsoever [*Première Semaine. Second Jour*, 11. 705-5]. Du Bartas's humorless American editors seriously maintain that the poet is here recording an incident of his youth when his mother was knocked unconscious by a bolt of lightning. *Works*, ed. Holmes et al., 1: 17.

[29] *Anne Bradstreet*, p. 237.

observed in Bartas as well. If Bradstreet acknowledged a literary model, she can hardly be faulted for following it.

As Hans Galinsky has shown, there is absolutely no agreement among critics about the merits of Bradstreet's poetry; one speaks disparagingly of the "Bartas disease" and another suggests that she is inferior precisely because she does not reproduce ingenious conceits. Most commentators now feel that her occasional poems written to and about members of her family are the ones with greatest poetic merit. Paradoxically the same critical climate of opinion that has rejected Anne Bradstreet's *The Tenth Muse* as contrived and artificial has at the same time highly applauded Edward Taylor's poems, charged as they are with bizarre imagery and conceits. Regardless of the prevailing attitude toward artificiality in verse, it must be recognized that Bradstreet, like Taylor, was the product of a literary period as well as of a geographical environment. Also it must not be forgotten that she originally acquired her place in literary history through the published edition of *The Tenth Muse*, while her personal verse remained in manuscript, and that the book that introduced her to her seventeenth-century contemporaries will always retain its significance as a register of colonial taste and a reminder of literary internationalism. The more *The Tenth Muse* resembles *La Semaine*, the closer it approaches the mainstream of literature. Both those who patronize Bradstreet as a victim of the "Bartas disease" and those who maintain that she had little to do with her French predecessor mistakenly look for significant signs of their relationship in "a contrived metaphor, a stilted image, or an overelaborate descriptive passage," to use the words of her biographer.[30] Far more significant resemblances are to be found in two major aspects of the Renaissance style, that is, the maintaining and extending of

[30] Ibid., p. 270.

a complex structure and the development of the theme
of the grandeur and magnificence of the universe. In this
regard, Bradstreet shares the poetic vision not only of her
French predecessor Bartas, but also of her Mexican successor Sor Juana Inés de la Cruz.

THREE

EDWARD TAYLOR AND THE AMERICAN BAROQUE

Anne Bradstreet and Edward Taylor are ordinarily considered as by far the two best poets of colonial America. Few links other than religious and geographical can be discerned between them, however, even though it appears that the only book of English poetry discovered in Taylor's library after his death was a copy of *The Tenth Muse*.[1] The subject matter of Taylor's verse is almost exclusively devotional, whereas Bradstreet's covers a variety of human concerns, including domestic relationships. Her simple diction and clear syntax contrast sharply with Taylor's elaborate verbal techniques. Although Taylor's artificial language may seem to be almost unique when compared with the plain style of his contemporary poets in the English colonies of America, his mannerisms seem less extravagant when seen as part of the widespread esthetic tradition throughout the major European literatures of the seventeenth century known as the baroque.

Critics have accepted the notion that the baroque style passed from Europe to Spanish America, and as a result the term a "Spanish-American baroque" is widespread. The designation in the Spanish language is either "El barroco de Indias" or "Barroco literario de Indias."[2] The cor-

---

[1] *The Poems of Edward Taylor*, ed. Donald E. Stanford (New Haven, 1960), p. xxvi.

[2] Mariano Picón-Salas, *De la conquista a la independencia* (México, 1944), pp. 99-109.

responding concept of an artificial style passing from Europe to English America has so far gained only moderate acceptance. It was formulated originally, appropriately enough, by a Czechoslovakian scholar, Zdeněk Vančura, who spoke in 1933 of "Baroque prose in America."[3] Eight years later Austin Warren used the phrase "Colonial Baroque" and a Japanese scholar, Ken Akiyama, more recently appropriated "belated baroque prose" to explain the phenomenon to the Orient.[4] Warren based his definition on the strictures of unfriendly critics: " 'Baroque' shall name such English poetry and prose antedating the neoclassical movement as would, by neoclassical standards, be judged 'false wit.' "[5] Warren's notion of an "American Baroque" was taken up and extended by Harold Jantz, an authority on German baroque literature and the pioneer anthologist of seventeenth-century American poetry.[6] Jantz also does not provide a comprehensive definition, but accepts with reservations a pejorative description by Moses Coit Tyler delivered over a century ago—not of baroque as such, but of one kind of English poetry fashionable early in the seventeenth century, "the degenerate euphuism of Donne, of Wither, of Quarles, of George Herbert." The advantage of these definitions is that they depart from conventional expositions of the baroque in Europe by eliminating all reference to art and architecture or to themes and ideologies and limit themselves entirely to linguistic and rhetorical characteristics.

There is no question that the concept of baroque de-

[3] René Wellek, *Concepts of Criticism* (New Haven, 1963), p. 88.

[4] Hans Galinsky, " 'Colonial Baroque,' A Concept Illustrating Dependence, Germinal Independence and New World Interdependence of Early American Literature" [a beautiful baroque title], in *Actes du VIIᵉ Congrès de l'Association Internationale de Littérature Comparée* (Stuttgart, 1979), 1: 44.

[5] *Rage for Order. Essays in Criticism* (Chicago, 1948), p. 2.

[6] In *Discoveries & Considerations*, ed. Calvin Israel (Albany, 1976), pp. 7-10.

veloped originally in the history of art and that criteria previously applied to painting, sculpture, and above all architecture came to be transferred to the literature of the seventeenth century. If there is a baroque presence in the Anglo-Saxon part of America, it is obviously exclusively literary, for New England and the other British colonies of America, unlike the Spanish colonies covering the territory of the present Mexico and Peru, produced very little before 1700 in the way of art and architecture except for the utilitarian and primitive. The Spanish colonies, on the other hand, not only erected magnificent cathedrals and splendid palaces, but created masterpieces in the decorative arts, which today are among the world's outstanding examples of intricacy and embellishment.

Another reason why the concept of baroque seems somewhat alien to the English colonies is that the earliest critics to establish its standards or criteria were German and Italian art historians. When the concept was first applied to literature, it was Italian, Spanish, and German writers who were considered relevant, and even now they are the ones to whom the designation seems most applicable. Many critics of French and English literature seem uncomfortable with baroque as a period concept, and it has certainly not been accepted in these literatures on an equal level with other terms such as Renaissance, neoclassicism, Enlightenment, or Romanticism. Indeed, during most of the nineteenth century, the term baroque, in its application to literature at least, was used as a synonym for bad taste.

Even contemporary critics who deal primarily with Spanish and Italian texts are by no means unanimous in identifying the particular elements that constitute the baroque, and few have attempted to apply any but the most general criteria in seeking common ground in all the literatures of Europe. Some major differences in philosophy or cosmic attitudes may be perceived, however, that distinguish the baroque from the Renaissance that preceded or in some instances coexisted with it. The Renaissance was the period of humanism, when man felt proud of his humanity, believed that each individual could excel in every form of knowledge and endeavor, tried to extend the limits of science and philosophy, and considered art to be inferior to nature as its mirror and servant. In literature, the Renaissance expressed the notion of ideal beauty, frequently associating it with Platonic philosophy. In the period of the baroque, however, man emphasized his limitations, both physical and mental; abandoned the notion of attaining competency in many disciplines; and looked to the spiritual rather than the natural world for knowledge and inspiration. Paradoxically, he placed art on an equal level with nature and even in some senses on a superior plane. Beauty was considered as something illusory or relative, and its physical manifestations were frequently described in crude and earthy language. In literature, content was subordinated to language, and words were frequently used for words' sake. Having abandoned the quest for new knowledge, the writer sought novelty in expression, not in content. The product of this activity, when successful, was known as *wit* in English, *ingegno* in Italian, *agudeza* in Spanish, and *esprit* in French. A famous English poem by Abraham Cowley, "Of Wit" (1656), defines and illustrates this elusive intellectual quality and also warns against its excesses, subsequently known as "false wit." Whether Taylor's wit is true or false or whether it is appropriate to consider his poetry under the heading baroque, he was certainly the leading exponent in the English colonies of the exuberant style. Indeed, the poets who resemble him most in the devising of verbal intricacies are not from either England or the English colonies of America, but from Italy, Spain, and Spanish America.

The outstanding Italian practitioner of the baroque style, Giambattista Marino, expressed his esthetic creed in one of his verses, "The aim of the poet is to create wonder" [È del poeta il fin la meraviglia]. By this, Marino meant that poetry should evoke a feeling of astonishment or amazement by means of its novelty, daring, or intricacy. For Marino as for other writers in the baroque tradition, the essence of good poetry is wit or acuity; its effectiveness depends upon the degree of wonder it produces; and its chief instruments are rhetorical figures and tropes, the most important of which is the metaphor.[7]

Marino's favorite metaphors are geological (jewels and precious metals such as rubies, pearls, crystal, silver, and gold), botanical (flowers, and the effects of the seasons and the elements), and biological (the natural functions of birth, death, and regeneration). He piles up nouns and adjectives in heaps or assembles them in clusters and uses structural devices such as the chiasmus, and balance and antithesis. He frequently uses carnal metaphors for spiritual themes, for example, describing the drops of blood exuding from Christ's wounds as tongues of love that work for the poet's benefit [Tanto son per mio ben lingue amorose].

The chief ingredient of the Marinistic style, however, is elaborate conceit. The more numerous the conceits, according to Marino, the better the poem. In one of his prose works, he accumulates the following expressions for the human tongue: "midwife of souls, forge of words, key of memory, bell of wit, hand of reason, curb of prudence, helmsman of the will, the stamp that presses conceits in others' ears, the pen that writes the letters of thought; brush that paints the images of the intellect, the battering ram assaulting the strongest hearts; trumpet making public the internal affections; arrow that wounds and heals; spear that kills and revives."[8]

---

[7] James Mirollo, *The Poet of the Marvelous, Giambattista Marino* (New York, 1963), p. 120.

[8] Ibid., pp. 153, 134-35, 148, 131, 33. Richard Crashaw, the English poet, translated a section of one of Marino's religious poems, *The Massacre of the Innocents [La Strage degl' Innocenti (1632)]*, and it was

Although Marino and his Spanish contemporary Luis de Góngora were acquainted with each other's works, there is no evidence that either borrowed from the other. In other words, they arrived independently at remarkably similar poetic styles, a statement that can be broadened to include Taylor as well. The poetry of Góngora and his school is commonly labelled Góngorism, and there are two other terms widely used in Spanish criticism to describe its primary elements. The first of these is *culteranismo* or "cultism," derived from the adjective *culto*, referring to people who are cultured or cultivated. Cultism designates esoteric language, consisting of such elements as recondite vocabulary, complicated syntax, and extravagant figures of speech. The second Spanish term, *conceptismo* or "conceptism," which derives from the noun *concepto*, designates intellectual formulations such as conceits, paradoxes, and ingenious antitheses. Although one term theoretically concerns words and the other ideas, it is almost impossible in practice to separate the two. A conceit, for example, may both create images and stimulate ideas. The terms cultism and conceptism are useful primarily in attributing a preponderance of one quality or another; that is, a poet who depends largely on vocabulary and verbal effects is considered cultist; one who regularly establishes intellectual relationships is considered conceptist. Both tendencies exist in Góngora, but it might be fair to say that he is less cultist than Marino and less conceptist than Sor Juana Inés de la Cruz. In the same way, Taylor is highly cultist, and hardly conceptist at all.

---

published as the longest piece in Crashaw's verse collection *Steps to the Temple* (1646), a matter of some significance to students of Taylor since the English poet whom he resembles most is considered to be Crashaw. L. C. Martin, the editor of Crashaw's *Poems*, gives 1610 rather than 1642 as the date of *La Strage*, and this error has been perpetuated by many critics of Crashaw. Other works of Crashaw showing indebtedness to Marino are treated by Mirollo, *Poet of the Marvelous*, pp. 248-49.

Like Marino, Góngora is noted for elaborate conceits and for using carnal metaphors to express spiritual themes. He also uses balance and antithesis, paradox, repetition, oxymoron, allegory and personification, and he alludes liberally to the *topoi* of Greek and Latin authors. Several other characteristics, all tending to make his work obscure, are so widespread in Góngora's work that they set him apart from other writers. His vocabulary is loaded with neologisms, slang, and foreign words. His analogies are often not only far-fetched, but almost unintelligible; he is, in other words, guilty of catachresis or recondite analogy. Spanish critics in the past have condemned him particularly for his *hipérbaton*, a word that may be translated as "hyperbate" or "hyperbaton," but which is almost never encountered in English. It refers to innovations in syntax, usually inversions in word order, which are considered a blemish in Spanish prosody, but which in English have been made respectable by the blank verse tradition.

A British scholar, fully cognizant of the parallel to Marino, argues that one of Góngora's major aims is the evocation of wonder through the description of nature and that this element in his poetry is inherently related to his verbal techniques of intricacy and novelty. The wonder that seventeenth-century poets perceived in nature does not resemble that associated with the sublime in the eighteenth century, which is more familiar to modern students. The Augustans felt that the sublime was inspired by the infinitude of the universe as reflected in such vast works as the ocean, the skies, and the mountains, but the wonder in Góngora stems from the perception of artistic arrangements in nature. According to one of Góngora's contemporaries, "What is most marvellous about the world is not the immensity of these Heavens, nor the number of stars there, nor the sheer bulk of essences, but its wit, its design, its framework, its order, its correspondences."[9]

Sor Juana Inés de la Cruz, although obviously affected by the techniques of Góngora, developed a unique and independent style. She shares with both Marino and Góngora the use of puns, paradox, and parallelism and antithesis, but uses conceits sparingly. Like Góngora, she derives her metaphors from the crudest parts of nature as well as from the pleasurable and the picturesque, attaining, in the words of a Spanish critic, "almost a preciosity of the gross."[10] In structure, her favorite device is the chiasmus, and she developed the art of the hyperbole to a height beyond that attained by any of her predecessors.

The English metaphysical poets obviously belong to the same tradition as these Italian and Hispanic writers, but there are important differences among them. Marino and Góngora may be considered as "practitioners of a style marked by sensuous imagery, exclamatory syntax, and an attempt to achieve the stupefying and the marvelous."[11] Donne, Crashaw, and other exponents of the metaphysical style, on the other hand, specialize in conceits that communicate intellectually rather than astonish or overwhelm. Equally important, their works are pervaded by a sense of irony and cosmic paradox.[12] Austin Warren has pointed out major characteristics of Taylor's poetry that are alien to the baroque style in England, "his downright coinages, his inversions and other awkward, sometimes unconstruable constructions."[13]

---

[9] Juan Eusebio Nieremberg, *Curiosa y oculta filosofía* (Madrid, 1643), p. 300. Cited by M. J. Woods, *The Poet and the Natural World in the Age of Góngora* (Oxford, 1978), p. 188.

[10] Picón-Salas, *De la conquista*, p. 100.

[11] Frank J. Warnke, *European Metaphysical Poetry* (New Haven, 1974), p. 3.

[12] Ibid., pp. 6-7.

[13] *Rage for Order*, p. 13.

These characteristics are part and parcel of the style of Góngora as well, indeed his distinguishing ones. Since the poetry of Taylor is sensuous and stupefying rather than intellectual and ironical, and since scholars have already pointed out the major resemblances between Taylor and the two English poets with whom he has greatest affinity, Herbert and Crashaw, the following pages will concentrate on analogies between Taylor and his Italian and Hispanic counterparts.

In one of Taylor's unpublished manuscripts appears the phrase, "I wrote these . . . not for the Wit sake nor for the Verse sake but for the History sake."[14] This sentence reveals that Taylor conceived of three separate elements in poetry, its substance or subject matter, "the History," and its two separate rhetorical adornments, "the wit" and "the verse." The latter can be considered as equivalent to the conceptism and cultism of Spanish criticism, both of which, in most of Taylor's poetry, take precedence over the history or subject matter.

One of Taylor's major aims, if not the primary one, is, like Marino's, to evoke wonder. Not only are nearly all of his verbal artifices directed toward this purpose, but he several times expressly evokes objects and sensations associated with the marvelous. In one poem of sixty-six lines, he uses some form of the word *wonder* six times together with *amazed* and *marvels* [125-126]. In other poems he cites "A Clew of Wonders!" together with "Big belli'd Wonders" [67]. He introduces another poem with the exclamation, "Stupendious Love! All Saints Astonishment!" [20]. And he celebrates the sacrament of communion because of its imparting "To mee to wonderment" [240].

In temporal affairs, the kind of wonder that intrigued

---

[14] *Poems*, p. 507. Future references to this edition will consist of page numbers within brackets after particular quotations.

Taylor was that derived from the mechanical, labeled in an Italian treatise on wit as *mirabili per arte*. He cites a number of wonders of the ancient and the modern worlds, including the hanging gardens of Babylon, the pyramids, the military engines of Archimedes, the clock with moving figures at Strasburg, and the artificial man of Albertus Magnus that could walk and speak [180]. Taylor's interest in the mechanical arts links him with two representatives of the Romantic movement who were also fascinated by mechanical creatures, E.T.A. Hoffmann and Nathaniel Hawthorne. In the dichotomy of Art-Nature, the baroque tradition accorded respect to art in greater measure than did preceding or subsequent historical periods. Taylor comes close to placing the two on an equal plane in his statements: "Nature doth better work than Art," and "Art, nature's Ape, hath many brave things done" [181, 179]. He even affirms, "An heap of Pearls is precious: but they shall / When set by Art Excell" [456]. He consistently proclaims, of course, that for him everything in both art and nature is inferior to the glories of God. In reference to Christ's redemption, therefore, he admonishes himself, "Wonder, my Soule, at this great Wonder bright" [157]. Spiritual phenomena he regards as a kind of artifice, superior to nature; he describes, for example, bread and wine turned into the flesh and blood of Christ as "not fram'd by natures acting, but by Art" [270]. As Austin Warren has pointed out, Taylor analogizes nature to the crafts,[15] exactly the reverse process associated with the Romantics. In a typical poem, he conceives the earth as laced and girded by rivers like green emerald ribbons, and compares it to "a Quilt Ball within a Silver Box." The stars he describes as "twinckling Lanthorns in the Sky."

It has been argued that Taylor's poetical theory bears an intimate relationship to his theology—that his view

---

[15] *Rage for Order*, p. 8.

of language, while consistent with Puritan literary theory in general, is at the same time based on "a close analogy between words and the Word."[16] Two German seventeenth-century philosophers, Böhme and Leibniz, did indeed develop such a theory of language as a manifestation of the Deity, viewing Hebrew as the language closest to that spoken in the Garden of Eden, but Taylor cannot be said to belong to their tradition, for he nowhere directly alludes to any kind of inherent relationship between language and the Divine Being except for quoting John 1:14, "The Word was made Flesh." Indeed, his practice indicates that, like Marino, he saw no special connection between words and metaphysics, but believed that the poet seeks to attain wonder, primarily through verbal effects that by their brilliance and novelty dazzle the reader's mind.

Kindred themes repeated consistently throughout Taylor's verses are the difficulties of poetic composition and his personal deficiencies as a writer of verse. These themes are united in a "Prologue" in which he asks whether a mere "Crumb of Dust" may have the power to outshine the earth, the mountains, and the sky by means of poetic creation. He then identifies himself as this crumb of dust and admits the dullness of his fancy, but concludes in a submerged proud conceit that if granted divine inspiration he could make the Lord's works shine like flowers or precious jewels. The phrase "Crumb of Dust" has been seen as a link between Taylor and George Herbert, who also uses the metaphor, but it could equally illustrate resemblance to any number of French and Spanish writers in the biblical tradition, who refer to man as *"poca tierra"* or *"dépouille de bou."*

In various poems, Taylor speaks about the inadequacy

---

[16] William J. Scheick, *The Will and the Word* (Athens, Ga., 1974), p. 103.

EDWARD TAYLOR

of "Quaint Metaphors" in general and terms his own "Quaintest Metaphors" as better fitted to criticize his own shortcomings than to praise God [25, 37]. His "tatter'd Fancy" and "Ragged Rymes," he affirms "Teeme leaden Metaphors" [233] which "are but dull Tacklings tag'd / With ragged Non-Sense" [149]. On other occasions, however, he seems content with his "sparkling Metaphors" [146] and admits the possibility of "Rich Metaphors" [267]. In one of these "rich" metaphors, he compares the travail of composing under divine inspiration to the agonies of a victim in a torture chamber being put to the question [51]. Sor Juana also treats the mental torments of the poet by comparing wit to fire, which the more matter it consumes, the more it flares up.[17] In lines which might be compared to Góngora's for their ambiguity, Taylor proposes,

> . . . Glory as a Metaphor, Il 'tende
> And lay it all on thee, my Lord!
> [262]

His meaning can be discerned only by the aid of a further poem in which he portrays a metaphor as a medium of communicating sensual as well as intellectual stimuli. Here he describes the glories of nature as themselves being a metaphor for God. In other words, he uses the word "metaphor" as itself a metaphor.

> . . . Lord . . . thou dost use
> This Metaphor to make thyself appeare.
> [263]

Superficially these lines seem to support the hypothesis that Taylor believed that language is inherently connected with divinity, but he is actually saying that the glories of

---

[17] *Obras escogidas*, ed. Juan Carlos Merlo (Barcelona, 1968), p. 111.

nature, not metaphor or any other aspect of language, reveal the Divine Presence.

In his commentary on the biblical verse, "The Word was made Flesh," he affirms,

> The Orator from Rhetorick gardens picks
> His Spangld Flowers of sweet-breathed Eloquence.

And in extending the metaphor, he suggests that the flowers are converted into earrings, the identical coupling of flowers with precious jewels that he introduced in his prologue. This blending of the animate and the inanimate and giving equal emphasis to the beauty of art and that of nature is also one of the chief characteristics of the style of both Góngora and Marino. Góngora, for example, devotes an entire stanza to a description of Dawn scattering red roses over a woman, embodying a carefully contrived balance between art and nature. He wonders whether snowy crimson or scarlet snow suits her best, suggests that the Abyssinian pearl enters into competition with her natural beauty, and portrays Cupid, whose anger is aroused by the presumption of the pearl, as condemning it for its brilliance and sentencing it to hang in gold from the mother-of-pearl of the woman's ear.[18] In a single one of his sonnets, Góngora introduces ivory, marble, ebony, amber, gold, silver, crystal, pearl, sapphire, and ruby. Equally significant in Marino, as we have already seen, is the basing of metaphors upon gems and precious metals, particularly "ruby, pearl, amber, sapphire, crystal, silver and gold."[19]

Taylor's favorite jewels are pearl, jasper, ruby, diamond (which he usually names carbuncle), and emerald (which he also names smaragdine). Pearl appears most frequently because of its biblical meanings of wisdom and experi-

[18] Lowry Nelson, *Baroque Lyric Poetry* (New Haven, 1963), p. 186.
[19] Mirollo, *Poet of the Marvelous*, p. 153.

ence, and other theological associations. Taylor uses the pearl as a symbol for Christ, grace, and life. In addition to specifying particular gems, Taylor employs general terms such as "precious stones" and "rich jewels." He also alludes frequently to crystal, silver, and gold. In his various poems over sixty different objects are described as golden, including gutters, bread, feathers, anvils, and rivets. Perfumes and aromatic spices are frequently introduced to represent the qualities of luxury and splendor as well as to embody the exotic flavor of the Old Testament. In one of his meditations, Taylor portrays Christ's garden as comprising beds of flowers beset with pearl, opal, gold, and silver, another example of the play between animate and inanimate [194]. In a further poem using jasper, ruby, and sapphire to represent the divine perfection and resplendence, Taylor refers to Christ as "Grace's chiefe Flower pot." In a separate reference to Christ and his "Deare Spouse," the Christian Church, Christ is her Flower, and "she thy flower pot" [148]. Elsewhere Taylor calls upon Christ, "Be thou my Flowers, I'le be thy Flower Pot" [15].

The use of carnal metaphors in a religious context represents another major link between Taylor and Marino. The latter, for example, describes the mouth of Mary Magdalen as the dwelling place of nectar between vivid pearls and fervid rubies and of pungent thorns in the midst of vermilion and odorous roses.[20] Innumerable parallels may be discerned in Taylor. His theological subject matter is based on analogies between the physical and the spiritual worlds. The largest part of his published work consists of over two hundred poetic *Meditations* on the Lord's Supper, and almost a quarter of these are based on passages from the Song of Solomon. The theology of the Lord's Supper obviously rests upon the metaphor of bread and wine as flesh and blood, and the Song of Solomon is in-

[20] Ibid., p. 291.

terpreted in Calvinistic theology as a metaphorical representation of the Christian Church as the Bride of Christ. Taylor's poetry, which is also metaphorical rather than ideological, does not reveal his personal interpretation of the doctrine of the Lord's Supper, although he specifically rejects transubstantiation and consubstantiation, and one would assume that he accepted the Calvinist concept of merely spiritual transference. This knotty theological question is dealt with by Ursula Brumm, but Taylor's verse is too cryptic to make a complete resolution possible even for this fine scholar. According to Brumm, Taylor draws on the notion of types and antitypes to explain the sacrament. "He is able to account for Christ's flesh and blood being bread and wine by establishing a typological connection of them with manna and the Paschal lamb."[21]

Taylor calls upon his soul to "Purge out and Vomit by Repentance" all ill humors [269]. He terms the human veins of Christ golden gutters and golden pipes which pour forth nectar or red wine into crystal vessels (divine ordinances) with sapphire taps [21]. He drinks Christ's health in his own blood-wine [46] and even proposes to use Christ's blood as a writing fluid [182]. He portrays God's flesh as a feast laid out on a banquet table [22] and suggests that human blood runs through the veins of Christ to extinguish the fires of Hell [5]. The latter conceit is based upon the doctrine of mystical union with Christ, who has "Marri'de our Manhood, making it its Bride." Taylor also emblemizes Christ as a vine that produces a wine to make things clear in contrast to ordinary wine that makes people drunk [258]. In elaborating a verse from the Song of Solomon, he asks why Christ bestowing "his lovely Love" should, nevertheless, mask his face, "allowing not a kiss?"

[21] *American Thought and Religious Typology* (New Brunswick, N.J., 1970), p. 75.

[254]. He also portrays Christ hugging him within his bosom [73], and asks his body

> Why hast thou done so ill
> To Court, and kiss my Soule, yet kissing kill?

This is very close to a paradox in one of Marino's erotic poems, "The Song of the Kisses" in which kissing, by depriving the poet of life, revives him.

> Quel bacio, che mi priva
> Di vita, mi raviva.

A good deal of Taylor's imagery is coarse and crude in the extreme, as in the above references to purging and vomiting. Elsewhere he refers to his "Members Dung-Carts that bedung at pleasure" [73], "Puddle Water Boyld by Sunn beams" [77], and "drops dropt in a Closestool pan" [78]. He lists loathsome diseases, including "Bad Stomach, Iliak, Colick Fever, . . . Scurvy, Dropsy, Gout, and Leprosy. . . . Itch, Botch Scab" [206]. Vocabulary such as this is not completely alien to Anglo-Saxon literature of Taylor's century, as witness Thomas Coryate's *Crudities* (1611), but it is not to be found in the English metaphysical poets, not even in Donne. There is none of it in Marino although parallels are to be found in Góngora and Sor Juana Inés de la Cruz. Góngora describes a native of Esgueva drinking that which has been emptied into the river from the toilet Cabinet "according to the laws of digestion,"[22] and Sor Juana ends single lines of a group of five burlesque sonnets with words describing biological functions, for example, offal [*caca*], coitional pleasure [*refocilo, regodeo, regüilo*], and bad breath [*tufo*], fine illustrations of the preciosity of grossness.[23]

Taylor goes further than any of his contemporaries in phallic and other sexual imagery. In reference to the erotic

---

[22] "Letrilla" No. 4, f. 68. *Obras en verso del Homero español, 1627*, facsimile edition (Madrid, 1963), folio 68.

[23] Picón-Salas, *De la conquista*, p. 106.

element in life, he asks his soul why it dwells in such "sensual Organs" which make it stray from its "noble end" [430]. Then he pursues the subject

> My nobler part, why dost thou laquy to
> The Carnal Whynings of my senses so.

"Nobler part" is a pun on high ideals and the male organ. In his most daring image, he describes the phallus of God as "thy royall Pipe" [88]. In one of his longer poems, "A Fig for Thee Oh! Death," he works out an elaborate sexual analogy describing his body as "my vile harlot" and "my strumpet" and looking forward to the General Resurrection when "The Soule and Body now, as two true Lovers / Every night . . . do hug and kiss each other." Although his body has sought to seduce him into sin, Taylor never has "Surprised been nor tumbled in such grave." This means in a general sense that he has never been victim to sensuality, but it also refers to tumbling as a sexual activity. A similar double meaning exists in the subsequent line, "Hence for my strumpet I'le ne'er draw my Sword." The sword has both theological and phallic connotations. Subsequently Taylor challenges Death to capture and rape the body (portrayed as a woman) "And grinde [her] to power in thy Mill the grave."[24]

Taylor's most distinctive feature, one that separates him from the English metaphysical poets, is the vast number of his deliberate innovations in language. He invents new words, resurrects obsolete ones, interweaves dialect and standard forms, and interchanges parts of speech. Al-

---

[24] This sexual imagery has been brought to light by Thomas M. Davies and Arthur Forslater in "Edward Taylor's 'A Fig for Thee Oh! Death,' " in *Discoveries & Considerations*, ed. Calvin Israel, pp. 67-77. They go too far, however, in interpreting the last line of the poem, "I still am where I was, a Fig for thee," as equivalent to making the sign of the *fica*, the thumb between two closed fingers. Although I am alert to all evidence of transatlantic relationships, I doubt that Taylor meant to suggest this Italian gesture. In my opinion, he was using *fig* merely in the biblical sense of the unproductive life.

though these linguistic techniques are typical of the baroque style, they are also associated with burlesque poetry, which flourished in England and on the continent during the sixteenth and seventeenth centuries, particularly in travesties of the classics. They are obvious adornments, moreover, of Samuel Butler's now neglected comic masterpiece *Hudibras* (1663). Taylor, however, has much more in common with Góngora, whose characteristic vocabulary has been extensively analyzed by Spanish critics. They have noted particularly neologisms, archaisms, erudite terms, vulgarisms, slang, colloquialisms, and foreign words. Góngora describes his verse style as "learned although bucolic" [culta sí, aunque bucólica],[25] a description that has equal application to Taylor's. Typical of Taylor are such colloquial expressions as Kerfe [99], saddlebackt [134], puking [137], fuddled [149], bedotcht [149], tittletattle [150], Bloomery [159], thrum [179], and muck [8]; such pedantic or esoteric ones as osculated [95], Conjues [157], Quintessenced [172], evigorate [177], Visive [203], Dicotomy [400], Secundine [448], facete [478], and verbous [478]; and such exotic ones as Spicknard [22], Citterns [135], Al-tashcketh Mictam [152], and Garzia Horti [12].

During the seventeenth century, esoteric and abstruse terms were commonly known as "hard words," Butler, for example ridiculing them as

> Words so debas'd and hard, no stone
> Was hard enough to touch them on.
> [*Hudibras*, Part I, Canto i.]

Sylvester's translation of Du Bartas conveniently supplied "An Index of the Hardest Words" or a "briefe explanation of most of the most-difficulties through the whole worke." If Taylor's poetry had been published early in the seven-

[25] "Al excelentisimo Señor Conde de Niebla," dedicatory poem to *Polifemo*, in *Obras en verso del Homero español*, folio 113.

teenth century, his learned and exotic vocabulary would have been considered as a fashionable display of hard words and accepted by the reading public in about the same way in which it viewed the pedantic affectations of the French *précieux*. A modern critic must, therefore, exercise considerable caution in attempting to determine how much of Taylor's strange diction should be interpreted as individual idiosyncrasy and how much as merely conforming to a literary convention—outmoded though the convention may have been while Taylor was writing.

One type of colloquial language to be found in Góngora is the proverb or folk saying in such forms as the following:

> Como estaba flaco,
> parecía cencerro.
> > [f 109][26]
>
> cantaba mis aleluyas
> > [f 105]
>
> pues conoce un galgo
> entre cien gallinas
> > [f 106]
>
> La vida es corta, y la esperança larga,
> > [f 86]
>
> Que se nos va la Pascua, mozas, que se nos va la Pascua.
> > [f 110]

One finds in Taylor a correspondingly large variety of popular idioms:

[26] The citation in brackets refers to a folio page (either recto or verso) in the facsimile edition of *Obras en verso del Homero español*. The same system of citation will be used in subsequent references to this work.

EDWARD TAYLOR

> a Bird in hand
> [21]
>
> full as is an Egg of meate
> [40]
>
> Out of the Frying Pan
> [482]
>
> Beggar upon horseback
> [394]
>
> Whosoever trust doth to his golden deed
> Doth rob a barren Garden for a Weed.
> [396][27]

Another trait of Taylor's verse which closely resembles that of Góngora is the extensive use of hyperbate or inversion. As previously indicated, Spanish critics are particularly attentive to this element in Góngora, and most consider it a blemish. A single example will suffice,

> Nuevos conoce oy día
> Troncos el bosque i piedras la montaña.[28]

Literally translated, this means: "New knows today / Trunks the thicket and stones the mountain"; the normal word order would, of course, be, "The thicket knows new trunks today; the mountain, stones." In English poetry, little attention is ordinarily paid to inversion, perhaps because of the influence of Milton, who used it exten-

---

[27] Benjamin Franklin remembered so well the latter "good old verse" in popular speech that he teased his sister by means of a mildly scatological paraphrase,
> A man of deeds and not of words
> Is like a garden full of . . .
Papers of Benjamin Franklin, ed. Leonard W. Labaree et al. (New Haven, 1965), 8: 155.

[28] Elisha Kent Kane, *Gongorism and the Golden Age* (Chapel Hill, N.C., 1928), p. 75.

sively both in *Paradise Lost* and in his sonnets. Inversion is coupled with syntactical confusion in the following typical lines by Taylor.

I kening through Astronomy Divine
  The Worlds bright Battlement, wherein I spy
A Golden Path my Pensill cannot line,
  From that bright Throne unto my Threshold ly.

Although the meaning of these lines cannot be completely unraveled, the normal word order would be the following: "I [am] kening through the world's bright battlement, divine astronomy, wherein I spy a golden path ly[ing] from that bright throne unto my threshold, [which] my pencil cannot line." This passage illustrates another characteristic of Taylor's poetry, its obscurity. Recondite metaphors such as "the World's bright Battlement" are common in Góngora, where they are classified according to formal rhetoric as catachresis. They also are in large measure responsible for the labeling of his poetry as cultist or intelligible only to the elite.

The only innovation in language developed by Góngora that Taylor does not also practice is the introduction of foreign words. Taylor favors colloquialisms, archaisms, and unusual forms of standard words, but only sparingly interjects Greek and Latin phrases. Among Anglo-Saxon poets, Butler in *Hudibras* excels in adapting foreign words to English, but the best single example of a parallel to Góngora's multilingual proclivities among contemporary English poets is the last four lines of Donne's "Upon Mr. Thomas Coryat's Crudities," which contains Latin, Old French, modern French, Spanish, and Italian and is printed in Black Letter as well as ordinary type. It may be compared to a sonnet of Góngora's utilizing Spanish, Latin, Italian, and Portuguese, and to a much earlier English poem of twenty-one lines by John Skelton, "Speke Parrot," containing phrases in Latin, Greek, French, Italian, and Dutch as well as English.

Taylor shares another essential element of Gongorism, a fondness for extravagant conceits. The Spanish poet typically makes comparisons or draws analogies between disparate objects and brings the pure, the noble, and the refined into contact with the base, the vulgar, and the crude. As a result, his conceits are often labeled grotesque, bizarre, or ludicrous.

Taylor's method is exactly the same, and most of his conceits are just as far-fetched. Whereas Góngora describes a cliff as urinating,[29] Taylor tells his readers that "the heavens in rain shed / Their Excrements upon our lofty heads" [471]. Taylor describes himself as God's "well-tuned instrument" [11], as a coin "new minted" by God's stamp [16], and as a sundial reflecting God's sunshine [140]. In a single poem, he compares himself to a bran, a chaff, a grain of barley, a husk, a shell, a thistle, a briar prickle, a thorn, a lump of lewdness, a pouch of sin, and a purse of naughtiness; he also compares his heart to a park and his head to a bowling alley [111]. He suggests that God is a coconut the size of the earth and then retracts the comparison as debasing [140], in effect convicting himself of false wit.

One of the elements in Góngora's style most difficult to define is that of word arrangement—the use of a variety of verbal tricks designed to amuse or to astonish. One of his sacred poems begins with the nursery rhyme:

A la dina dana dina, la dina dana
[f. 74]

In a sonnet composed of a single sentence, he uses the interrogative *qual* eleven times in seven lines [f. 16]. In

---

[29] Ibid., p. 79.

another he associates the similar sounds of *libros* and *libres* and the forms *passo* and *paseo*. "Con pocos libros libres . . . / . . . passo, y me paseo" [f. 26]. In like manner, he couples *con grasa buena* and *con buen gracia* [f. 26].

Taylor's word games are similar, but not identical. He plays, for example, on "form" in the couplet,

> Thou dost it Form, Inform, Reform, and Try
> Conform to thee, marre her Deformity.
>
> [150]

In four stanzas of one poem he uses some form of the word *crown* twelve times [70-71]. In six lines from another poem he combines repetition with punning [448].

> The'Uncharitable Soul oft thus reflects,
>   After each Birth a second birth doth Come.
> Your Second Birth no Second Birth ejects,
>   The Babe of Grace then's strangld in the Womb.
> There's no new Birth born in thy Soul thou'lt find
> If that the after Birth abide behinde.

Taylor plays elsewhere with "mite" and "might," using some form of the homonym thirty-seven times [167-69]. In another segment of fifteen lines, he uses some form of the verb "do" twenty-two times [147]. I could cite innumerable other examples. Taylor was obviously conscious of the artificiality of these verbal effects, once referring to his poetry as "Acrostick Rhimes" [473].

Other easily recognizable rhetorical devices in Taylor's style are hyperbole, oxymoron, pun, alliteration, and the chiasmus. These techniques can be found in several literary periods or styles, but they are so widespread in seventeenth-century verse that they have come to be associated with the baroque, particularly when two or three of them together appear in the same poem.

Góngora, in a hyperbole, states that a nightingale sings

with such force that the sound of a hundred thousand birds issues from her throat ("que tiene otros cien mil dentro del pecho" [Soneto LXIX]). Taylor has the same hyperbole, but draws it out over thirty lines. In treating the inadequacy of human praise of God, he imagines the entire world broken up into its constituent atoms, then each atom as a world populated by as many men as the world can hold, and finally each of these men praising God with as many tongues as there are men in the world [451-52]. In another place, he affirms that the glory of Christ's apparel darkens by contrast "Ten thousand suns at once ten thousand wayes" [24]. This type of contrast Sor Juana treats in one of her poems as in itself a rhetorical device. Things are seen better by means of their extreme opposites, she maintains, and whiteness shines more brightly when placed next to blackness.

> Las cosas se ven mejor
> por sus contrarios extremos,
> y lo blanco luce más,
> si se pone junto al negro.[30]

Naturally this doctrine of contraries is applied pragmatically throughout Sor Juana's works. There are many instances in Taylor as well. Christ's glory, for example, makes a shine that benights the sun [25], and the "glory seen, to that unseen's a Smut" [21].

Oxymoron, or the juxtaposing of opposites, another way of presenting contraries, is illustrated in Góngora by the phrase "rhetoric of silence" ("*retórico silencio*" [1. 259, *Polifemo*]) and in Marino by "loquacious silence" ("*silenzio loquace*" [*Poesie varie*, p. 135]).[31] Taylor speaks of "Fireless Flame" and "Chilly Love" [5] and declares, "Hell

---

[30] *Obras escogidas*, p. 120.
[31] Mirollo, *Poet of the Marvelous*, p. 136.

Heaven is, Heaven hell, yea Bitter Sweet" [50]. The lowly pun appears in various poems by Góngora, including one on money in which he brings out the second meaning of each of the following coins: *cruzados* (crosses), *escudos* (nobles), *dados* (earls), *ducados* (dukes) and *coronas* (crowns).[32] Taylor represents Christ saying "Fight not for prey, but Pray and Fight" [405]. In a funeral elegy for a minister named Hooker, he writes, "That thou callst home thy Hooker with his Hook" [482].

Alliteration is so common in all baroque poets that a single line will serve as illustration, one from Sor Juana Inés de la Cruz, "que a cada cual tocarle considera."[33] In Taylor, we find "The Girths of Griefe alone / Do gird my heart till Gust of Sorrows groan" [472]. As well as:

What shall Mote up to a Monarch rise?
An Emmet match an Emperor in might?
[252]

The chiasmus is a structural device used sparingly by Góngora, moderately by Marino, and lavishly by Sor Juana Inés de la Cruz. Twelve of the fourteen lines of one of her sonnets, for example, contain a chiasmus, and in another the chiasmus is present in ten out of fourteen.[34] The intellectual crossing from one word to another which is called chiasmus may take place in a single line, but it more frequently occurs in two consecutive lines. Both types are illustrated in a single poem by Sor Juana.

Amo a Dios y siento en Dios;
[I love God and feel well in God]
que si son penas las culpas
que no sean culpas las penas

[32] Kane, *Gongorism*, p. 78.
[33] *Obras escogidas*, p. 271.
[34] Ibid., pp. 190-91.

> [That if the penalties are sins
> That the sins are not penalties][35]

In the single line, *amo* crosses with *siento* and *Dios* with *Dios*. In the doublet, *penas* crosses with *penas* and *culpas* with *culpas*. Another of Sor Juana's single lines has a striking resemblance to one of Taylor's, not only in the use of the chiasmus, but also in its concept.

> muerto a la vida y a la muerte vivo[36]

> [I am dead toward life and toward death I live]

Taylor expresses it as

> A Dying Life, and Living Death by
> Sin.
> > [390]

Since Taylor's lines are regularly longer than Sor Juana's, his crossings are less compressed.

> Oh! that thou wast on Earth below with mee!
> Or that I was in Heaven above with thee.
> > [10]

> Such as are Gracious grow in Grace therefore
> Such as have Grace, are Gracious evermore.
> > [438]

> Thy Grace will Grace unto a Poem bee
> Although a Poem be no grace to thee.
> > [473]

The only one of all the major characteristics uniting Marino, Góngora, and Sor Juana Inés de la Cruz that Taylor does not share is that of constant allusion to the literary traditions of Greek and Latin antiquity. All three of

[35] Ibid., pp. 131-32.
[36] Ibid., p. 270.

Taylor's forerunners were immersed in the classics, and their works incorporate on almost every page either a verbal echo of some celebrated passage or some reference to the ancients, whether to an author, literary personage, or mythological situation. Even though Taylor was a "learned man who kept his Theocritus and Origen, his Augustine and Horace, with him in the wilderness,"[37] he makes no effort to display this classical background in his poetry. Out of thousands of lines of verse, one may discover hardly a dozen classical allusions, and these are the most rudimentary such as "Mercury" [207], "promethius' filching" [226], "Pandora's box" [226], and "Sapphick Slippers" [488].

Submerged under the surface of Taylor's verse, however, exists a classical mode that he shares with Marino and Góngora, that of the pastoral. Marino's most important poem *Adone* is an idyllic treatment of the myth of Adonis, and one of his most delightful short works is *La Pastorella* [*The Shepherdess*], both a pastoral and an erotic masterpiece. Góngora describes his most popular work *Polifemo*, which treats the love between the shepherd Acis and the nymph Galatea, as bucolic rhymes sung to the sound of a rustic flute [stanza 1]. Taylor similarly describes his *Meditations* in terms of the pastoral, but his symbols are those of the Hebrew Old Testament rather

[37] *Poems*, ed. Stanford, p. xviii. A manuscript translation of the Daedalus-Icarus story in Ovid's *Art of Love* written about 1700 has recently been attributed to Taylor. Mukhtar Ali Isari, "Edward Taylor and Ovid's *Art of Love*: The Text of a Newly-Discovered Manuscript," *Early American Literature* 10 (1975): 67-74. If indeed from his hand, this fragment not only reveals a connection between Taylor's poetic vocation and the Latin classics, but also indicates that his earliest experiments were in the neoclassical vein. The diction of this translation has more resemblance to Dryden's *Virgil* or Pope's *Homer* than to the devotional works of Herbert or Crashaw. In other words, Taylor seems anachronistically to have explored the neoclassical vein before specializing in the baroque.

EDWARD TAYLOR

than those of Theocritus and Virgil. He accompanies himself on a harp, described in one poem as "brassy wire" and "jews trump" [177], and in another as "my Shoshannim's sweetest Well tun'de string" [209]. He calls upon God to "blow this Oaten Straw of mine" [162], and apologizes, in the tradition of scores of other literary shepherds, for his "unskilfull ditty" "piped through my sorry quill" [175].

Certain other differences may be noted between Taylor and his Italian and Hispanic predecessors. Taylor sets forth his various tropes in rapid succession, producing a kind of cornucopia effect; whereas Marino and Góngora intersperse their conceits between passages of narrative or description. The conceits of Marino and Góngora are rich and subtle, the most sophisticated of which are double in the sense of combining linguistically almost incompatible elements, a process that one of Marino's contemporaries described as a "supermarvelous" product of human wit.[38] An example from Marino cited by James Mirollo is *Donna che cuce*, literally "woman who sews," which refers in its context to the beams of contact between a woman's eyes and her lover; the doubling consists in converting the sight beams to a thread that binds the two together.[39] Essentially the same figure may be noticed in Donne's well-known "The Ecstasy":

> Our eye-beames twisted, and did thread
> Our eyes upon one double string.

Milton, in one of his Italian sonnets, "Diodati, e te'l diro," develops a similar metaphor, portraying the fire that darts from the eyes of his mistress as so powerful that filling his ears with wax has little efficacy in blunting the effect.

[38] E. Tesauro, *Il Cannocchiale Aristotelico* (Torino, 1670), p. 446.
[39] *Poet of the Marvelous*, p. 155.

> E dagli occhi suoi avventa si'gran fuoco,
> Che l'incernar gli orecchi mi fia poco.

The doubling here consists in transferring the sensation of sight to hearing. The same process takes place in a phrase of merely two words in Milton's *Lycidas*, "Blind mouths" [l. 118]. An English scholar, M. J. Woods, gives a number of examples from Góngora of the transference from one element to another.[40] "Winds of crystal" refers to showers of water; "a Libya of waves" portrays the ocean in terms of desert sands; "feathery fishing" represents falconry; and "nautical venery" describes girls engaged in hunting seals, the latter metaphor incorporating in addition a play on the two senses of venery—hunting and sexual desire. Taylor's metaphors, in contrast, are for the most part single-edged rather than double, and his conceits rarely involve intricate patterns of antithesis and paradox such as are found in Marino, Góngora, and Sor Juana. As Austin Warren has said in another context, the humbler ingenuities were what the New Englanders could reproduce.[41]

Taylor's eighth meditation, which Warren considers one of his best, has an example of multiple meanings, although not metaphorical doubling. Here Taylor compares his soul to a bird of paradise that has been put into a wicker cage, his body, and suggests that the bird also represents Adam in the cage of the Garden of Eden. This metaphor might be considered a double one only if the bird of paradise were taken in the Renaissance sense as a representation of Venus or carnal love. There is no reason for assuming that Taylor intended this connection, but if he did, the

[40] *The Poet and the Natural World in the Age of Góngora*, pp. 124-27.

[41] *Rage for Order*, p. 5.

metaphor could be taken also as a major baroque symbol in which the peacock represents ostentatious profusion.[42]

Taylor should certainly not be considered to be a poet of ideas, even though he makes considerable intellectual demands upon his readers. His *Determinations* touches upon a few basic points of theology and doctrine, but his *Meditations* consists primarily of word play, sensuous description, and emotion. The debate which various critics have carried on over the relative merits of the *Determinations* and the *Meditations* depends largely on whether the function of poetry is to convey meaning, which would place the *Determinations* ahead, or to dazzle by verbal effects, which would give the preference to the *Meditations*. Although individual poems in both collections involve a complex theology, Taylor never treats ideas systematically, but at most implies them or introduces them in fragments. The following typical lines, for example, are said to delineate the concept of the Great Chain of Being.[43]

> Life Vegetative now hatcht in the Egge,
>   Flourishing some things nobler than the rest.
> Life sensitive gives some of these its Head,
>   Inspiring them with honour next the best.
>   And some of which Life Rationall Enfires,
>   Cloathd with a Spiritualizing Life, aspires.
>
> This Life thy Fingers freely dropt into
>   The Humane shaped Elements and made
> The same Excell the Rest and nobler goe
>   Enspirited with Heavenizing trade.
>   [*Meditations* 2.89. 13-22]

---

[42] A Swiss scholar, Jean Rousset, argues that the two major symbols of the French baroque are Circe and the peacock, representing respectively metamorphosis and ostentation or "domination du décor." *La Littérature de l'âge baroque en France. Circé et le paon* (Paris, 1954).

[43] Scheick, *The Will and the Word*, pp. 13-14.

Glory lin'de out a Paradise in Power
    Where e'ry seed a Royall Coach became
For Life to ride in, to each shining Flower.
    And made mans Flower with glory all ore flame
                            [*Meditations* 1.33 19-22]

These lines indubitably depict four stages of existence,
the vegetative, the sensitive, the rational, and the spiritual, but they do not imply that the four are related to each
other in any kind of hierarchical system. They are taken
from two unconnected poems and do not portray the notions of gradation, continuity, and plenitude that represent the essence of the doctrine of the Chain of Being as
set forth by A. O. Lovejoy and found in such poetic rep-
resentations as Alexander Pope's *An Essay on Man*.

One of the few extended ideological passages in Taylor's
works appears in a funeral elegy on his wife. The second
of its three parts takes up the question of whether true
grief may be expressed through the artificiality of meas-
ured verses and whether poetry is an appropriate medium
for the display of such grief, a theme common to other
elegies, including Tennyson's *In Memoriam*. On the neg-
ative side, Taylor suggests that work and music suit each
other better than do sorrow and music, that deep emotion
cannot be expressed in contrived verbal patterns ("Frisk
in Acrostick Rimes"), that ostentation of grief reduces its
sincerity ("Break a salt tear to pieces as it drops"), that
David's lamentation for Jonathan had provoked no poetic
display, and that many heads of state are buried without
poetic tributes. He observes, on the other side, that his
duty requires him to memorialize his wife's virtues, that
otherwise her progeny will remain ignorant of her excellence, that the enumeration of her qualities will lend distinction to his poem, that she may in heaven learn of his
poem and derive pleasure from it, and that the act of

writing may help to assuage his deep sorrow. This poem is notable also for three paradoxes, rhetorical devices that are elsewhere rare in Taylor's poetry. Death is ordinarily considered as the untying of the knot of true love, but Taylor finds his love increased: "Oh strange Untying! it ti'th harder." He is reconciled to his wife's passing since he expects that she will join the Lord in heaven: "thou tookst her into thine / Out of my bosom, yet she dwells in mine." His wife contributes to his poem although it does nothing for her: "Thy Grace will Grace unto a Poem be / Although a Poem be no grace to thee."

In subject matter, Taylor's lament for his deceased wife resembles Sor Juana's portrayal of the grief of a wife for her departed husband, which we have commented upon in the preceding chapter. Paradoxically the tone of neither poem conforms to its rhetorical devices. Sor Juana's diction is restrained, apart from a series of extreme hyperboles, but she, nevertheless, gives rein to her emotions or to what she calls "the rhetoric of tears."[44] Taylor's poem, on the other hand, is a melange of conceit, paradox, alliteration, chiasmus, hyperbole, and bizarre vocabulary; yet his feelings are held in check. Sor Juana communicates bitterness and inconsolable grief; Taylor, Christian resignation.

It has been said that poetry like Taylor's could not have been written in England because the cultural milieu of that intimate island would impose itself upon the artist's creativeness, thus stifling his individuality. Taylor's poems, according to this view, could have been produced only in a frontier wilderness where no curbs existed on the poet's imagination. It would seem to the contrary, however, that the baroque elements of Taylor's style which we have been examining are the products of an artificial society, no matter what the conditions of the poet's daily life.

[44] Picón-Salas, *De la conquista*, p. 120.

Taylor's poetry, moreover, is just as barren of allusions to things typically American as is Bradstreet's. The qualities that make his verse seem un-English are primarily the exotic ones derived from the Old Testament—such elements as an alien vocabulary (for instance, smaragdine for emerald, carbuncle for diamond) and references to the birds and rare products of the East. There is an English poet also embodying these qualities who resembles Taylor strongly, but he is not Herbert, Crashaw, or any other of the metaphysicals, but a product of the eighteenth century—the partly mad Christopher Smart, whose highly sensuous *Song of David* (1763) draws on many of the exotic biblical images and symbols that are typical of Taylor.

Both Smart and Taylor were anachronistic. Smart's poetry found its way into print because he lived in the second half of the eighteenth century, when various precursors of romantic attitudes made other deviations from neoclassical standards acceptable. Taylor, however, was writing in the age of Pope and Swift when Herbert was ridiculed and even Donne looked down upon. Since his poems were conceived in New England, an environment in which the baroque had not only never flourished, but had come to be regarded with hostility, it is not strange that his verse had to wait until the twentieth century for its initial printing. In German literature, anachronistically delayed writers in the baroque style are sometimes classified under the rubric late or high baroque, but such terms would make no sense in reference to Taylor since the baroque presence in North America is not extensive enough to justify chronological subdivisions.

The literary career of Sor Juana Inés de la Cruz helps explain the fortunes or misfortunes of Taylor. He was born a few years prior to Sor Juana near the midpoint of the seventeenth century, but survived her for more than thirty years into the second quarter of the eighteenth. This chronology is significant when considered in relation to publishing history. Sor Juana's poems were written and published while the taste for linguistic exuberance was still fashionable in her literary milieu. There were nineteen editions of her works under various titles between 1689 and 1725, but not a single one after 1725 until 1865, almost a century and a half later. During the period prior to 1725, Sor Juana was more widely read than any other poet of Spain or Spanish America,[45] but the penetration of neoclassicism and French critical standards into Hispanic culture during the eighteenth century brought her style of poetry into disfavor and caused her works to be almost completely forgotten. Neoclassicism arrived much earlier in England—concomitant with the Restoration in 1660—and as a result Taylor's poems were out of date before they were written. Early in the twentieth century a myth arose that Taylor had given instructions in his will forbidding the publication of his poetry, and a critical debate ensued concerning the nature of his motives for doing so. One of the most imaginative embroideries on the topic appeared in a thick book published as late as 1977, ornately, but falsely, informing its readers of the "pastor-physician of the frontier village of Westfield having left orders with his heirs that his four hundred pages of poetry not be published, lest their rich, sensuous warmth corrupt his brethren or his own reputation."[46] Some myths die hard or never. A clear-headed scholar has investigated the source of the myth and discovered that no will exists which mentions Taylor's poetry.[47] It would seem, therefore, that the only reason why Taylor's works remained in manuscript is the same that explains why Sor Juana's

---

[45] *Obras escogidas*, p. 63.

[46] Arthur Bernon Tourtellot, *Benjamin Franklin The Shaping of Genius* (Garden City, N.Y., 1977), p. 306.

[47] Francis Murphy, "Edward Taylor's Attitude toward Publication: A Question concerning Authority," *American Literature* 34 (1962): 393-94.

fell into obscurity after 1725—that they were completely
alien to prevailing neoclassical standards and consequently had no appeal in the marketplace. When Taylor's
works were finally published and hailed in the twentieth
century, it was because the baroque had by then gained
new understanding and a new generation of adherents.[48]

[48] The latest development in the study of comparative literature consists in showing relationships between works of the West [Europe and
America] and those of the East [Asia and Africa]. Convincing parallels
have been established between sartorial imagery or the "clothing conceit" in Taylor and similar rhetoric in Indian and Persian devotional
poetry. Mohan Lai Sharma, "Of Spinning, Weaving and Mystical Poetry:
The Fine Yarn of Taylor, Indian Yogis, and Persian Sufis," *Mahfil* 6
(1970): 51-61.

PART II

THEME
AND
IDEOLOGY

ONE OF THE MAJOR concerns of comparative literature is the tracing of themes in the thought, folklore, and imaginative literature of various nations, in the process of which both major and minor writers are taken into consideration. The two best known of the themes in Western literature derive from purely imaginary characters, Faust and Don Juan. Both of these are far more important to Latin American than to North American letters, perhaps because the story of Don Juan originated in Spain and is closely linked to that of Faust, each having at its core the problem of evil. North American literature touches on the Faust theme in the works of Increase Mather and his grandson Thomas Walter. The latter published a theological pamphlet in Boston in 1720, *A Choice Dialogue between John Faustus, a Conjurer, and Jack*

Tory, His Friend.[1] A century later Washington Irving introduced the Hispanic symbol of sexual exploitation in his sketch "Don Juan: A Spectral Research." The classical theme of the Golden Age was also transplanted to the New World. Adventurers such as Gonzalo Jiménez de Queseda and Sir Walter Raleigh located the utopian land of Eldorado in South America, and it later acquired universal recognition through Voltaire's ironical portrayal in *Candide*. William Byrd of Westover sought a "Land of Eden" and Thomas Morton of Merrymount a "New Canaan" in North America.

Purely North American themes that originated before 1800 include those featuring three heroines, embodying typically American virtues, Pocahontas, Polly Baker, and Jane McCrae. The dramatic episodes with which they are associated arose from the historical periods of exploration, colonization, and revolution respectively. Pocahontas and Jane McCrae were actual living figures, but Polly Baker, so far as can be determined, was a pure invention by Franklin, even though she eventually came to be accepted in both Europe and the United States as an actual historical personage.

The most widely known of the three heroines is Pocahontas, probably because her story has become part of the mythology regularly imparted to American schoolchildren. She is essentially the literary creation of Captain John Smith, one of the early explorers of the Virginia territory. In his early reports, he mentions Pocahontas only casually, and it was not until many years after his return to England that he portrayed her as his rescuer. According to his *Generall Historie of Virginia* (1624) he was captured by a group of Powhatan Indians while seeking food on a journey up the James River. After being exhibited to sev-

---

[1] André Dabezies, "The First American *Faust* (1720)," *Comparative Literature Studies* 8 (1971): 303-9.

eral camps of Indians over a period of several days, he was prepared for a ceremony of execution. Suddenly the daughter of the Indian chieftain emerged from the crowd of onlookers, took his "head in her armes and laid her owne upon his to save him from death" [*Historie*, 3: 46-49]. The original Pocahontas eventually married one of Smith's subordinates and was taken to London. As a literary legend, the story of her gallant rescue of Smith, apart from its intrinsic drama, served to vindicate the conquest of the Indians by portraying a native princess as the benefactor of an English adventurer.

The third of the three archetypes of feminine initiative, Jane McCrae, is the least known even though she is the only one whose story can be authenticated by contemporary documents. Her tragic tale figures in several English and American poems and in a French historical novel, *Mis Mac Rae*, by Hilliard d'Auberteuil, published in 1784. The author was an acquaintance of Franklin and fellow member of the Masonic lodge of the Seven Sisters in Paris. Jane McCrae also appears as Lucinda in Joel Barlow's *The Columbiad*. A Loyalist sympathizer during the American Revolution, she was engaged to be married to an American soldier fighting on the Loyalist side. En route to an army camp where the marriage ceremony was to be performed, she was abducted by a group of Indians, who shot and scalped her and then demanded payment for her scalp from the British General Burgoyne, who had offered a bounty on American scalps. The story of Jane McCrae made Burgoyne's policy seem inhuman and barbaric and was useful in stirring American patriotic sentiments against the enemy.

The stories of Pocahontas and Jane McCrae, however, lack the universal human elements and ideological overtones that have elevated the European themes of Faust and Don Juan to the preeminence that they have enjoyed for at least three centuries. Faust epitomizes the spirit of

Western man in his quest for knowledge, power, and technological prowess and Don Juan explores the fundamental problems involving the sexual nature of mankind. Both themes raise questions about the existence of God, the nature of good and evil, and the possibility of salvation or damnation. Franklin's apparently artless comic anecdote of the speech of Polly Baker does not invoke quite such an extensive range of philosophical problems and notions, but her simple narrative has important ramifications in theology and theories of human rights.

The transition from the study of themes to the study of the history of ideas is almost imperceptible. Ideologies, in contrast to separate ideas, represent combinations of notions that are joined together in a pattern or sequence leading to particular conclusions. The first person to go through the process is an original thinker; anyone who later repeats the same system is reflecting an ideology. Organized groups, or individuals in common with other individuals, may reflect ideologies, and there may even be personal ideologies or systems of belief held by single individuals.

During the eighteenth century, among the major concepts inspired by political developments there were two of particular consequence to the American colonies, those of natural rights and those of the state of nature. Both concepts were fundamental in the writings of Paine, Dickinson, and Franklin. Indeed, the speech of Polly Baker represents a combination discourse-apologue on the doctrine of natural rights. The earliest literary manifestation of the notion that the individual has rights that transcend the body politic appears in Sophocles' play *Antigone* in the fifth century B.C., in which Antigone defies Creon's edict forbidding the burial of her brother. Her justification of her action may be interpreted as either a vindication of the law of nature over positive law or as a placing of a moral imperative over obedience to the civil power. Polly

Baker's defense of her breaking the laws against adultery may be interpreted in exactly the same manner, and as a person she may be compared to Antigone as an exponent of human rights and, secondarily, women's rights.

One of the major Enlightenment statements of the doctrine of human rights was that of Diderot in the article "Natural Law" of the *Encyclopédie*. In essence, according to Diderot, "You have the most sacred *natural right* to everything which is not challenged by the entire race. . . . Everything which you shall conceive, everything which you shall meditate, will be good, great, elevated and sublime if it is to the general and common interest." In the key passage of the article, Diderot exhorts his readers: "Say to yourselves often, I am a human being, and I have no other *natural rights* truly inalienable except those of humanity." The importance of Diderot's argument is that he defines rights in terms of humanity, establishing their human, not divine, origins. The weakness of his argument is that the notion of a general will upon which rights are supposed to depend is an abstraction of little value to the average man. Diderot's affirmation, moreover, is severely limited to merely generic rights (those belonging to all humanity in the aggregate). Paine later attempted to transcend these limitations. He not only defined rights in concrete terms, but also distinguished between civil and individual rights. In contrast to Diderot, he not only stressed those rights belonging to single persons, but maintained that the rights of physical liberty and liberty of conscience are held immediately from God rather than being granted by a human leader or even acknowledged by common assent.

Throughout the eighteenth century, many theorists had speculated about a period in the history of mankind known as the state of nature, a period before the institution of social life. Classical literature, by means of the pastoral idyll and the legend of the Golden Age, had celebrated the age of innocence when man lived close to nature, eating nuts and drinking pure water, sharing all things in common, and knowing neither anger nor war. The notion was revived in the eighteenth century and applied to political theory by various European writers, including Rousseau. In their theories, the crucial moment was when man left the state of nature for organized relationships. According to Rousseau's *Discours sur l'origine et les fondements de l'inégalité* (1755), the period just at the brink of entering society, that period "of the development of human faculties, maintaining a golden mean between the indolence of the primitive state and the petulant activity of our vanity," must have been "the happiest and most durable epoch" of human existence. Rousseau does not make clear whether in the transition from the state of nature to society the process involves the domination of a leader or whether the social order is decided by an agreement among equals. Paine does not refer to the state of nature, but he uses another expression for the same concept, the "state of natural liberty." He opens *Common Sense* with the complaint that "some writers have so confounded government with society as to leave little or no distinction between them." In addition to characterizing society as good and government as bad, he suggests that the earliest societies were formed by the association of equals.

Writers who cherished nostalgic feelings for the lost state of nature were likely to accept a cluster of ideas now known as primitivism. Essentially this is the view that the earliest stage of human history was better than any following ones and that whatever developments have occurred after the state of nature have been pernicious. Linked with this view in art and literary criticism is the opinion that the earliest specimens of any artistic genre are the models for later ones and, therefore, superior to later productions. A passionate dispute over this opinion developed in the Renaissance and flared up again in the eighteenth century. Those who maintained the preeminence of past traditions were designated symbolically as the ancients, in contrast to the defenders of the present known as the moderns. The main arguments on both sides were reproduced in the Western Hemisphere in discussions on the nature of epic poetry and on the truth of the doctrine of progress. A closely related theme of even more venerable lineage is that of *translatio studii*, the passage of the arts and sciences from one place or milieu to another. This theme is to be found in America throughout the entire eighteenth century. The American version of the Golden Age was nearly always located in the future. In the patriotic euphoria that followed political independence, writers who adopted the opinion that no place or culture in the past could be compared to America in the present were enlisting themselves on the side of the moderns, whether consciously or not.

It was certainly consistent for partisans of the moderns and advocates of the doctrine of progress to join in celebrating the glories of the newly proclaimed national literature of the United States, but logically the defenders of the ancients might have been expected to be somewhat more reticent. Apparently aware of the risk of contradiction, most of the latter praised the classical heritage in such a way as to enlist it as one of the elements contributing to the luster of emerging American letters. In similar fashion, the European tradition of republican government was commonly regarded as a major component of the new American state, but nevertheless overshadowed by the modern superstructure. The self-congratulatory attitude of many literary voices of the period anticipated an attitude that Goethe epitomized for his own purposes in 1827, "Amerika du hast es besser."

Few of the authors who expounded the theme of American superiority were known outside the United States, but earlier ones such as Franklin, Dickinson, and Paine, who espoused natural rights and reported democratic political aspirations, were read and taken seriously in Europe. The study of literary relations involving these later figures registers actual contact, not merely analogies and resemblances.

FOUR

THE MANY VERSIONS OF POLLY BAKER: DEISM AND HUMAN RIGHTS

FRANKLIN has been called "a greater and more influential writer than Dr. Samuel Johnson."[1] The comparison is certainly provocative, and there is no question about its truth from the perspective of comparative literature. Dr. Johnson was a scholar trained in the classics, who progressed through journalism to become a professional man of letters. Dr. Franklin, who was almost entirely self-taught, took up journalism as an adjunct to the printing trade, and developed his literary talents as an aid in his careers in science, politics, and statesmanship. Johnson wrote poetry and literary criticism vastly superior to Franklin's; Franklin drew upon the proverbial wisdom of all the literatures of Europe for his *Way to Wealth;* he wrote an autobiography that is one of the world's masterpieces in the genre, and a literary hoax "Polly Baker" to which the greatest authors in the French Enlightenment paid tribute. Most students of English literature, who call the second half of the eighteenth century the Age of Johnson, know Franklin merely as one of the Founding Fathers of the American nation and have never read a page of his work. But outside of the Anglo-Saxon hegemony, where few readers would even recognize Johnson's name, Franklin is still being studied at all levels

[1] J. A. Leo Lemay, "Franklin and the Autobiography. An Essay on Recent Scholarship," *Eighteenth-Century Studies* 1 (1968): 185.

from secondary school to the seminar. In the realm of universal literature, comprising the masterpieces known and admired throughout the world, Johnson has no place at all, but Franklin is securely represented by his autobiography, his *Way to Wealth*, and his story of Polly Baker.

As early as 1762 David Hume remarked that Franklin was "the first Philosopher, and indeed the first Great Man of Letters" in the English part of the Western Hemisphere.[2] At this time Franklin's major literary works had either not been published or were not known to be Franklin's, and Hume was, therefore, basing his highly flattering estimate of Franklin's literary distinction upon his personal and political letters and upon his descriptions of scientific experiments, particularly the famous electrical ones. Franklin had not even embarked upon his autobiography, and although *The Way to Wealth* was already widely known, it was not associated with Franklin. It was nowhere attributed to him in print until 1773, when it was included in a French edition of his works under the title of "Father Abraham's Speech." A version in English bearing Franklin's name did not appear until 1779. French sources, as we shall see later in this chapter, were also the first to associate Franklin with Polly Baker, but not until the period of the American Revolution. Hume, therefore, appears to have been gifted with extraordinary prescience or intuition.

Of Franklin's three masterpieces, we shall be concerned only with his "Speech of Polly Baker." When considered as the prototype of a literary genre in which semiserious courtroom rhetoric invests unconventional sexual behavior with comic overtones, Polly's speech is unique in American letters, but it has one illustrious European predecessor and several equally distinguished progeny. As every

---

[2] *Papers of Benjamin Franklin*, ed. Leonard W. Labaree et al. (New Haven, 1966), 10: 82.

student of Franklin knows, Polly is accused of bearing five bastard children. She defends herself in an impassioned protest that she has always been ready to marry the man who had betrayed her and that in bearing children she has been carrying out the religious and civic duty of replenishing the population. Several ideological themes animate her discourse, varying in importance according to the printed text in which it is presented (Franklin's original not being extant) or to the interpretation of editors and commentators.

The archetype of Franklin's serio-comical legal plea is a tale from the Italian Renaissance in Boccaccio's *Decameron*. In a story entitled "Lady Filippa against the Statute of Prato," a dynamic and intelligent young woman charged with a sex offense defends herself by attacking the injustice of the law. This lady, Filippa de Pugliese, having been discovered in bed with her lover, has been charged with violating a strict law that every woman found by her husband in the act of adultery should be put to death by fire. Against the advice of her family and friends, Filippa refuses to save her life by denying the charge, but prefers to appear in court to answer it. She admits to her judge without shame and hesitation that she has many times slept with her lover, but argues against the validity of the law by which she is condemned. She maintains that laws should apply to all citizens equally and be enacted by common consent, but the law by which she is accused applies only to women, not to men, and no women, furthermore, had been involved in forming it. She then asks her husband whether she had ever declined to gratify his physical needs or been the least reluctant to do so, and the husband admits that she has always been willing to indulge him, indeed more often than he had himself desired. Filippa then asks the judge what release she should be expected to find for her sexual needs that still remain after her husband has been fully satisfied. Is it not more fitting, she asks, for her to share her pleasures with a worthy gentleman who loves her exceedingly than to let them be wasted or to be lost entirely? The judge and audience are convinced by her arguments, and after much laughter the edict is modified to concern henceforth only those women who disgrace their husbands by accepting money from their lovers.

Exactly the same primary elements exist in the speeches of Filippa and Polly Baker: 1) the situation of a resourceful woman addressing a bar of justice in her own behalf; 2) the defense of women's rights as equally valid as men's; 3) the palliation of sexual indulgence; and 4) the appeal to good sense over tradition, or natural law over civil law. Both speeches illustrate equally the principle supplied as a heading in the 1620 English translation of *Il Decameron*, but not present in Boccaccio's original text, "What worth it is to confesse a trueth, with a facetious and witty excuse."[3] To be sure, the two ladies are accused of different crimes, Filippa of adultery and Polly of bearing illegitimate children, but both defendants are impelled to satisfy overpowering physical needs, and are in the end vindicated on the grounds of natural law. The two ladies have the same termperament or personality; that is, they are lusty, enterprising, audacious, spirited, and candid. Even physically they seem to be alike, although here the evidence is scant. Filippa is described as *bellissima*, translated in 1620 as of "singular beautie and praise-worthy parts." One might suspect that Polly, after bearing five bastard children, would have but a faded beauty at best. The first known text is completely silent concerning Polly's physical features, but in later printings in both *The Gentleman's Magazine* and the *Irish London Magazine* she is described as "the beautiful Polly Baker." The pri-

[3] *The Decameron . . . Translated into English Anno 1620 with an Introduction by Edward Hutton* (London, 1909), III: 131.

mary link between the two narratives, however, is the formal one—the courtroom setting, a beautiful woman on trial, and a speech delivered by the accused in her own defense.

Franklin had an opportunity of reading the *Decameron* during his youthful sojourn in England for a period of nearly two full years in 1725 and 1726. Here he worked in a printing house, and, in addition to consorting with other press hands and minor poets, enjoyed in his leisure hours the company of an alehouse coterie presided over by the cynical and jovial Dr. Bernard Mandeville, author of *The Fable of the Bees*. In this society, it is possible that Franklin had access to an English translation of *The Decameron*, or that during one of his drinking sessions he heard the story of the beautiful and audacious Filippa narrated as a good story by some tavern companion.

Although the connection between Boccaccio and Franklin is merely conjectural, that between Franklin and the next contributor to the genre of the salacious legal memoir, Voltaire, is clear, direct, and specific. In 1774 Voltaire published two closely parallel fictitious courtroom speeches, one by a husband, the other by a wife, but both complaining that the laws and customs of their times permitted them no redress of the sexual injustices that they had respectively suffered. That Polly Baker provided Voltaire the inspiration for the wife's speech has already been suggested by a writer in the French newspaper *Le Figaro* (1 June 1976). Polly's speech had appeared in French as early as 1770 in a celebrated work that Voltaire read and discussed immediately after its appearance, the abbé Raynal's *Histoire philosophique et politique des deux Indes* (1770). Not only does it seem probable that Voltaire became acquainted with Polly's speech in 1770, but it is clear that he eventually learned the secret of its authorship, for the collected edition of his works published posthumously at Kehl in 1785-1786 provides the first attribution of Polly's speech to Franklin to appear anywhere in print. In the article "Ana, Anecdotes," originally published in *Questions sur l'Encyclopédie* in 1774, but now included as part of the *Dictionnaire philosophique*, appears the statement that the story of Polly Baker "is a pleasantry, a pamphlet of the illustrious Franklin." This statement did not appear in the original publication of "Ana, Anecdotes" in the *Questions*, but was added sometime between 1774 and 1785 either by Voltaire himself or by the editors of the Kehl edition. It is highly unlikely that the Kehl editors would have tampered with Voltaire's text, for in the notes to their edition they make a scrupulous distinction between those of Voltaire and their own. Voltaire himself probably added the information concerning Franklin's authorship, acquiring it from one of his longstanding admirers, the abbé Morellet, who was intimately associated with Franklin during his residence in Paris during the American Revolution. Morellet's "Ana" manuscript, which is now in the British Museum, includes an interesting section on Polly Baker in which Franklin is identified as her creator.

Voltaire's two courtroom speeches in the tradition of Boccaccio and Franklin also appeared in the original *Questions sur l'Encyclopédie*, but in a separate article, that on "Adultère." Both were as fictitious as the speech of Polly Baker, and both were designed to protest against the irrationality and inflexibility of marriage laws in Catholic countries. One was presumably delivered by a French magistrate to the ecclesiastical authorities of his city, complaining that the laws prevented him from divorcing a wife who had repeatedly made him a cuckold; the other was allegedly delivered by a Portuguese countess to the municipal council of Lisbon protesting against the rigorous penalties she faced for a single indiscretion despite her husband having gone unpunished for scores of them.

In the speech of the injured husband, whose wife has

created a public scandal by her promiscuity, Voltaire typically attributes to a priest her original loss of chastity before marriage. The aggrieved husband, only forty years old and still handsome and vigorous, has separated in disgust from his wife, but is kept by scruples from seducing the wife of another man, or from consorting with willing girls or pliant widows. He wishes a second marriage, the only honorable solution to his plight, but precisely the one that is forbidden him by his Church and its dominance over French society. He affirms then in a formal plea to the Church authorities that his wife is the criminal, but that he is the one who is being punished. Just as Polly has "debauched no other Woman's Husband," he is "too scrupulous to seek to seduce the spouse of another." His sense of virtue and propriety requires that he continue to satisfy his sexual needs, but the Church prohibits him from marriage with an honorable woman. In his words, "Today's civil laws, unfortunately founded upon canon law, deprive me of the rights of humanity." This recourse to human rights, which in the eighteenth century were identical with natural rights, is parallel to Polly's complaint that the laws of New England go contrary to natural law in that they keep her from performing "the Duty of the first and great Command of Nature, and of Nature's God, *Encrease and Multiply*." Voltaire's aggrieved husband also suggests the principle more clearly affirmed by Polly that Church and state be kept separate, that if hers is a religious offense, it should be left to religious punishments. Voltaire's husband, moreover, observes that social customs based upon theology go contrary to the teaching of the Scriptures; as Polly appeals to natural law or the command of nature's God, the aggrieved husband cites the verse in Matthew (14:9) in which Christ sanctions divorce on the grounds of adultery. In his words, "God allows me to remarry, but the Bishop of Rome does not allow it." After a brief summary of historical episodes in which divorce has been allowed in Europe, he returns in his peroration to a stronger wording of his principle: "the Church does not have the right to deprive me of a blessing which God grants to me."

Voltaire's second address, that of the adulterous wife, has even stronger formal resemblances to the speeches of Lady Filippa and Miss Baker. The complainant, a Portuguese countess accused of adultery, admits her guilt, but argues in extenuation that her husband has carried on with impunity with the lowest sluts of the court and the town whereas she has imitated him only a single time and then with the handsomest young man of Lisbon. Like Polly, the countess argues that theology is irrelevant. Polly says to her accusers "You believe I have offended Heaven, and must suffer eternal Fire." Significantly she refers to the belief of her judges, but does not say that she shares this belief. The countess also refers to a religious belief, but is equally careful not to say that she accepts it. She makes the additional point that whatever punishment religion places upon her must also be her husband's lot: "The Scriptures have forbidden adultery to my husband as well as to me: he will be damned like me, nothing is more clear." Polly also adduces the sharing of guilt by affirming that all of the members of the court are acquainted with "that very Person," her seducer. He has in the meantime become advanced to honor and power in the government whereas she has been punished "with Stripes and Infamy." She complains of their contrary situations as being "unjust and unequal." The countess similarly affirms that "in matters of justice, things must be equal." Yet her husband goes unchallenged by the civil authorities for his host of infidelities, while she for her single one is liable to have her head shaved, to be shut up in a convent, and to have her dowry taken away and given to her husband. She asks, therefore, whether these things are just and whether it is not evident that cuckolds have made the laws.

Voltaire's speeches were in their own way as humorous as Franklin's and their purpose was equally serious, for they broached three of the major topics prohibited by French censorship of the time, and they took the unorthodox side. These fundamental topics were the right of reason, the limits of authority and Revelation, and the foundation of Christianity and its relationship to the state.[4]

Voltaire's heroine in one way is closer to Boccaccio's Lady Filippa than to Polly Baker, for the Portuguese and the Italian ladies are both on trial for committing adultery, whereas the crime of the unmarried Polly is merely fornication aggravated by the offense of giving birth to children out of wedlock. The Portuguese and the Italian ladies are, of course, not accused of producing illegitimate children. All three admit committing the act for which they are condemned, but deny that they are guilty of any crime. And all three criticize the laws under which they are brought to trial as unjust. Boccaccio's heroine commits adultery because her husband does not provide her sexual satisfaction; Voltaire's does so because her husband is promiscuous in pursuing other women. Although neither Voltaire nor Franklin was an outstanding advocate of women's rights, both used the argument that a double standard is unjust—that women should not be condemned for behavior that is condoned in men. In this sense, therefore, Voltaire's Portuguese countess is more closely related to Polly Baker than to Lady Filippa.

One further example of the influence of Polly Baker upon a major French author of the eighteenth century is a speech in the written text of Beaumarchais's famous play, *Le Mariage de Figaro* (1776), the source, of course,

---

[4] Ira O. Wade, *The Clandestine Organization and Diffusion of Philosophic Ideas in France from 1700 to 1750* (Princeton, 1938), *passim*.

of the opera of that name by Mozart.[5] This speech even in our day is omitted from staged versions of the play, presumably for the reason given by Beaumarchais in his preface, that the actors feared that its severe philosophical outlook would darken the gaiety of the action.

In the speech, Marceline, the mother of Figaro, appears before a tribunal presided over by a judge and the Count Almaviva in order to defend herself for all of the faults of her youth, including a single illegitimate birth, a somewhat modest score in contrast to Polly's five offspring. Here there is no comedy, no deism, and no philoprogenitiveness, but in place of them a passionate statement of the principle that men are to blame for the lapses of the women they pursue and that it is men and not women who should be punished. Marceline's words advocate the cause of all women who have ever been accused of lapses from virtue.

In the age of illusions, of inexperience, and of physical necessities, when seducers besiege us while poverty wounds us what weapons can a child wield against so many united enemies? Such a one judges us here severely who perhaps in his life has been responsible for the loss of ten unfortunate ones. . . . Men, worse than ungrateful, who brand with scorn your victims, the playthings of your passions! It is you who should be punished for the errors of our youth; you and your magistrates, so vain of the right to condemn us, those who through their guilty negligence allow all honest means of subsistence to be taken away from us. . . . Even among the highest ranks women obtain from you only a derisive respect; trapped [as they are] with superficial esteem into a real servitude; considered as minors with

---

[5] I am basing my account of Beaumarchais on Agnes G. Raymond, "Figaro, fils naturel de Polly Baker? ou la Réhabilitation de Marceline," *Comparative Literature Studies* 12 (1975): 34-43.

regard to our property, punished as adults in regard to our faults, your conduct toward us inspires horror or pity.

This is, of course, not a translation of Polly Baker's speech, but a parallel to her situation, and the reference to property also suggests Voltaire's countess. Marceline's reproach to her accusers and to her judge, who may himself have corrupted ten women, is, nevertheless, essentially the same as Polly's. The latter complains of injustice and inequality in that her "Betrayer and Undoer," the first cause of all her "Faults and Miscarriages . . . should be advanced to Honour and Power, in the same Government that punishes" her "Misfortunes with Stripes and Infamy." Beaumarchais, like Boccaccio, appears as an outspoken feminist and presents the male sex as the persecutor of the female. Franklin never went this far in his own ideology, perhaps because he was not completely free from offenses against women in his own life.

Beaumarchais's Marceline may be linked to Polly Baker through Voltaire's twin discourses in his article "Adultère," published two years before *Le Mariage de Figaro*. Beaumarchais, moreover, was the major entrepreneur and joint editor with Condorcet of the notable Kehl edition of Voltaire's works, which, as we have indicated above, first attributed the story of Polly Baker to Franklin. To be sure, this proves merely that Beaumarchais was aware of Polly's history in 1785, not in 1775 or 1776 when he wrote the speech of Marceline, but the parallels indicate his awareness at the earlier date.

The legend of Polly Baker grew and shaped itself not only by means of imitations and adaptations of the story, but also by translations and interpretations of its earliest known printing. Two years after its publication in the London newspaper *The General Advertiser* in April 1747, an annotated text was reprinted in a London tract by Peter

POLLY BAKER

Annet entitled *Social Bliss Considered: In Marriage and Divorce; Cohabiting unmarried, and Public Whoring.* The author used the example of Polly to underscore his disapproval of divorce and premarital sex together with his advocacy of the social benefits of public prostitution.

Full-scale ideological development of the Polly Baker theme took place, however, in an expanded French translation, which we have already indicated appeared in the abbé Raynal's *Histoire philosophique et politique des deux Indes*, one of the most famous contemporary books about the American continent. Raynal incorporated the speech in his book under the impression that it was a genuine historical document, and he was later amazed to learn, on a visit to Franklin's apartments in Paris when Franklin was serving as commissioner from the United States, that his host had written the speech as a hoax. Upon hearing this from Franklin's own lips, the French philosophe replied, "My word, . . . I am more pleased to have included your tales in my work than the truths of others."[6]

The great liberties that Raynal takes with Franklin's original text are all the more remarkable considering that he at first believed he was reporting an actual speech. He completely rewrote entire sections of his alleged translation in order to strengthen the deism of the original and to add principles of feminine equalitarianism, which are certainly not dominant in Franklin's version. Raynal shifts the emphasis from the duty of augmenting population to the pleasure in the sexual act itself, in a sense combining the arguments of Polly with those of Boccaccio's Filippa. Raynal's heroine complains, therefore, of masculine injustice in condemning the female partner from whom the male derives pleasure and companionship. "Let him," she says, "not crush with opprobrium a sex which he has

[6] A. O. Aldridge, *Franklin and His French Contemporaries* (New York, 1957), p. 96. Subsequent remarks on abbé Raynal are based on this book.

himself corrupted; let him not infuse shame and misery into the pleasure which thou hast given him as the consolation of his affliction; let him not be ungrateful and cruel to the very seat of happiness in delivering to torture the victim of his voluptuousness." Polly's speech is incorporated into the chapter of Raynal's work bearing the title, "Severity which still exists in the laws of New England," ostensibly an attack on the excesses of Puritanism.

By and large Raynal transforms Franklin's basically comic discourse into a deistic sermon. Raynal's heroine, for example, in her introductory remarks, independently acknowledges reason as her guide and arbiter. "I am going to make Reason speak. As she alone has the right to dictate the laws, she can examine them all." In speaking of the education she has given to her illegitimate offspring, an extention of the situation that had not occurred to Franklin, she again praises reason as her moving principle. "I have formed them to virtue, which is merely reason. They will be citizens as yourselves unless you take away from them by new fines the basis of their maintenance and force them to flee a region which has spurned them from the cradle."

Franklin's Polly complains of the severity of the laws, but argues merely that their rigidity should sometimes be relaxed in particular circumstances, that "there is left a power somewhere to dispense with the execution of them." Raynal's Polly unequivocally sets forth the Rousseauean precept of the supremacy of conscience over law. "I defy my enemies, if I have any which I have not merited, to accuse me of the least injustice. I examine my conscience and my conduct; the one and the other, I say it boldly, both appear pure as the day which gives me light, and when I look for my crime, I find it only in the law."

Franklin's Polly is not a prude; yet she justifies her cohabitation solely on the grounds of procreation. Raynal's Polly, as we have seen, frankly admits the force of carnal urges, and, perhaps because of the tolerant attitude toward gallantry in the French milieu, justifies these urges as part of the nature of things.

> In order not to betray nature, [she says,] I do not fear to expose myself to unjust dishonor, to shameful punishments. I should prefer to suffer everything than to foreswear the vows of propagation, than to suppress my children either before or after conceiving them. I have not been able, I admit it, after losing my virginity, to remain celibate in a secret and sterile prostitution, and I ask for the punishment which awaits me rather than to hide the fruits of the fecundity which heaven has given to man and woman as its principal benediction.

Raynal's alterations are not limited to the intellectual content of the original text; they embrace also a fundamental change in the integral form or structure of the narrative. Where Franklin's original piece consists entirely of Polly's speech directed to her judges and accusers, Raynal's version contains an additional dramatic peroration addressed to the Divine Being Himself. After repeating Franklin's argument that God could not be angry at her deed since He had endowed her progeny with immortal souls, she turns from her accusers to address God directly.

After Raynal, Polly appeared in another major work of the French Enlightenment, Diderot's *Supplément au voyage de Bougainville [Supplement to the Voyage of Bougainville]*, which was written soon after Raynal's *Histoire* but not published until 1796. Diderot made an independent translation of Polly's speech, following his original somewhat more closely than had Raynal. After Polly admits bringing five handsome children into the world, Diderot has her affirm that "I have nourished them with my milk." This reference to the then popular practice in France of breast-feeding may have been due to the influence of

Rousseau.[7] Diderot also echoed Peter Annet by adding a denunciation of unmarried men who seduce virtuous women and start them on the road to prostitution. Diderot excluded, on the other hand, Polly's view that failing to have children is a crime of the same nature as assassination, her proposal to tax bachelors, and her claim to have deserved a monument for her procreative activities.

Franklin's motive in writing "Polly Baker" may still be obscure; although it is obvious that he was interested in both an entertaining situation and a platform for his ideas, we cannot tell which was of primary importance. Also we cannot be sure which of the ideas incorporated in the story he considered to be the most vital. With Diderot no such doubts exist. He used the situation to illustrate the philosophical principle which had been introduced into Raynal's 1780 edition, perhaps by Diderot himself, and which Diderot later adapted as the subtitle of his *Voyage*: that is, "On the Inconvenience of attaching moral considerations to certain physical actions to which they are not appropriate." As a principle it is actually not far removed from Polly's objection to laws which "turn natural and useful Actions into Crimes." Nearly everything in Diderot's *Voyage* concerns the natives of Tahiti, who were handsome and gracious in physique and completely free and uninhibited in their sexual behavior. They illustrated, therefore, for Diderot, living proof that the puritanical notions of jealousy, fidelity, chastity, and modesty associated in Europe with sexual gratification represent moral concepts improperly attached to a physical act. He rebuked his European compatriots, therefore: "Busy yourself, if you wish, in the dark forest with the perverse companion of your pleasures, but allow the good and simple Tahitians to reproduce without shame in the sight of heaven in broad daylight." Diderot's idyllic portrayal of the un-

---

[7] Raymond, "Figaro, fils naturel," p. 40.

inhibited sexual behavior of the inhabitants of the South
Seas represents an Enlightenment refurbishing of the classical pastoral tradition in which Arcadia and the Golden
Age represented the myth of the ideal society.[8] Franklin's
Polly Baker may seem quite remote from ancient Arcadia
or eighteenth-century Tahiti, but she certainly illustrates
Diderot's (and Raynal's) principle that moral considerations are artificially attached to physical actions. The law
under which she is condemned she repudiates as unrea-
sonable in itself; the entire body of laws of this kind she
condemns as turning natural and useful actions into crimes;
and the particular law which she has been accused of
violating, she affirms, contradicts the first and great command of nature, to increase and multiply.

No reference to Polly Baker in German literature has
hitherto been noted prior to the twentieth century. Eleven
years before Franklin's death, however, Polly was cited by
a German philosopher, August Hennings, in a treatise
published in Copenhagen, *August Hennings Philosophische Versuche*.[9] The author occupies a respected place
in the annals of American-European comparative literature because of a poem in the epic genre (also published
in Copenhagen in 1799) entitled *Olavides*, devoted to the
trials and victories of a Peruvian hero of the Enlightenment, Pablo de Olavide.[10] Hennings is also important in
Franklin scholarship as probably the first writer in Germany to draw attention to Franklin's "Standing Queries
for the Junto," which, several years before Herder, he published in both English and German in his *Philosophische
Versuche*.[11] He indicates that the Junto papers are to be

[8] Renato Poggioli, *The Oaten Flute* (Cambridge, Mass., 1975), p. 60.

[9] 2 vols. (Copenhagen, 1779), 2: 205. A second edition was published
in the following year.

[10] Estuardo Nuñez, *El nuevo Olavide* (Lima, 1970), p. 28.

[11] 1: 355-361. Information on Herder's use of Franklin is found in
Papers, ed. Labaree (1959), 1: 259.

found in Franklin's *Political, Miscellaneous and Philosophical Pieces* (London, 1779) and that they are extracted in the *Monthly Review* for March 1780. The latter rather than the printed volume was probably Hennings's source as well as Herder's later on. Hennings treats Polly in connection with the emotional effect of the experiences of other people, presenting her as an illustration of the manner in which the distress of others operates upon one's feelings. "Who can read the story of Polly Baker," he writes, "one of these unfortunates in New England without emotion? Who would not consider her innocent and admire the gentleman who recognized virtue in her offence?" According to Hennings, the perverted view of female honor in the case of Polly Baker was almost as horrible as that which required widows in Indostan to immolate themselves upon the funeral pyres of their husbands. No doubt Hennings had read about Polly in the sentimentalized version of Raynal because he echoes Raynal's implied praise of the judge who marries her, by that action illustrating the primacy of reason over the courts of law.

After this survey of the European metamorphoses of Polly Baker, we are in a position to analyze the ideological and literary elements in Franklin's original creation. We may hope to decide, for example, to what degree Franklin was attempting to convey a serious message and to what degree he was being facetious. On the serious side we may investigate the ideas he was seeking to present. We may inquire whether he felt that women were being discriminated against in the society of his day, that the stigma against bastard children should be removed, or that maximum population was so desirable in a "new country" such as America that any means to obtain it was legitimate? It is self-evident that Franklin's purpose was both comical and serious and that he was concerned with all of the forementioned ideas.

The basic elements of "Polly Baker" that elevated it

above its provincial colonial milieu and led to its international renown may be considered under the headings of eroticism and ideology. Eroticism is used in the sense of deriving pleasure from contemplation of the human sexual act and its accompaniments. In "The Speech of Polly Baker" this type of pleasure blends with the comic as it does in the tradition of bawdy tales from the period of Boccaccio and Chaucer to the present. In the Puritanical setting of colonial New England the notion of a woman being tried in public five times consecutively for having an illegitimate child creates a comic shock in the ludicrousness of the situation. J. A. Leo Lemay has recently pointed out the scattering of a number of salacious puns throughout Polly's speech.[12] She remarks, for example, "I cannot conceive . . . what the Nature of my Offense is" and refers to "the first Cause of all my Faults and Miscarriages," deliberately emphasizing the words "conceive" and "Miscarriages," by inserting parenthetical phrases immediately after them. The man who originally seduced her, she declares, is "now a Magistrate of this Country," recalling the anatomical overtones in Hamlet's phrase "country matters." To be sure, these puns are not as obvious in the present day as they would have been to many of Franklin's contemporary readers. The scholar who first noted these double meanings vindicated his perceptions by observing that Franklin at the age of sixteen printed in his brother's newspaper, *The New-England Courant*, the bland statement that "Women are prime Causes of a great many Male Enormities." One might also suggest that Franklin discerned sexual overtones in one of his favorite proverbs, which he put forward conspicuously in his autobiography and elsewhere: "it is hard for an empty Sack to stand upright." He indulged in the openly sca-

---

[12] "The Text, Rhetorical Strategies, and Themes of 'The Speech of Miss Polly Baker,' " in *The Oldest Revolutionary. Essays on Benjamin Franklin*, ed. J. A. Leo Lemay (Philadelphia, 1976), p. 109.

tological, moreover, in his surreptitious *To the Royal Academy of Brussels*, a parody of Enlightenment academia in which he proposes research into converting to perfume the noxious effluvia caused by breaking wind.[13] Whatever puns exist in "Polly Baker," therefore, are probably intentional.

Franklin, like Polly, was not a prude in any sense of the word, and he believed that the sexual act is a good in itself, not only as a means to procreate. In a famous letter to Joseph Priestley, written toward the close of the Revolutionary War, he dramatically elaborated the modern philosophy of "Make Love, Not War." With supreme disgust he condemned the human race, "for without a Blush they assemble in great armies at Noon Day to destroy, and when they have kill'd as many as they can, they exaggerate the Number to augment the fancied Glory; but they creep into Corners, or cover themselves with the Darkness of night, when they mean to beget, as being asham'd of a virtuous Action." Modern scholarship has discovered that Franklin is here paraphrasing the great Renaissance skeptic Montaigne,[14] but the sentiments were nonetheless his own. They were repeated by Diderot, in the remark already quoted, "Busy yourself, if you wish, in the dark forest with the perverse companion of your pleasures, but allow the good and simple Tahitians to reproduce without shame in the sight of heaven in broad daylight."

During all periods of his life, Franklin believed that a healthy eroticism was superior to Puritanical morality that stressed the subduing of sexual impulses. This is one of the themes of "Polly Baker." To show that Franklin was presenting Polly sympathetically in order to condone

[13] Richard E. Amacher, *Franklin's Wit and Folly. The Bagatelles* (New Brunswick, N.J., 1953), pp. 66-69.

[14] Robert Newcomb, "Benjamin Franklin and Montaigne," *Modern Language Notes* 72 (1957): 489-91.

her breaches of the traditional sexual code rather than to condemn her, it is sufficient to point to parallel treatments of the theme in his other works. Carl Van Doren associates Polly Baker with his surreptitious "Advice to a Young Man on the Choice of a Mistress," both presumably written when he was entering his fortieth year, and suggests that Franklin's acute sexual awareness at this time was the result of the normal life cycle.[15] With Franklin, however, there is no need to isolate a particular "salty year," for eroticism may be found in his works in all periods. During his sojourn in Paris during his seventies, for example, he composed several libidinous *jeux d'esprit* for Mme Catherine Helvétius, widow of the noted *philosophe*. Two of them were printed on his private press, and one was soon afterward reprinted in the famous *Correspondance littéraire* of Melchior Grimm.[16] In the first, entitled *The Flies*, Franklin converts the buzzing sounds of the insects in his apartment into a plea for the separate households of Franklin and Mme Helvétius to merge into a single one. The second bagatelle, entitled *The Elysian Fields*, ventures on a theme which is called in our day wife-swapping. Here Franklin reports a dream that he has been transported to paradise, where he meets Helvétius, now married to Franklin's late wife. Franklin thereupon returns to the good Earth, reports his adventure to Mme Helvétius, and challenges her, "Let us take our revenge." The nineteenth-century French critic Sainte-Beuve, writing at the height of the French Romantic movement, felt that in the *Elysian Fields* "one can sense a deep emotion underlying the playful surface,"[17] but seen as a companion piece to Polly Baker, the facetiousness is more apparent. After Franklin's return to America, Mme Helvétius wrote a reminiscing letter about Franklin's dream of the Elysian

[15] *Benjamin Franklin* (New York, 1938), pp. 150-54.
[16] Ed. Maurice Tourneux, 16 vols. (Paris, 1877-1882), 12: 385-86.
[17] Claude-Anne Lopez, *Mon Cher Papa* (New Haven, 1966), p. 268.

Fields and remarked, "I believe you have been a rascal and will find more than one wife up there!"[18]

When Franklin wrote the *Elysian Fields*, Mrs. Franklin had been dead for several years, but even during her lifetime he had treated the same theme of marital exchanges. He once reported that one of the young ladies in his English social circle whom he described as an "amiable and delectable Companion" had vowed to marry either Franklin or his friend John Hawkesworth, depending on "whose Wife should first depart this Life." As a consequence both Franklin and Hawkesworth "sincerely wished Health & long Life to the other's Wife."[19]

The explicit theme of these bagatelles is that constancy or fidelity to a single mate is a questionable virtue. This is implicit also in "Polly Baker," and it seems to have been a reflection of Franklin's own personality. One of his French friends, in commentary on his popularity with the ladies of Paris, remarked that he treated all of them with an amiable coquettishness that they loved. "When one particular lady, eager for his preference, asked him if he did not care for her more than for the others, he would answer: 'Yes, when you are closest to me, because of the force of attraction.' "

In all of Franklin's bagatelles in which eroticism appears, the situation being described usually has some unrealistic element, for example, talking flies, a visit to the Elysian Fields, and five consecutive trials for bearing bastard children. It is hard to discern a serious purpose in the bagatelles for Mme Helvétius, but there are a number of them in Polly Baker.

The theme of the equality of the sexes, or at least equal justice, may be discerned in Franklin's "Polly Baker" text as distinguished from adapters such as Hennings, Diderot,

[18] Ibid.
[19] A. O. Aldridge, *Benjamin Franklin Philosopher and Man* (New York, 1965), p. 212.

and Peter Annet, who emphasized other notions. Even in Franklin, feminism is not as dominant as it is in Voltaire and Beaumarchais, for Franklin's Polly merely complains that for her to be prosecuted while her partner in crime becomes a magistrate is "unjust and unequal." Probably Franklin himself believed that men and women should not be treated disproportionately for the same transgression of the law, which is essentially all that Polly is saying, but at no time in his life did he ever suggest women's equality in any other sense. When one considers Polly's speech in conjunction with the briefs of Boccaccio's Filippa and Voltaire's countess, however, it becomes difficult not to read feminist ideology into it. Boccaccio's Filippa is forthright in her demand for sexual equality. She declares as a universally acknowledged principle "that the Lawes enacted in any Country, ought to be common, and made with consent of them whom they concerne." The edict under which she is accused, however, "is rigorous against none, but poore women onely." It is unjust, moreover, since when it was made, "there was not any woman that gave consent to it, neither were they called to like or allow thereof." Voltaire's countess echoes this principle in inquiring "whether it is not evident that it is cuckolds who have made the laws." Polly's speech was overtly associated with feminism in March 1778, when it was incorporated in one of the earliest French feminist periodicals, the *Journal des Dames*.[20]

---

[20] Evelyne Sullerot, *Histoire de la presse féminine en France, des origines à 1848* (Paris, 1966), pp. 24-25. This author explains in a footnote that she had completed her description of the Polly Baker text as found in the *Journal des Dames* with no knowledge whatsoever of its source or previous history when she mentioned it by chance to an acquaintance who was writing a thesis on Diderot and who then explained that it had been included in the *Supplément au Voyage de Bougainville*. After comparing the two texts, Mme Sullerot concluded that without being word for word, the two versions are identical in facts, arguments, and entire phrases.

Another serious topic that Franklin's Polly Baker embraces is religion. Her speech serves the double purpose of holding up to ridicule the Puritan morality associated with New England and presenting for approval the rational deism that Franklin embraced as his personal religion throughout his entire life. He had previously derided the Puritan spirit in print, condemning particularly its dismal outlook. In 1734, for example, he published in the *Pennsylvania Gazette* a ribald parody of the clerical style of contemplative ascetic gloom, concluding that we should "rejoice and bless God, that we are neither Oysters, Hogs, nor Dray-Horses; and not stand repining that He has not made us Angels."[21] A few years later Franklin wrote for his *Gazette* a series of essays defending a liberal Presbyterian minister against the other clergymen of his synod who had accused the minister of heterodoxy because of his preaching morality and good works instead of salvation by faith alone.[22] To be sure, Polly Baker in her speech says nothing about the clergy, since she is being judged by civil lawyers and magistrates. She cleverly blends or equates the religious and the secular, however, by suggesting that both base their dedication to the sacredness of the marriage ceremony upon its usefulness as a source of income. In her words, only "the Minister, or the Justice" could have any complaint "because I have had Children without being Married, by which they have miss'd a Wedding Fee." Also she remarks parenthetically, "I am no Divine." She argues convincingly for the principle that eventually became a pillar of the American Revolution, the separation of church and state. "If mine, then, is a religious Offence," she states, "leave it, Gentlemen, to religious Punishments." She also directly attacks the laws that turn what she considers normal sexual behavior

---

[21] A. O. Aldridge, "A Religious Hoax by Benjamin Franklin," *American Literature* 36 (1964): 204-9.

[22] *Papers*, ed. Labaree (1960), 2: 27-33, 37-126.

into crime. "Abstracted from the Law," she says, "I cannot
. . . conceive what the Nature of my Offence is." Franklin
is here hitting at all of the laws in New England regulating
private morality, not only those against fornication. Since
Franklin draws particular attention to the circumstance
that her speech was uttered "before a Court of Judicature,
at Connecticut near Boston in New England," we can be
sure that it is the rigorous morality of Puritanism associated with this region of America that is his target.

Along with the ridicule of Puritan theology, Franklin
blended into Polly's speech one or two elements of deism.
A modern scholar has suggested that "the satire of the
speech was directed both at the orthodox religionists who
wished to impose their own moral ideas on others and
the unorthodox who were forever appealing to Nature."[23]
If this is true, Franklin was indulging in self-satire, for the
deistical strains are to be found duplicated with utter seriousness in many other passages in Franklin's works.
These deistic elements are so important that subsequent
writers, such as Peter Annet in England and the abbé Raynal
in France, revised the speech in such a way as to eliminate
its comedy altogether and present it as a document of
deist propaganda.

In her speech Polly refers to "the Nature of Things" as
an absolute standard, and in the same manner in which
a clergyman would cite a biblical text, she points to "the
first and great Command of Nature, and of Nature's God,
Increase and multiply." Polly's reference to the "Command of Nature, and of Nature's God" is the second most
famous use of the phrase in all American letters. It is more
widely known only in the version "Laws of Nature and
of Nature's God," which appears in the Declaration of
Independence. Before the publication of Polly's speech,

---

[23] Max Hall, *Benjamin Franklin and Polly Baker* (Chapel Hill, N.C.,
1960), p. 111.

Pope in *An Essay on Man* had praised the independent
spirit who "looks through Nature up to Nature's God"
[IV. 331] and Bolingbroke echoed that "one follows Nature
and Nature's God" [*Letter to Mr. Pope*, 1753].

Polly also uses the teleological argument for the existence of God; that is, the view that a creator may be discerned in the regularity and order of the universe. In a
lecture "On the Providence of God in the Government of
the World," which he had delivered in his youth, Franklin
had marveled at "the admirable Structure of Animal Bodies of such infinite Variety, and yet every one adapted to
its Nature, and the Way of Life it is to be placed in, Whether
on Earth, in the Air or in the Waters, and so exactly that
the highest and most exquisite human Reason, cannot
find a fault and say this would have been better so or in
another Manner."[24] Polly is falling back on this mode of
reasoning when she asks, "How can it be believed that
Heaven is angry at my having Children, when to the little
done by me towards it, God has been pleased to add his
divine skill and admirable Workmanship in the Formation
of their Bodies, and crown'd it by furnishing them with
rational and immortal souls." Polly adds an element that
has nothing to do with the teleological argument or with
Franklin's religious opinions expressed elsewhere in his
works—immortal souls. There is no evidence whatsoever
in Franklin's works to show that he ever believed that
human beings have souls, although he often expressed the
hope of immortality.

Another dominant theme in Polly's speech is the attempt to erase in some measure the stigma from unwed
mothers and illegitimate children, a theme that was first
noted in 1926 by one of Franklin's biographers, Phillips
Russell. Alluding to Franklin's own illegitimate son, William Franklin, Russell interpreted Polly's defense of her-

---

[24] *Papers*, ed. Labaree, 1: 264-69.

self as the mother of natural children as "in reality Franklin's own defense of himself made for the benefit of those
critics in Philadelphia who had been saying nasty things
about him."[25] Although this opinion has been challenged
by the argument that "such an attempt might boomerang
by simply calling attention to a painful situation,"[26] there
can be no question that Franklin felt that being born out
of wedlock should not be considered a disgrace. He once
confided to the physician-philosopher Cabanis that he attached very little importance to the wedding ceremony.
"To the contrary, he regarded it, especially in countries
where divorce has not been established, as an institution
equally immoral and absurd. He also considered as extremely unjust those laws which placed in a special category children born outside of marriage."[27] Franklin, by
the way, was not alone in the eighteenth century in this
opinion. The prime minister of Denmark, Struensee,
worked persistently to rehabilitate the image of illegitimate offspring and before his execution in 1772 for treason
succeeded in forcing the repeal of laws in his country
making it a crime to have a bastard child.

Franklin introduces two other ideological topics by means
of Polly's question, "Can it be a Crime (in the Nature of
Things I mean) to add to the Number of the King's Subjects in a new Country that really wants People?" Here
she makes a distinction between positive and natural law,
that is, between the standards of artificial society and
those of nature, and the necessity of maximum population
for the political benefit of a nation. The distinction between positive and natural law is the basis of the later
Raynal-Diderot principle concerning "the Inconvenience
of attaching moral considerations to certain physical ac-

[25] Cited by Hall, *Franklin and Polly Baker*, p. 109.
[26] Ibid.
[27] Jean P. G. Cabanis, *Oeuvres philosophiques*. Edited by Claude Lehec
and Jean Cazaneuve. 2 vols. (Paris, 1956), 1: 348.

tions to which they are not appropriate." The conviction of the economic benefits of a growing population comprises one of the elements of philoprogenitiveness (or love of progeny), along with erotic pleasure and participation in the joys of family life, which may also be traced in Franklin's private ideology. Hundreds of novels, like Richardson's *Pamela*, stressed the personal pleasure to be derived from pregnant wives and healthy babies; sermons invoked the divine imperative implicit in Proverbs 14:28, "In the multitude of people, is the king's honor"; and treatises on political and economic theory upheld the maxim that "in proportion to the numbers of useful subjects, will be the strength and riches of a state." Nobody revealed a greater fondness than Franklin for fecundity and procreation as such. In 1755 he published, for example, *Observations concerning the Increase of Mankind, Peopling of Countries*, a tract that was reprinted and widely circulated throughout America and Europe and gained for Franklin the reputation of being the outstanding demographer in the British colonies. His argument runs: People increase in proportion to the ease and convenience of supporting a family. This economic facility exists to a high degree in unsettled countries like America. Whatever increases production increases population, and those citizens who aid in the process deserve to be called "Fathers of their Nation." In the American colonies the population doubles in twenty to twenty-five years, but the process requires about 350 years in Europe. In another century, the colonies will outstrip the mother country. All of the presuppositions of this argument are found in Polly Baker's speech. Voltaire shared Franklin's notions concerning the advantages to a state of maximum population, and in the speech of his cuckolded husband he inserted one of his perpetual complaints against the clergy, that its mandatory celibacy was an affront against population.

After the abbé Raynal's adaptation of Polly's speech, it became for Franklin a symbol of the unreliability of history. In a conversation with one of his intimate associates in Paris, abbé André Morellet, Franklin cited his hoax as an example of the short time in which a contrived tale could be converted into historical fact. The literary genre in which Morellet places Polly's speech—"un petit roman politique et moral" [a short political and moral piece of fiction]—provides a clue toward Franklin's own interpretation of the work. Franklin related to Morellet the chief circumstances of the circulation of the speech—that it was composed around 1740, inserted into the newspapers of the time, its authenticity debated until public interest declined, revived by Raynal, and since then firmly believed. "Thirty years had been sufficient to convert the tale into history."[28] While still in France, Franklin cited as an example of the errors in Raynal's *Histoire philosophique* the charge that "the people of Massachusetts Bay preserve their Fanaticism," a strong indication that he felt either that fanatical Puritanism no longer existed in New England or that this aspect of Polly's speech had been distorted.[29]

In a sense, Franklin's objections to the converting of Polly's speech into a historical document show that he considered it as a work of the imagination, as a revelation of human character and behavior as well as a vehicle for moral and political ideas. When the analogies between Franklin's Polly and Boccaccio's Filippa are perceived, Polly's character transcends the New England setting. Her speech becomes less important for its portrayal of Puritanical rigor and the quaintness of some colonial customs than for its exposition of psychological attitudes and a social situation of universal application, of equal rele-

[28] A. O. Aldridge, *Benjamin Franklin et ses contemporains français* (Paris, 1963), p. 92.
[29] Hall, *Franklin and Polly Baker*, p. 125.

vance to Renaissance Italy as to Colonial America. Probably the elements of broad application in the story of Polly Baker had as much to do with the decision of Diderot and abbé Raynal to repeat and embellish it as had the elements of deism and primitivism, which are generally considered to have had primary appeal to the French *philosophes*. This consideration points to an important paradox in their portrayals of Polly. By translating her speech into French they seem to lift her from provincial boundaries, but at the same time, by associating her with primitivism, they put her back again. Diderot in particular seems to place Polly apart from the stream of advanced civilization by associating her with the natives of Tahiti as outstanding examples of nonconformity to a characteristic of social development that Diderot condemns, the attaching of "moral concepts to physical actions which do not correspond with them." The example of Filippa would have suited Diderot's purpose just as well, but the connotations of ribaldry and bawdiness associated with *Il Decameron* would have made the Italian heroine inappropriate for his serious purpose.

Franklin's achievement in the indirect portrayal of character may also be given greater recognition than it has received in the past by comparing his method with Boccaccio's. If literary characters are considered on a scale, with wooden types like the personae of fables and fairy tales at one end and sophisticated and complex personalities like those in *Les Liaisons dangereuses* and *Anna Karenina* on the other, Boccaccio occupies a position close to the middle. Thanks to his artistic skill, Filippa is a vital and realistic character. The reader has no difficulties in imagining her either in the arms of her lover or pleading her case before her judge. Polly Baker has equally apparent human dimensions despite the fact that her speech lacks any kind of narrative framework. Polly lives as a real personage because of the psychological acuity and credibility

POLLY BAKER

of her reasoning, which portrays a personality as well as an ideology.

Despite the ready acceptance by Franklin's contemporaries of the authenticity of Polly's speech, some twentieth-century critics have condemned the basic human situation on which it is predicated as far-fetched or even ludicrous. They cannot accept the coincidence of a man who has been responsible for the ruin of a young virgin recognizing her many years later when he is a judge at her trial and then proposing marriage to her. This situation, whether presented by Franklin with adequate literary verisimilitude or not, actually happened at least once in real life and provided the basis for a full-length novel by one of the masters of world fiction—a writer in the class of Goethe, Dickens, and Stendhal. The novel, published at the very end of the nineteenth century, is *Resurrection* (1899), and its author is Tolstoy. Its plot was suggested by an incident in Russian society—the plight of a girl of sixteen, who was seduced and then deserted by her lover, forced into prostitution, and eventually rescued by her seducer, who recognized her while acting as a juryman at her trial on a charge of prostitution. In the novel, Tolstoy deviates from the circumstances of the real incident, thereby bringing the story of the unfortunate victim, Katúsha Máslova, even closer to that of Polly Baker. The seducer is the protagonist of the novel, a member of the aristocracy, Prince Dmítri Neklúdoff, and Katúsha is a servant girl at his aunt's estate. On a brief visit, he takes advantage of her in a moment of delirious passion, thrusts a bank note upon her, and then disappears. Ten years afterwards, during which time she has completely vanished from his mind, he is summoned for jury duty and recognizes her in the prisoner's dock. She has spent the intervening years in a brothel and is on trial for poisoning a patron of the establishment. She does not recognize Neklúdoff as her seducer, but the latter is so overwhelmed by the encounter that he determines to secure her legal vindication and to marry her in order to atone for the great wrong he has committed against her. He later learns that Katúsha had carried his child, but that it died at birth. He succeeds in having the judgment against her modified, but in the end she refuses his offer of marriage. *Resurrection* is an ideological vehicle for the presentation of Tolstoy's religion (based on Christian socialism) and of his economic theories (based on Henry George's single tax) in the same way that the "Speech of Polly Baker" is designed to portray Franklin's principles of deism and philoprogenitiveness. But the plot elements in the two narratives are essentially the same.

I had already written the above section on Tolstoy when my attention was drawn to an article, also treating the subject of the relations between "Polly Baker" and *Resurrection*, in a Festschrift for a Soviet comparatist. The author, G. M. Fridlender, surveys Tolstoy's interest in the Enlightenment, provides documentary evidence of Tolstoy's acquaintance with Franklin's autobiography, and underscores the similarity of plot lines in *Resurrection* and the novella-pastiche of Franklin, Raynal, and Diderot.[30] Fridlender is unable to prove any more than I, however, that Tolstoy had read the story of Polly Baker in any of its multitudinous versions. I mention his article primarily to indicate that he and I independently arrived at a similar conclusion. According to Fridlender's interpretation, the *philosophes* of the eighteenth century emphasized Polly's maternal role in presenting to the government five useful new citizens; whereas Tolstoy stressed the theme of the seducer-judge (or juryman in *Resurrection*) from the ruling class confronting the girl of the common people who had been abandoned by him. A polemic

[30] " 'Voskresenie' L'va Tolstogo i 'Reč Polli Beker' B. Franklina," in *Sravnitel'noe izučenie literatur [The Comparative Study of Literatures]*, ed. E. A. Smirnova (Leningrad, 1976), pp. 304-8.

has developed in American scholarship over whether Tolstoy had ever read Franklin's works, even his autobiography, and whether the latter work had exercised a significant influence upon the Russian novelist.[31] Fridlender seems to have settled the question by reporting that Tolstoy recommended the publishing of an edition for the common reader of Franklin's autobiography, Swift's *Gulliver's Travels*, and Lessing's *Nathan der Weise*.

From the perspective of bare plot or the theme of the seducer-judge, Polly's basic situation is identical to that of the protagonist of a major American novel of the nineteenth century, Hawthorne's *Scarlet Letter*. Both Polly and Hester Prynne are accused of a sexual offense, both are brought to judgment before a tribunal of which the partner in the offense is a member, and both remain silent instead of revealing their identities.

Comparison of Polly Baker with other fictional heroines brings up the question of whether the Polly who is on trial in Connecticut should be considered an actual prostitute or merely an oversexed or normally sexed woman. One must decide whether she earns her living through selling her favors, or whether she provides for her economic existence through ordinary means and satisfies overwhelming erotic needs in her leisure moments as best she can. I have always held the latter interpretation, which is both the more plausible and the more comical, and I know of only one critic who calls Polly a whore.[32] The latter designation gives her a greater resemblance to Tolstoy's Katúsha, but at the same time makes her, like Katúsha, a tragic figure and, therefore, not the comic personality that Franklin probably intended. If she is merely an ordinary woman whose sexual drive has driven her to

[31] Henry Hill Walsh, "On the Putative Influence of Benjamin Franklin on Tolstoi," *Canadian-American Slavic Studies* 13 (1979): 306-9.

[32] Leo Lemay, *Oldest Revolutionary*, p. 109, remarks "we see a direct reference to her livelihood, gained by soliciting the men."

throw caution to the winds, she is entirely comic—almost a caricature. If she is a prostitute she cannot be regarded, like Boccaccio's Filippa, as a crusading opponent of the double standard in sexual relations, an attitude that she certainly expresses.

Leo Lemay believes that "Franklin has deliberately created an ironic obtuse persona in Polly Baker,"[33] but such an opinion can hardly be reconciled with the view that Polly is Franklin's spokesman on serious points of ideology, as she certainly is. If she were vulgar and stupid, moreover, her speech would not have obtained the international celebrity with which it was almost immediately rewarded. The novelist Balzac was so impressed with Polly Baker that he gave Franklin credit for inventing the literary genre of the canard along with the lightning rod and republican government. This is exaggerated praise in reference to both literature and politics—Swift and Voltaire had previously perpetrated equally successful journalistic hoaxes.[34] That which distinguishes the Polly Baker story from other masterpieces of the kind is its extraordinary degree of verisimilitude. Other hoaxes were soon exposed and moved from the realm of actuality to that of fiction. Polly Baker, however, not only kept her credibility throughout the entire eighteenth century, but even in the twentieth continued to be cited as an actual historical figure, for example, in *A Social History of the American Family* published during World War I.[35]

Polly's fame depends upon three separate elements: the

[33] Ibid., p. 103.

[34] *Les Illusions perdues*, Pt. II, chap. 23. Balzac was off the mark, moreover, in attributing to Franklin at the same time another anecdote from Raynal's *Histoire*, that of an "Englishman who sold a negress who had saved his life, but first . . . got with child in order to make more money out of the sale." Voltaire correctly pointed out that this tale is no other than the famous story of Inkle and Jarico, originally told by Steele in *Spectator* no. 11.

[35] Hall, *Franklin and Polly Baker*, p. 153.

verisimilitude of Franklin's style, the eroticism associated with Polly's situation, and her forthright character. It is probably the last that has contributed most to her universal appeal. Because of the seriousness of attention given to her character and predicament by eminent European writers, Polly Baker transcends the genre of the canard of literary hoax and attains the rank of a literary theme, joining the company of such celebrated fictional legends as Faust, Don Juan, and Dracula.

FIVE

PAINE AND DICKINSON: POLITICS AND LITERATURE

Balzac in one of his novels establishes a parallel in French letters between conservative political philosophy and Romanticism on one side and between liberal philosophy and classicism on the other.[1] "By a strange anomaly," he observes, "the romantic royalists call for literary freedom and the abrogation of laws which provide our literature with its conventional forms; while the liberals cling to the unities, regular rhythms in the alexandrine line and classical themes." It would be difficult to establish for the American Revolutionary and Federal periods a similar relationship between political philosophy and literary theory and practice although ethical ideals obviously contributed to political ideologies of all shades. Among classicists, Joseph Dennie believed that government should be in the hands of an aristocratic elite and Joel Barlow believed that it should be controlled by the people; among Romanticists, James Fenimore Cooper took the conservative side in politics and William Cullen Bryant the liberal.

The two men who have generally been considered to be the foremost propagandists of the American Revolution, John Dickinson and Thomas Paine, seem on the surface to illustrate the contrary of Balzac's paradox. Paine's literary style embodies many Romantic characteristics with its irregularity, impulsiveness, and flamboyance, and his

[1] *Les Illusions perdues*, Pt. II, chap. 8.

political opinions were certainly in the vanguard of the radicalism of his time, combining as they do the ideals of republicanism and natural rights. Dickinson's literary style, on the other hand, embodies neoclassical standards of careful organization, restraint, and decorum. To this extent there does exist a substantial difference between the two propagandists, but this contrast cannot be extended to comprise political attitudes as well. Dickinson has traditionally been portrayed as highly conservative, but in actuality he and Paine shared the same fundamental ideology. Indeed the only major intellectual difference separating the two men is their attitude toward the Greek and Roman classics, Dickinson establishing them as models for almost his entire way of life, and Paine rejecting them in favor of the languages and cultural ideals of the modern world.

My primary concern in this chapter will be with American political ideas rather than universal literature, but I shall retain the comparative method in treating the manner in which the works of Dickinson and Paine were received in France.

Although Dickinson and Paine knew each other personally and both ended their political careers as staunch defenders of the administration of their mutual friend Thomas Jefferson, they are practically never considered as kindred figures in political or intellectual history. Biographers of either man uniformly ignore the other. The notable exception is Moncure D. Conway, a graduate of Dickinson College and the author of the first biography of Paine to be based on extensive original research. Conway told how "honest John Dickinson" helped obtain a financial grant for Paine from the state of Pennsylvania. Most modern historical works that make any comparisons between Paine and Dickinson, however, erroneously suggest that their political systems were antithetical.

It cannot be denied that historical figures frequently

become symbols of economic and political ideologies. Franklin and Jefferson on one side, Hamilton and Adams on the other, do represent concrete political attitudes, and their followers in political life have magnified their differences by forming opposing factions. These are not dichotomies artificially imposed by historians many years after the events in which these figures participated. To their contemporaries and near-contemporaries, these men stood for separate political philosophies as different from each other as the systems of Thomas Paine and Edmund Burke. On the American scene, Paine may without much discussion be ranked on the side of Franklin and Jefferson. Historians have had difficulty in correctly placing Dickinson because of one major event in his life, his decision not to support the Declaration of Independence in the Second Continental Congress. This decision, Dickinson later maintained, was based primarily on timing, on his personal appraisal of the wretched state of unpreparedness of the colonies.[2] By voting against independence, Dickinson indeed temporarily enrolled himself in a camp opposite from that of Thomas Paine. Because of the cautious legalism of much of his writing, moreover, Dickinson has frequently been compared to Burke, and it is easy to understand what created the impression that his thought is inimical to Paine's. The related belief has grown up that throughout his career Dickinson habitually appealed to history and legal precedent rather than to natural law and natural rights. This interpretation is not supported by the facts. Not only was Dickinson not the American Burke, but his mature political philosophy was essentially the same as that of Thomas Paine. Dickinson himself recognized the similarity in their fundamental views, and he declared it emphatically.

[2] "Vindication" in Charles J. Stillé, *The Life and Times of John Dickinson* (Philadelphia, 1891), p. 367.

At first glance the two men seem to have resembled each other only in their life span. Dickinson was born in 1732, Paine five years later. Dickinson died in 1808 and Paine the following year. But Dickinson saw the light in surroundings of ease and affluence, Paine amid poverty and proletarian strife. Dickinson during most of his life held high political office and his prestige was never challenged. Even his political opponents treated him with the utmost deference. Paine, however, was as much reviled as respected throughout his entire public career. Although he exerted considerable political influence at various times and places, he worked almost invariably behind the scenes, and he never held an elected office in America. Early in the Revolution he served as the paid secretary of the committee of foreign affairs of the Congress and later as clerk of the Assembly of Pennsylvania. Dickinson held any number of elected offices including that of president of the Supreme Executive Council of Pennsylvania. Paine was on close enough terms to be invited to dine at the President's table at least once when the question of the recompense for his services during the Revolution was being considered. Dickinson reported to the Council of the state that he and Washington had discussed Paine's financial status and that both desired that provision be made for him. On another occasion both Paine and Dickinson were present at a spectacular fête in Philadelphia to celebrate the birth of the Dauphin of France. Benjamin Rush, who reported their presence, added that Paine "retired frequently from company to analyze his thoughts and to enjoy the repast of his own original ideas."[3]

A minor episode involving the return of Congress from Princeton to Philadelphia in 1783 reveals Paine's support of Dickinson in local politics. In a letter to Rush con-

---

[3] *Letters of Benjamin Rush*, ed. L. H. Butterfield, 2 vols. (Princeton, 1951), 1: 280.

cerning rival addresses to the citizens of Philadelphia, Paine
described one that he had himself drawn up as initiated
by "those whom Mr. Dickinson have very good reason to
believe his friends, and who intend it as a softening heal-
ing measure to all sides."[4] In 1805 after Paine returned to
the United States from France, he paid a merited tribute
to Dickinson. In the midst of his attacks on the politicans
"who once figured as leaders under the assumed and fraud-
ulent name of *federalism*," he particularly complimented
those who had since gone "into honorable and peaceable
retirement, like *John Dickinson* and *Charles Thomson*."[5]

Both Paine and Dickinson were at one time associated
with a Quaker environment, and in mature life both questioned conventional Christian doctrine. Paine's religion
is a complicated subject, but one may certainly say that
during most of his adult years he accepted deist principles.
Dickinson late in his career expressed belief in Christianity, but also admitted, "I am not, and probably never
shall be, united to any religious Society, because each of
them, as a society, holds principles which I cannot adopt."[6]

As early as 1765 in his writings on the Stamp Act, Dickinson revealed traces of the political ideology that would
make him comfortable with the system of Paine and Jefferson at the end of the century. A recent scholar has
pointed out that in opposing the Stamp Act, Dickinson
did not, as most historians maintain, depend upon legalistic logic or appeals to precedent, but offered instead "a
clearly articulated theory of natural rights—to be happy,

---

[4] *Complete Writings of Thomas Paine*, ed. Philip S. Foner, 2 vols. (New York, 1945), 2: 1219.

[5] Ibid., p. 949.

[6] Samuel Miller Papers, Princeton University Library, cited by David L. Jacobson in *John Dickinson and the Revolution in Pennsylvania 1764-1776*. University of California Publications in History (Berkeley and Los Angeles, 1965), p. 2.

to be free, and to be secure in one's property."[7] His various defenses of American rights were not based upon charters or compacts, but upon "immutable maxims of reason and justice." In a work of 1766 written under the pseudonym of a "North American," Dickinson described rights in the following terms: "They are created in us by the decrees of Providence, which establish the laws of our nature. They are born with us; exist within us; and cannot be taken away from us by any human power."[8] One could readily accept these words as being taken from the works of Thomas Paine.

Exactly the same presuppositions figure in Dickinson's *Letters from a Farmer in Pennsylvania* of 1768, and many of the phrases in this, his most popular work, recall his arguments of the preceding years. "The colonists, and men everywhere, enjoyed a basic right to be happy, they could not 'be happy, without being free,' and they could not be free unless secure in their property. Dickinson argued, as he had three years before, that American rights had been 'created . . . by the decrees of Providence, which establish the laws of our nature.' "[9] Despite many recent interpretations which see very little in the Farmer's *Letters* except resistance to Parliamentary taxation for the purpose of revenue rather than for the control of trade, the *Letters* actually stress freedom and natural rights. They make use of standard Whig themes such as the threat to liberty by executive control over assemblies, the danger of losing the right of voluntary taxation, the evils inherent in establishing the precedent of a revenue tax, the record of ministerial injustice, and the horrors of bureaucracy, corruption, and a standing army. Dickinson states his argument forthrightly and does not hedge it with legalistic refinements, and whenever he cites precedents he does so in order to show that traditions may be wrong and per-

[7] Ibid., p. 39.
[8] *An Address . . . Barbadoes*, 1776, cited by Jacobson, ibid., p. 262.
[9] Jacobson, *John Dickinson*, p. 55.

nicious. In other words, Dickinson even in the 1760s shows little resemblance to Edmund Burke of the 1790s. So forceful was Dickinson's style that the Tory *Critical Review* in England "accused the Farmer of inciting the colonies to independence."[10]

Although the Farmer's *Letters* and *Common Sense* are based on similar presuppositions and are rightly considered as the two most successful propaganda pieces of the American Revolution, their stylistic techniques reveal important differences. Dickinson writes in the vein of an Addisonian essay; Paine in that of a Swiftian tract. Dickinson adopts the device of an invented character as the presumed author; in the words of his opening sentence, he is "a farmer settled after a variety of fortunes, near the banks of the river Delaware, in the province of Pennsylvania." Paine in contrary fashion bluntly asserts, "Who the Author of this Production is, is wholly unnecessary to the Public, as the Object for Attention is the *Doctrine itself*, not the *Man*."

As Dickinson introduces himself in the character of the Pennsylvania farmer, he seems to be a colonial Montesquieu. He casually reveals that his servants are few and that he spends most of his time in his library, which is the most valuable part of his small estate. These details put his readers at ease by explaining, as he subsequently indicates, how it is that he has acquired more knowledge in history, law, and the constitution of his country than most men of his class. Paine keeps his personality as the author completely submerged, but he uses a style and vocabulary to suggest that he is a common man as well as an exponent of common sense.

Dickinson's style is in its way as forceful as Paine's, but it incorporates a different manner of insistence. Dickinson announces his themes, states them, and comes back

[10] Carl F. Kaestle, "The Public Reaction to John Dickinson's *Farmer's Letters*," *Proceedings of the American Antiquarian Society* 78 (1968): 345.

to them repeatedly. Paine relies on single presentations, occasionally drawn out, but usually short and self-contained. He makes one point and then passes on rapidly to another.

Without question Paine's subject matter is more philosophical and of more universal interest than Dickinson's. Much of *Common Sense* represents pure ideology, based on theoretical reasoning and abstract principles. The Farmer's *Letters*, on the other hand, are entirely pragmatic, treating issues, conditions, and personalities of the immediate time and specific place. Paine probes such basic concepts as the presumed state of nature, the origin of government, and the basic principles of monarchy, hereditary succession, and republicanism. Dickinson confines himself to such particular and specific issues as taxation without representation, the authority of Parliament to regulate trade but not to raise revenue, the distinction between external and internal taxes, and the relationship between virtue and liberty. Dickinson's letters have exclusive and continuous reference to the thirteen British colonies in America. Paine's pamphlet interprets the situation of the colonies as an illustration of principles that relate to the fundamental interests of all mankind. The two writers touch common ground mainly in attempting to rouse their countrymen to contemplate the imminent ruin confronting them; to take immediate action, not wait for the future; and to recognize the common bond of unity joining the thirteen colonies. The major example of verbal similarity between the Farmer's *Letters* and *Common Sense* exists in their common expression of the principle of solidarity. Dickinson says of the colonies, "the cause of one is the cause of all" [Letter I]. Paine enlarges the prospect, declaring "the cause of America is in a great measure the cause of all mankind."[11]

[11] *Complete Writings*, 1: 3.

Most hortatory works published in colonial America were oriented toward either the Greek and Roman classics or the Christian Scriptures, and many authors leaned alternately in both directions. Since Dickinson was one of the most dedicated classicists on the American continent, it is not strange that he should embellish his letters with appropriate allusions to the ancients. Indeed, every one of his twelve letters concludes with a Latin phrase or sentence, followed by an elegant translation into English. Dickinson also adorns his text with quotations from Plutarch, Tacitus, Sallust, Cicero, Demosthenes, and Virgil. These quotations are overweighed, however, by others from European and English authors, including Machiavelli, Rapin, Montesquieu, Locke, Pitt, Cambden, Hume, Pope, and Shakespeare. In his footnotes, Dickinson learnedly cites relevant legal decisions, but he keeps his main text completely free of these documentary authorities.

Even though historians associate Dickinson with the religious sect to which his wife belonged, the Quakers, he was, as we have already seen, not a particularly religious man. He nevertheless incorporates a fair number of biblical quotations in his *Letters*, and he particularly praises "the beautiful and emphatic language of the sacred scriptures" [Letter V]. Here and elsewhere when he cites biblical passages, however, he does not imply any authority in his texts, but uses them, as he does his classical sources, entirely for their language or their meaning. Paine, who had close associations with Quakers in early life, is usually considered by critics as anticlerical in all his writings, but in *Common Sense* he cites Scripture passages much more extensively than does Dickinson, and he appeals to these texts, moreover, as representing divine authority. He several times refers to "the will of the Almighty" and speaks of "the King of America" who "reigns above." In comparison to his scriptural quotations, Paine's references to secular literature are sparse indeed. They are limited to Milton; to three English political writers, Sir William Meredith, James Burgh, and Sir John Dalrymple; to a naval historian, John Entick; to a Quaker pamphleteer, Richard Barclay; and to an Italian moralist, Dragonetti.

Dickinson flatters his readers and countrymen, actually describing the inhabitants of the colonies as in general "more intelligent than any other people whatever" [Letter VII]. Paine in some of his other works writes in a similar ingratiating strain, but in *Common Sense* he limits himself to praising the material strength of the colonies and the advantages inherent on the American continent. Dickinson's style, which has reconciliation as its aim, is appropriate for urging resistance to oppression and injustice, but it remains squarely within the limits of propriety and decorum. Dickinson does indeed make such appeals as "my dear countrymen, ROUSE yourselves, and behold the ruin hanging over your heads," but he advises these same countrymen to "exert themselves in the most firm, but most peaceable manner, for obtaining relief" [Letters II and III]. Paine unequivocally places independence over reconciliation, and he adopts an extreme style to suit his message. As Dickinson's words are appropriate for resistance, Paine's are keyed to revolution. Paine does not seek merely to incite sporadic riots and tumults, but rather to turn every citizen of America against British rule. He castigates all Crown officials as murderers and colonists friendly to them as cowards and sycophants. He affirms that "thousands are already ruined by British barbarity," and denounces George III as "the Royal Brute." Paine's free use of invective is completely alien to Dickinson's sober restraint. Both propagandists, however, appeal to feeling. After Dickinson reviles those colonists who attempted to enforce the Stamp Act as "base-spirited wretches," the closest he comes to personal abuse, he remarks that "every honest bosom, on their being mentioned, will feel what cannot be *expressed*." Paine subjects the record of British atrocities to "those feelings and affections which nature justifies, and without which, we should be incapable of discharging the social duties of life." Parenthetically, Dickinson's style in private correspondence is much less reticent than it is in his public writings. In reference to the fall in public esteem which he suffered consequent to his voting against independence, he affirmed in a personal letter, "no youthfull Lover ever stript off his Clothes to step into Bed to his blooming beautiful Bride with more delight than I have cast off my Popularity."[12]

The publishing histories of the Farmer's *Letters* and *Common Sense* are completely different. Dickinson wrote the entire series of letters as a unit, but divided his material into twelve parts as a promotional device, assuming that they would obtain greater circulation and visibility if put out as twelve installments in newspapers rather than a single pamphlet. He carefully orchestrated the serial publication, fabricating objections to previous letters by fictitious readers and then providing his own answers.[13] Paine adopted the contrary method of publishing his entire work at one time as a pamphlet. His material is even less unified or homogeneous than that of the Farmer's *Letters* and would have been equally suited to serial publication. No one knows why he chose the pamphlet form, but it may be that he was dissatisfied with the results he had obtained from previous contributions to Philadelphia newspapers. Dickinson's *Letters* appeared in "nineteen of the twenty-three English-language newspapers published in the colonies in early 1768," and seven American pam-

[12] To Charles Thompson, 7 August 1776, in New York Historical Society, *Collections* 11 (187): 29.
[13] Kaestle, "Public Reaction," p. 339.

phlet editions followed in two years.[14] A modern scholar has estimated that the various newspaper printings had 75,000 readers and the pamphlets an additional 27,000.[15] *Common Sense* appeared in at least twenty-nine issues in the colonies during the single year of 1776, and Paine himself estimated that 120,000 copies were printed within three months.

In August 1776, Silas Deane reported from Paris to the American Committee of Secret Correspondence that "Common Sense has been translated, and has a greater run, if possible, here than in America." Deane also quotes from a letter to a French official which affirms that the author of *Common Sense* "is one of the greatest legislators [political experts] among the millions of writers whom we know; without question if the Americans follow the fine program which their compatriot has outlined for them, they will become the most flourishing and happy nation that has ever existed."[16] Paine's pamphlet was indeed well received in France, but Deane may have exaggerated the degree of its popularity. It originally appeared in translation in a periodical devoted to furthering the American cause, *Affaires de l'Angleterre et de l'Amérique*. It was mentioned there first in May 1776 in a letter from a mythical London banker, which included scattered sections in paraphrase. In the next month, large extracts were given, interwoven with commentary. Since *Common Sense* had appeared anonymously in Philadelphia and Paine was totally unknown anywhere else in the world, the *Affaires* mentioned Dickinson, Franklin and John Adams as possible authors. A complete translation—the only one in French to appear during the American Revolution—was published in Rotterdam in 1776. It was based on an Eng-

[14] Ibid, pp. 325-26.
[15] Ibid., p. 353.
[16] Francis Wharton, ed., *Revolutionary Diplomatic Correspondence*, 6 vols. (Washington, 1889), 2: 124.

lish edition and, therefore, had blank spaces wherever the original text refers to the British monarch.

Paine did not become personally known in France until after the publication of his *Rights of Man*, which defended the French Revolution against the attacks of Burke. He took up temporary residence in Paris in the spring of 1791, where he collaborated with Condorcet in editing an incendiary journal *Le Républicain*. Another of his associates, François Xavier Lanthenas, translated *Common Sense* in this year along with *Rights of Man*. A second edition came out in the same year and a third in 1793-94. Another publisher, Buisson, the same who published the first edition of Franklin's *Mémoires*, brought out in 1793 a new translation by A. G. Griffet de la Baume, but unfortunately based upon an English edition in which the most energetic passages of the original had been replaced by asterisks. Hence it was inferior to the translation of Lanthenas, which was based on a presentation copy to Turgot in which Paine himself had filled in all the blank spaces. A fourth translation, anonymous, was brought out by a later publisher, Poulet, in 1822.[17]

Although *Common Sense* was thus more widely known in France than were the Farmer's *Letters*, Dickinson's pamphlet was reviewed by one of the most eminent representatives of the French Enlightenment, an honor not accorded to *Common Sense*, although Brissot praised Paine's *Rights of Man* in a discourse on the floor of the French Convention and Condorcet also eulogized it in print.[18] The eminent French *philosophe* who reviewed the

[17] Further details may be found in A. O. Aldridge, "The Influence of Thomas Paine in the United States, England, France, Germany and South America," in *Proceedings of the Second Congress of the International Comparative Literature Association*, ed. W. P. Friederich (Chapel Hill, N.C., 1959), 2: 369-83.

[18] *Bibliothèque de l'homme publique . . . par M. Condorcet*, Seconde Année, Tome Neuvième (Paris, 1791), p. 3n.

Farmer's *Letters* was Diderot. Before treating his review, I shall summarize the antecedents of the French translation.

Dickinson owed this distinction entirely to the influence of Benjamin Franklin, who had also been responsible for the publication of a London edition of the *Letters*. Franklin sent a copy of the English edition to one of his most ardent French disciples, a deistic physician, Dr. Jacques Barbeu Dubourg, an associate of Turgot, Mirabeau, and other physiocrats, who immediately began turning it into French. While engaged in this task in his apartment in Saint Germain de Prés, he was visited by Benjamin Rush, carrying a letter of introduction from Franklin.[19] The first question Dubourg asked was whether Rush knew the author of the *Letters*, and when he learned that Rush was indeed acquainted with Dickinson, Dubourg broke into warm praise, saying "that in his opinion the Roman Orator Cicero was less eloquent than the Pennsylvania Farmer," a remark that Dubourg subsequently included in the preface to his translation. Dubourg later introduced Rush to his physiocratic associates and arranged for him to attend the weekly gatherings of the Marquis de Mirabeau. Rush reported that at his first visit to the Marquis's salon, one of the subjects of conversation was the recent translation of the Farmer's *Letters*. "They were praised with enthusiasm by all the company." Rush was then able to answer many questions about their author. He told Dubourg that Dickinson had been called the Demosthenes of America and that in consideration of his patriotic zeal a generous ecclesiastic of Virginia, whose name he had forgotten, had made Dickinson a present of ten thousand pounds sterling. Rush was probably also re-

[19] For documentation on the relations between Rush and Dubourg see A. O. Aldridge, "Jacques Barbeu-Dubourg, a French Disciple of Benjamin Franklin," *Proceedings of the American Philosophical Society* 5 (1951): 344-47.

sponsible for the equally unreliable statement in Dubourg's preface that the *Letters* had had thirty editions in America in six months, a number larger than the combined newspaper and pamphlet printings during two years.

As soon as Dubourg's translation appeared, the physiocrats published lengthy extracts in their literary organ, *Ephémérides du citoyen, ou bibliothèque raisonnée des sciences morales et politiques*.[20] Their comments represent Dickinson's most substantial influence in France. The editors cited the writings of Franklin and Dickinson as evidence to refute the popular European theory of biological degeneration, the notion that all species—including the human—tend to deteriorate in the American climate. Noble works such as those of Franklin and Dickinson, they argued, can be developed and can flourish only among a courageous, moderate, and wise people. The editors presented a summary of each of Dickinson's twelve letters supplemented with generous extracts, but then devoted most attention to the ninth concerning the problem of taxation. In their discussion they disagreed completely with Dickinson's fundamental tenet—which he shared with English Whigs—that a free people must hold the government purse-strings in their own hands.

Other published references to Dickinson in France are few indeed. In the last decade of the century, a Swiss writer on the American Revolution, although making no mention of the Farmer's *Letters*, gave Dickinson credit for being the single voice in America that brought about the independence of the United States. Jefferson, in France when the Swiss writer's book was being reviewed, actually wrote a letter to the editor of a literary periodical protesting against this gross misinterpretation, but he never

---

[20] The extracts from Dickinson, which appeared throughout the year 1769, were translated by Dubourg.

sent the letter and, presumably, the error was never corrected.[21]

Diderot read Dubourg's translation of the Farmer's *Letters* as soon at it appeared and immediately wrote a review, which he intended for the *Correspondance littéraire*. Grimm, the editor of the *Correspondance*, mentioned Diderot's review in November 1769, but did not publish it, considering it perhaps, as Diderot's modern editors suggest, too libertarian (*éleuthéromane*). It remained in manuscript until after Diderot's death, when it was published in 1798 by his friend and associate Naigeon. In contrast to most modern historians, Diderot considered the *Letters* to be bold and outspoken. He believed that even though Dickinson was speakng to Americans, his principles were addressed to all men. Diderot was particularly impressed by the last letter, summarized in the French edition by the phrase "Assoupissement, avant-coureur de l'esclavage," a rendering of Dickinson's maxim, "SLAVERY IS EVER PRECEDED BY SLEEP." Diderot quoted two paragraphs that he found bold and inspiring and suggested that they contained the potential for a tremendous impact upon French society. In his words:

> We are allowed to read such things as this, and then people are amazed to find us at the end of a dozen years become other men. Can it be that they do not understand how easily spirits with a little generosity must imbibe these principles and be intoxicated by them? Oh, my friend, happily the tyrants are still more stupid than they are wicked; they will disappear; the lessons of great men will bear fruit, and the spirit of a nation will expand.

If Diderot was right about the boldness and inspirational potential of the Farmer's *Letters*, Dickinson's words prob-

[21] Saul K. Padover, ed., *The Complete Jefferson* (New York, 1943), p. 74.

ably had more to do than modern historians are willing to admit with preparing public opinion in America for the somewhat more inflammatory message of *Common Sense*, which appeared, in Diderot's phrase, precisely "at the end of a dozen years."

No American historians or literary critics have hitherto pointed out the significance of Diderot's comments, but there has been, nevertheless, considerable attention to the alleged vogue in France of the Farmer's *Letters*, a vogue that has been greatly exaggerated. The *Literary History of the United States*, edited by Robert E. Spiller, states that "in France . . . two editions were published" [p. 136]. The *Literature of the American People*, edited by Arthur Hobson Quinn, remarks that "In Europe the 'essays . . . became, for a time, the fashion,' 'Voltaire praised them,' 'they were talked of in the salons of Paris,' and 'the Farmer himself was likened to Cicero' " [p. 147]. I would not recommend that anyone spend much time looking for the second French edition or for praise of the *Letters* in the works of Voltaire. Both are completely fictitious. Except for Franklin, the only American author whom Voltaire is known to have commented upon is Phillis Wheatley. In a letter to Constant Rebeque, 11 April 1774, shortly after the London publication of her *Poems on Various Subjects* (1773), Voltaire affirmed: "Fontenelle was wrong in saying there could never be poets among the Negroes. There is at this time a Negress who writes very good verses in English."[22] Incidentally, a contemporary French tribute to Wheatley appeared in *De la littérature des Nègres* (Paris, 1808) by the legislator and former Bishop of Blois, Henri Grégoire. Grégoire's work, the world's first study of black literature, was later translated by D. B. Warden and published in Brooklyn in 1810 under the title *An Enquiry*

[22] *Complete Works of Voltaire*, ed. Theodore Besterman et al. (Geneva, Banbury, and Toronto, 1968-   ), Correspondence D. 17781.

concerning the Intellectual and Moral Faculties and Literature of Negroes. Grégoire refutes Jefferson's disparaging opinion of Wheatley, stresses her knowledge of Horace and praise her sentimental melancholy. While serving in the French Convention, Grégoire had ordered the translation of Joel Barlow's *Letter to the National Convention* (1792) and had proposed that Barlow, like Paine, be accorded the title and rights of French citizenship. After the publication of *The Columbiad*, however, he wrote a pamphlet against its anticlerical bias, which was translated as *Critical Observations on the poem of Mr. Joel Barlow* (Washington, 1809).

Responsibility for introducing Voltaire into the bibliographical history of John Dickinson may be traced to Charles J. Stillé, author of the only full-length biography of Dickinson, which was published almost a century ago. Stillé quoted a passage from George Bancroft's *History of the United States*, concluding with the statement: "Translated into French, they [the Farmer's letters] were much read in Parisian saloons [*sic*]; and their author was compared with Cicero." This comment is based entirely on Dubourg's preface to the single French edition of the letters, and in this sense it is accurate. But Dickinson's biographer engrafted upon this passage an additional sentence of his own, enclosing it within the same quotation marks which surround the previous one: "Voltaire joined the praise of the farmer of Pennsylvania and that of the Russians who aspired to liberate Greece." This sentence is embellishment, not quotation—and its only source is the author's imagination. Moses C. Tyler quoted Stillé in his famous *Literary History of the American Revolution*, and our twentieth-century literary historian quoted Tyler.

A period of over twenty years and the stirring events of the American Revolution intervened between Dickinson's Farmer's *Letters* and the first series of his *Letters of Fabius*. The latter reveal extensive and basic resemblances to Paine's *Rights of Man*. In these later essays, Dickinson abandoned his pose of a gentleman farmer alerting his neighbors to the pressing issues of the moment and in its place adopted the character of a moralist and philosopher. As such he incorporated the method of reasoning that Paine had introduced in *Common Sense* and developed in *Rights of Man*. The resemblance goes much further than similarity of method; not only are the essential principles of the *Letters of Fabius* the same as those of *Rights of Man*, but the two authors expressed themselves in language remarkable for its affinity.

Dickinson wrote two series of Fabius letters, one in 1788 advocating the adoption of the Federal Constitution and the other in 1797, defending the pro-French position of the Democrats against the anti-French attitudes of the Federalists. The first series was published originally in a Wilmington newspaper and was later combined with the second series in book form in 1797. The collected edition contains a number of footnotes, pointing out parallels between Dickinson's letters on the Constitution and Paine's *Rights of Man*. The editor, moreover, specifically draws attention to the close ideological and linguistic relationship between Paine and Dickinson. He explains that he has added

> some notes . . . of extracts from "The Rights of Man," published about three years after these Letters, containing similar sentiments, expressed with a remarkable resemblance of language, especially on the two great subjects—the *organization* of a CONSTITUTION from *original* rights, and the FORMATION of GOVERNMENT from *contributed* rights, both of so much importance in laying regular FOUNDATIONS of civil society, and consequently in securing the advancement of HUMAN HAPPINESS.

Dickinson himself almost certainly added these extracts as well as some others that are included from Joel Barlow and miscellaneous sources. But even if someone other than Dickinson may have been responsible for these editorial comments, Dickinson himself indicated his recognition of their appropriateness by allowing them to be reprinted in his *Political Writings* in 1801.

Many of the appended quotations from *Rights of Man* concern the necessity of a constitution—and it is not strange that Dickinson would use similar arguments in supporting the ratification of the document drawn up by the American Constitutional Convention. Before we may affirm that Dickinson was in the same camp with Paine, however, we need to decide exactly what each meant by the term "constitution."

Paine meant a drafted document or written code setting forth in detail the principles upon which a particular political society was to be governed. Edmund Burke, as is well known, maintained on the other hand that a constitution comprises the complex of laws, charters, and precedents that the members of the political society accept as a standard for the regulation of conduct which had grown up gradually rather than being adopted at a precise moment in history. Practically everyone in the eighteenth century admitted the value of some kind of constitution, with the notable exception of William Godwin, who regarded Paine's assertion that England possessed no constitution as an unmerited eulogium. Godwin believed that England did have a constitution, and as an opponent of government as such he felt that to say that it had not was undeserved praise.

More important than the form of a constitution is its spirit. The basic issues, as formulated by Paine and Burke, were the purposes for which a constitution exists. Is its main function to regulate those rights and privileges of individual men and classes of society, which have been acquired by tradition; or is it to protect the rights of all men, which were acquired at birth? The debate between Paine and Burke concerned precedent versus natural rights. Dickinson declared himself forthrightly with Paine on the side of natural rights against Burke and historical precedent. In a stirring passage, he proclaimed,

> Trial by jury, and the dependence of taxation upon representation, those corner stones of liberty, were not obtained by *a bill of rights* or any other RECORDS, and have not been and cannot be preserved by them. They and all other rights must be preserved, by *soundness* of *sense* and *honesty of heart.*—Compared with *these*, what are a bill of rights or any characters drawn upon PAPER or PARCHMENT, those frail remembrancers? Do we want to be reminded, that the sun enlightens, warms, invigorates, and cheers? or how horrid it would be, to have his rays intercepted by our being thrust for life, into mines or dungeons? Liberty is the sun of society. Rights are the rays.

The 1797 edition of Dickinson points out a parallel passage in *Rights of Man*—Paine's encomium of Lafayette's address to the French National Assembly. "Instead of referring to musty RECORDS and mouldy PARCHMENTS to prove that the rights of the living are lost, 'renounced, and abdicated for ever,' by those who are now no more," the French hero "applies to the living world, and says—'Call to mind the sentiments which *nature* has engraved in the heart of every citizen, and which take a new face when they are solemnly *recognized by all*. For a nation to love *liberty*, it is sufficient that she knows it; and to be free, it is sufficient that she wills it.' " A fundamental step in Paine's argument was to trace the process by which man evolved from an individual in the state of nature to a member of civil society. Dickinson went over the same process. In his words, "Each individual—

must contribute such a share of his rights, as is necessary for attaining that *security* that is essential to freedom; and he is bound to make this contribution by the law of his nature, which prompts him to *a participated happiness*; that is, by the command of his *Creator*; therefore, *he must submit his will in what concerns all, to the will of all, that is of the whole society.*" This passage is footnoted in the 1797 edition with Paine's remark that after the transformation of man from a natural individual to a member of society, "civil power, properly considered as such, is made up of the aggregate of that class of the natural rights of man, which becomes defective in the individual in point of power, and answers not his purpose, but when collected to a focus, becomes competent to the purpose of every one."

Other passages, not indicated by footnotes, reveal even closer verbal parallels. Paine distinguished between "that class of natural rights which man retains after entering into society, and those which he throws into the common stock as a member of society." Dickinson remarks that "in forming a political society, each individual contributes some of his rights, in order that he may, from a *common stock* of rights, derive *greater benefits*, than he would from merely his own." In supporting the Constitution, Dickinson compared the federated states to individual men forming a society. Constantly Dickinson emphasized the individual. "A confederation is but an assemblage of *individuals*. The auspicious influence of that *law* of his nature, upon which the happiness of MAN depends in society, must attend him in confederation, or he becomes unhappy; for confederation should promote the happiness of *individuals*, or it does not *answer the intended purpose*." The footnote refers us to Paine's observation that "*individuals, themselves*, each in his own personal and sovereign right, *entered into a compact with each other* to produce a government: and this is the only mode in which governments have a right to arise, and the only principle on which they have a right to exist."

In this letter, Dickinson quotes a verse from the Old Testament which he had formerly used to good effect in the Farmer's *Letters*. When the individual realizes that his own happiness comes through submitting himself to the will of the whole society, he gains a perfect repose. Figuratively this state exists "When every man shall sit under his vine, and under his fig tree, and none shall make him afraid." In the Farmer's letters Dickinson had emphasized a somewhat different sentiment [Letter V]. Man could sit in repose under his fig tree when assured of the rights inherent in the relationship of the mother country to the colonies, particularly that great one, "the foundation of all the rest—that their property acquired with so much pain and hazard, should be disposed of by none but themselves." Paine in his last *Crisis* was much less materialistic. He depicted America "Descending to the scenes of quiet and domestic life . . . to enjoy in her own land, and under her own vine, the sweet of her labors."

In his Fabius letters Dickinson stressed the necessity of tracing every social right to its ultimate source as a natural right. Even citizenship in the federal union could be so traced.

As MAN, he becomes a *citizen*; as a citizen, he becomes a *federalist*. The generation of one, *is not the destruction* of the other. He *carries* into society the naked rights received from nature. *These* thereby improved, he *carries* still forward into confederation. If that sacred law before mentioned, is not here observed, the confederation would not be *real*, but *pretended*. He would confide, and be deceived.

This principle is supported in the footnotes by three separate passages from Paine. The first is a famous denunciation of "the error of those who reason by precedent, drawn from antiquity, respecting the rights of man." They "do not go far enough into antiquity. They do not go the whole way. They stop in some of the intermediate stages of an hundred or a thousand years." In showing how civil rights originated from natural rights, Paine declared that "Man did not enter into society to become worse than he was before, nor to have fewer rights than he had before, but to have those rights better secured. His natural rights are the foundation of all his civil rights."

Dickinson in his fourth letter turned to the subject of the relationship of a constitution to civil rights. This is the most fundamental point in Paine's debate with Burke. Dickinson declared that a constitution possesses its grave and sacred character because it is a rational creation of man, designed to preserve his natural and civil rights. According to Dickinson,

A *constitution* is the *organization of the contributed rights* in society. GOVERNMENT is the EXERCISE of them. It is intended for the benefit of *the governed*; of course [it] can have no just powers but what conduce to *that end*; and the awfulness of the *trust* is demonstrated in this—that it is founded on the nature of man, that is, on the will of his MAKER, and is *therefore* sacred. It is then an offence against heaven, to violate that *trust*.

The footnotes cite Paine's insistence that

A constitution is not a thing in name only, but in fact. It has not an ideal, but a real existence; and wherever it cannot be produced in a visible form, there is none. A constitution is a thing ANTECEDENT to a government, and a government is only the creature of a constitution. The constitution of a country is not the act of its government, but of the people constituting a government.

In principle, if not in language, Dickinson's *Letters of Fabius* were just as revolutionary as Paine's *Rights of Man*. Paine is famous in history for advocating revolution in America, England, and France. Dickinson, by placing final authority in the people, recognized the right of revolution as firmly and openly as ever Paine did. If the organization of a constitution were defective, he argued, it could be amended. "A good constitution promotes, but not always produces a good administration." But in the event that despite everything, a bad administration should come into control, Dickinson's answer was unequivocal: "Let the *fasces* be *lowered* before—the *supreme sovereignty* of the people. It *is their duty to watch, and their right to take care, that the constitution be preserved;* or in the Roman phrase on perilous occasions—*to provide, that the republic receive no damage.*" This is buttressed in the notes by a quotation from Locke as well as one from the second part of *Rights of Man*. According to Paine, when the controlling power is vested in a constitution, "it has the nation for its support, and the natural and controlling powers are together. The laws which are enacted by governments, control men only as individuals, but the nation, through its constitution, controls the whole government, and has a natural ability so to do. The final controlling power, therefore, and the original constituting power, are one and the same power."

In addition to these similarities in ideas, the language of Paine and Dickinson reveals a strong resemblance in treating the subject of the origin of political union. Both speak of it as a natural process of cohesion and both use the somewhat unusual verb (in this sense) "to condense." In speaking of the coming into being of modern republics, Dickinson remarked that

> their institutions consist of old errors tissued with hasty inventions, somewhat excusable, as the will of the Ro-

mans, made with arms in their hands. Some of them
were *condensed*, by dangers. They are still compressed
by them into a sort of union. Their well-known trans-
actions witness, that *their connection is not enough
compact and arranged*. They have all suffered, or *are
suffering* through *that defect*. Their existence seems to
depend more upon others, than upon themselves.

Paine used the same imagery: "If we consider what the
principles are that first *condense* man into society, and
what the motive is that regulates their mutual intercourse
afterward, we shall find, by the time we arrive at what is
called government, that nearly the whole of the business
is performed by the natural operation of the parts upon
each other."[23]

Previous writers on Dickinson, assuming that the first
series of Fabius letters represents a conservative Federalist
point of view, have been at a loss to understand Dickinson's presumed conversion to Jeffersonian liberalism in
the second series written in 1797. One cannot doubt that
when the Constitution was presented for ratification,
Dickinson was indeed a pronounced Federalist. But he was
a Federalist in Paine's sense of one who believed in "ce-
menting the Union by a general government operating
equally over all the States, in all matters that embraced
the common interest." In this sense, Paine declared that
he himself "ought to stand first on the list of Federalists."
Even though frontier farmers in western Pennsylvania
condemned the Constitution and its advocates as "the
pillars of slavery, tyranny and despotism," other citizens
of the state such as Paine, equally concerned for the wel-

---

[23] Even though Dickinson's first series of letters was originally printed
before *Rights of Man*, the publishing of parallel passages in 1797 was
not intended to suggest that Paine had written in any way under the
influence of Dickinson. Paine left for France in April 1787, and there is
little likelihood that Dickinson's letters, written in the following year,
were known anywhere in Europe.

fare of the common man, saw the necessity of the Constitution and campaigned energetically in its behalf. Dickinson and Paine based their support of the Constitution on identical grounds. There is no contradiction, therefore, between Dickinson supporting the principles of federalism in 1788 and enlisting himself nine years later among the proponents of Jeffersonian philosophy. The parallels with the *Rights of Man* in the first series of Fabius letters show that Dickinson did not go through a drastic conversion between 1788 and 1797. Indeed, there was little change in his essential political philosophy ever since the publication of his *Letters from a Pennsylvania Farmer* in 1767-68. Paine and Dickinson, therefore, were philosophical allies and joint campaigners for the humanitarian ideals of the Enlightenment.

SIX

THE CONCEPT OF ANCIENTS AND MODERNS IN AMERICAN POETRY OF THE FEDERAL PERIOD

ORDINARILY the expression Augustan Age when applied to the modern world comprises English literature during the first half of the eighteenth century, but an essayist under the name of the Meddler in a Connecticut newspaper of 1791 remarked that "the Augustan age bears greater resemblance to the present, than to any intermediate period."[1] In reference to what is now called the Federal period of American literature, the Meddler observed, "Under a similarity of circumstances, America has at length become the seat of science, and the great mirror of freedom and politics. Her Attica has produced a Homer, who leads the way; a Virgil, who was the pupil of that great master, and a Horace, who resides at the seat of Augustus."[2] The American Homer here referred to is Timothy Dwight, author of a Biblical epic *The Conquest of Canaan* (1785); the American Virgil is Joel Barlow, author of a patriotic epic, *The Vision of Columbus* (1787); and the American Horace is Philip Freneau, author

[1] The English background is fully explored by James William Johnson, "The Meaning of 'Augustan,' " *Journal of the History of Ideas* 19 (1958): 507-22. Charles Perrault in 1687 drew the parallel with France in the seventeenth century in a poem "Le Siècle de Louis-le-Grand."

Et l'on peut comparer, sans crainte d'être injuste,
Le siècle de Louis au beau siècle d'Auguste.

[2] *New Haven Gazette* (26 January 1791).

of miscellaneous lyrics and satires.³ These three are generally considered to be the outstanding poets of the Federal period, a roster completed with the addition of two other New England names, David Humphreys and Robert Treat Paine.

A similar description of American letters in terms of the ancients appeared in a Massachusetts poem of 1789 entitled *Anticipation of the Literary Fame of America*. The anonymous author predicted the rising in the near future of "Columbian *Livies*," "countless *Cicero's*," "another Plato," "another Stagyrite," "some new Euripides," "some future *Virgil*," and "some modern Ovid." As a consequence of this emergence of counterparts of Greek and Latin authors, the anonymous poet forecast that

> The brilliant treasure of the Attick mine,
> Shall glow refulgent in our western clime.⁴

Although Dwight, Barlow, and Freneau were the outstanding American poets of their time, they are read today less for esthetic pleasure than for the ideological and social riches they contain. Their relative lack of emotional and esthetic appeal has been attributed in large measure to the tradition of classical rhetoric to which they belong. According to one modern critic, they tended in practice to obscure the dichotomy in the adage "Poeta nascitur, orator fit," and classical forms and figures became their stock in trade. One is hard put to decide today, therefore, "whether the works of such men as Robert Treat Paine are more properly described as declamatory poems or poetic orations."⁵ Other critics have charged that most of

---

³ *Rising Glory of America* (1772), had made the same connection between American literature and the ancients, "I see a Homer and a Milton rise."

⁴ *Massachusetts Magazine* 1 (February 1789): 117-18.

⁵ Gordon E. Bigelow, *Rhetoric and American Poetry of the Early National Period*, University of Florida Monographs, Humanities No. 4, 1960, Gainesville, Fla., p. 28.

the American poets of the Federal period slavishly imitated the neoclassical rhetoric of Pope and the Augustan English poets. Sometimes the classical and the neoclassical traditions are indistinguishable in their work, as are the images and symbols associated with one or the other style. Frequently a reference to a neoclassical author could be substituted for a classical one without changing the fundamental meaning. An example is the following line from a lyric by Freneau.

To such wild scenes as Plato lov'd.

In a later version of the poem, Freneau simply inserted Shenstone for Plato.

It is not my purpose, however, to discuss the quality of Federal poetry or to affirm or deny the thesis that either classical or neoclassical rhetoric is responsible for its alleged deficiencies. I intend rather to investigate the literary traditions affirmed by these poets and to attempt to ascertain whether their outward subservience to classical models was accompanied by the kind of ideological commitment to the ancient world which is associated with the Augustan Age of English literature at the beginning of the eighteenth century. A definite pattern may be discerned among these poets, consisting of superficial discipleship combined with fundamental rejection. They imitated the style of the ancients and conformed to Aristotelian notions of genre, but repudiated many of the intellectual traditions associated with antiquity. This is the first principle that I hope to establish. The second is that the verse and critical writings of these poets contain close parallels with concepts in the European quarrel between the ancients and moderns.

The formal stage of this famous polemic belongs to the seventeenth and eighteenth centuries and concerns French literature primarily, but the attempt to decide the relative merits of the intellectual achievements of the ancient world and those of later ages goes back at least as far as the Renaissance. The question is one part of the idea of progress, and treatments of it exist in all Western European literatures. A parallel to one of the esthetic aspects of the question—consideration of the degree to which literary works should conform to critical standards of the past—has even been shown to exist in the thought of ancient China.

American writers in the Federal period, in common with almost all authors in Western culture after the Renaissance, drew upon both a generally accepted literary tradition from the past and a less orthodox but nonetheless familiar body of writings from their own century. Insofar as America is concerned, these connections may be represented graphically by horizontal and vertical lines, the horizontal one going back to the Greek and Latin classics, and the vertical extending across the Atlantic to the European continent. Nobody doubts the influence in eighteenth-century America of the social theories of Montesquieu, the sentimental psychology of Richardson, or the poetic structure of Pope. It seems logical to assume that many of the issues in the quarrel of the ancients and moderns should also be debated in the New World even though the French treatises of La Motte, Fontenelle, and Perrault may not have been available in American libraries. It is true that none of the poets I mention refers to the ancients-moderns quarrel as such or cites its main protagonists, but the relevant passages in the works of such English combatants as Sir William Temple, Jonathan Swift, Joseph Addison, and Oliver Goldsmith were probably as well known to the American literati of the eighteenth century as they are today.

A striking illustration may be found in the critical theories of the so-called American Homer, Timothy Dwight, and the American Virgil, Joel Barlow. Both wrote prose essays attempting to dislodge Homer from his pedestal and using arguments strongly resembling those of the moderns in the French phase of the quarrel of the ancients and moderns. Dwight in a *Dissertation on the History, Eloquence, and Poetry of the Bible* (1772), published thirteen years before his *The Conquest of Canaan*, argued that the beauties of the Bible are at least equal to those of the greatest classical writers and in many passages greatly superior to them. After observing that Homer has been praised for giving life to every object which he attempts to describe, Dwight maintains that he is excelled by the Old and New Testaments. There, according to Dwight, "objects are not barely endued with life; they breathe, they think, they speak, love, hate, fear, adore, & exercise all the most extraordinary emotions of rational beings. *Homer* or *Virgil* can make the mountains tremble, or the sea shake, at the appearance of a God; in the *Bible* the mountains melt like wax, or flee away; the Deep utters his voice, and lifts up his hands on high, at the presence of the LORD of the whole earth" [p. 5].

Admitting that the Scriptures would be found wanting were they to be judged by the rules associated with classical criticism, Dwight had no hesitation in disparaging these rules. Confronting an imaginary critic, Dwight replied: "When you can convince me that *Homer* and *Virgil* . . . were sent into the world to give Laws to all other authors; when you can convince me that every beauty of fine writing is to be found, in its highest perfection, in their works, I will allow the beauties of the divine writers to be faults. 'Till that can be demonstrated, I must continue to admire the most shining instances of Genius, unparallel'd in force, or sublimity" [p. 5]. Sentiments such as this explain why Dwight selected as the subject matter of his own epic, not a secular theme such as Camoëns and Voltaire had exploited, but one based on the Old Testament account of the gory victory of Joshua over the Canaanites. In the structure of his poem, Dwight prided himself on giving unity to the entire action, but in doing so he grossly garbled the facts of his historical source. He tended as a consequence "to dilute, to render garrulous, and to cheapen, the noble reticence, the graphic simplicity, of the antique chronicle"—the model that he had taken pains to exalt above the Greek and Roman epics precisely because of its noble sublimity of style.[6] But we are not concerned with esthetic achievement, but with ideas, the reasons for Dwight's choosing biblical subject matter over pagan and historical themes. He was following not only the example of Milton, but also the arguments of a French champion of the moderns, Desmarets de Saint-Sorlin, in a prose *Discourse to Prove that Only Christian Subjects are Appropriate to Heroic Poetry* (1673). [*Discours pour prouver que les sujets chrétiens sont seuls propres à la poésie héroïque*].

Joel Barlow also adopted the form of the classical epic while rejecting the authority of Homer and Virgil, but his objections to the ancient poets were based not on subject matter, but on political ideology. Barlow published his *Vision of Columbus* in 1787 and twenty years later brought out a revised and greatly expanded version under the more Virgilian title of *The Columbiad*. In the preface to the latter, Barlow drew a distinction between the poetical object of an epic and its moral object, the first representing the fictitious design of the action; the latter, the real design or ideological purpose. Since the poetical object of the *Iliad*, which is to portray the anger of Achilles, excites a high degree of interest, it is extremely important, according to Barlow, that the real design should be beneficial to society. In reality, however, the real design has just the reverse effect. "Its obvious tendency was to inflame the minds of young readers with an enthusiastic ardor for

[6] Moses Coit Tyler, *Three Men of Letters* (1895), quoted in *Major Poems of Timothy Dwight*, ed. William J. McTaggart and William K. Bottorff (Gainesville, Fla., 1969), p. vii.

military fame; to inculcate the pernicious doctrine of the divine right of kings; to teach both prince and people that military plunder was the most honorable mode of acquiring property; and that conquest, violence and war were the best employment of nations, the most glorious prerogative of bodily strength and of cultivated mind" [p. ix]. Barlow found the moral tendency of the *Aeneid* to be "nearly as pernicious." Virgil's real design, in Barlow's opinion, "was to increase the veneration of the people for a master, whoever he might be, and to encourage like Homer the great system of military depredation" [p. x]. The only ancient epic poet whom Barlow would accept as a republican was Lucan. The ancients in general, and the Greeks in particular, were widely appealed to throughout the eighteenth century in both Europe and America as noble examples of republican virtues. The Whig historian Catherine Macaulay, for example, attributed her liberal political philosophy to the spirit of liberty in classical literature. It is somewhat unusual to see an American poet condemning both Homer and Virgil for inculcating political sentiments which allegedly enforce subjection and constraint. In judging the ancients by modern moral and sociological standards, Barlow was following the practice of the *Discourse on Homer* [*Discours sur Homère* (1714)] of abbé La Motte, who, as a leading exponent of the moderns, insisted that criticism had the right to condemn the barbarous conditions portrayed in the *Iliad*.

One of the subsidiary questions discussed in the quarrel of ancients and moderns was that of the comparative beauty of the classical and modern languages and their relative fitness for poetry. On this question, Barlow affirmed that when writing *The Vision of Columbus* he had labored under "the error of supposing that the ancients had a poetical advantage over us in respect to the dignity of the names of the weapons used in war," but that he became convinced that the advantage is actually on the side of the moderns. "There are better sounding names and more variety in the instruments, works, strategems and other artifices employed in our war system than in theirs. In short, the modern military dictionary is more copious than the ancient, and the words at least as poetical" [p. xv]. The circumstances of battle in ancient times, Barlow admitted, gave the ancients an advantage in the description of single combats, but in "a general engagement, the shock of modern armies is, beyond comparison, more magnificent, more sonorous and more discoloring to the face of nature, than the ancient could have been; it is consequently susceptible of more pomp and variety of description" [p. xvi].

In keeping with his dichotomy of the narrative design and the real design of an epic, Barlow indicated that the superficial object of *The Columbiad* was to survey the labors and achievements of Columbus and to portray him as "the author of the greatest benefits to the human race" [p. xii]. The real object of the poem, however, was "to inculcate the love of rational liberty," to "discountenance the deleterious passion for violence and war," to show that all good morals as well as all good government must be founded on republican principles, and to persuade that "the theoretical question of the future advancement of human society" remains unsettled only because of the lack of experience of organized liberty in the government of nations [p. xii]. In other words, *The Columbiad* was designed to teach the doctrine of progress, an essential notion of the moderns. In his notes to the poem, Barlow particularly rejected the notion of a Golden Age "or the idea that men were more perfect, more moral and more happy in some early stage of their intercourse," as well as the related doctrine that the world has been perpetually degenerating or growing worse [no. 50]. Both doctrines were widely used by the ancients in their quarrel with

the moderns. In another note connected with the controversy, Barlow admits that the ancients may perhaps claim
to be unrivalled in some of the arts which depend upon
the imagination, those such as architecture, statuary,
painting, eloquence, and poetry, but he points out that
these are not the arts which "tend the most to the general
improvement of society" [no. 47]. In particular reference
to Homer, Barlow repeated the accusation of his preface
that the *Iliad* was filled with the pernicious doctrine of
the divine right of kings [no. 42].

Even stronger evidence of Barlow's adherence to the
moderns may be found in his earlier *Vision of Columbus*
(1787), but this evidence requires interpretation. Barlow
followed as one of the models for this poem a modern
rather than a classical epic—a sixteenth-century work in
Spanish, *La Araucana* by Alonso de Ercilla—and he did
so because of reading a description of it in an essay by
Voltaire, the author of another modern epic, *La Henriade*.
In order to prepare advance publicity for a London edition
of *La Henriade*, Voltaire published in English an essay,
*Epick Poetry of the European Nations from Homer down
to Milton* (1727), a pioneer treatment of the study of literary genres. Barlow explained in the notes to his *Vision*
that it was entirely due to Voltaire's essay (probably in a
later French version) that his mind had been opened to "a
new field of Poetry, rich with uncommon elements." In
treating the preliminary section of *La Araucana*, a description of the geography, manners, and customs of Chile,
Voltaire had argued that the strangeness of the American
continent to European readers made the introduction of
this type of material necessary, although otherwise it would
have been quite out of place. This justification inspired
Barlow to include geographical and sociological passages
in his own epic, as well as a treatment of South America
and its native population. In his notes Barlow also complained bitterly about not being able to procure a copy of

either *La Araucana* or the parallel Portuguese epic, *Os Lusiadas* by Luis de Camoëns, considering the lack of materials one of the "disadvantages that an Author, in a new country, and in moderate circumstances, must have to encounter."

Besides its indebtedness to Voltaire and Ercilla, *The Vision of Columbus* is important internationally because of a dedication to Louis XVI of France, who returned the compliment by subscribing for twenty-five copies.

In a sense, Voltaire, in acquainting Barlow with Ercilla and Camoëns, was posthumously repaying a debt to Anglo-Saxon letters. The English poet William Collins told Joseph Warton that the former's uncle, Col. Martin Bladen, "had given to Voltaire, all that account of Camoëns inserted in his essay on the Epic Poets of all Nations, and that Voltaire seemed before entirely ignorant of the name and character of Camoëns" [*Works of Alexander Pope*, ed. W. L. Bowles, 10 vols. (London, 1806), 5: 322]. Nothing is known about Voltaire's first acquaintance with Ercilla, but it may equally have been through the agency of Colonel Bladen, who had served as an officer in Spain.

On the surface there seems to be a close relationship, ideological if not historical, between the doctrine of progress and the poetic themes of *translatio studii* and *translatio empirii*, which flourished in classical times and in the Middle Ages and have been widely recognized by scholars of early American literature. The most famous English version is, of course, Bishop George Berkeley's "Verses on the Prospect of Planting Arts and Learning in America," written in 1726, but not published until 1752. Joining *translatio studii* with the imagery of the stage and the theological doctrine of the millennium, he predicted that the fifth act of the human drama would take place in the West and affirmed that "Time's noblest offspring is the last." Later in the century the theme of *translatio studii* was joined to that of the rising glory of America, but it flourished in the colonies long before either the Revolution or the publication of Berkeley's verses. A single example will suffice, one taken from a Pennsylvania almanac of 1729 and reprinted in the *Gentleman's Magazine*.

> Rome shall lament her ancient Fame declin'd
> And Philadelphia be the Athens of mankind.[7]

Other examples from the Federal period are given in a later chapter on nationalistic fervor.

Superficially it would appear that the *translatio* theme represents evidence of the dedication of early American literature to its classical heritage, but analysis reveals that classical antecedents are consistently portrayed as inferior to contemporary manifestations. The *translatio* theme is one aspect of the idea of progress and as such weighs on the side of the moderns rather than the ancients. In other words, whatever salutary concept is considered as originating in Greece and Rome, it is always improved or brought to perfection in the West. Indeed, if the theme were carried to the extreme, future development could be envisaged as even transcending the European settlements of America. The same author who compared Dwight, Barlow and Freneau to their classical counterparts reminded his readers that the descendants of the barbarians who had overturned the Roman Empire had become the modern cherishers of the arts and sciences. The Americans, he observed, are the posterity of "those whom the Romans once held in as little esteem, as that in which we at present hold the [Indian] nations of the West." While considering the likelihood extremely remote, he nevertheless expressed the possibility that America, like the Roman Empire, might in the future "be again re-peopled and governed by her

---

[7] J. A. Leo Lemay, *A Calendar of American Poetry* (Worcester, Mass., 1972), p. 162.

native inhabitants" [Meddler no. II]. The only aspect of the *translatio* theme which may be effectively counted as a tribute to the ancients is that which treats political liberty as their contribution to civilization. There existed another widespread notion throughout the Enlightenment that liberty, as manifested in European thought, had not emerged from the Greeks at all, but had developed instead from the nations of northern Europe.[8] Any motif, such as *translatio*, that would restore liberty to the ancients could in this sense legitimately be considered as supporting the prestige of the Greeks and Romans. A pseudonymous poem in the *Pennsylvania Gazette*, 30 May 1778, neatly resolved the question by assuming an autochthonous origin.

> Even Liberty herself from Heaven shall come,
> And fair America shall rival Rome.

One of the most extreme statements against the Old World came from the pen of the lexicographer Noah Webster, who instead of treating *translatio studii* in the conventional sense, suggested in the preface to his *Spelling Book* (1783) that it would be better to reject everything from the past and make a completely new beginning. In his words, "Europe is grown old in folly, corruption and tyranny—in that country laws are perverted, manners are licentious, literature is declining and human nature debased. For America in her infancy to adopt the present maxims of the Old World, would be to stamp the wrinkles of decrepit age upon the bloom of youth and to plant the seeds of decay in a vigorous constitution."[9] In a sense,

---

[8] The concept of the superiority of northern or Germanic culture to that of the Mediterranean is treated from different perspectives in two excellent surveys: Thor J. Beck, *Northern Antiquities in French Learning and Literature (1755-1855)*, 2 vols. (New York, 1934-1935); J.G.A. Pocock, *The Ancient Constitution and the Feudal Law* (New York, 1967).

[9] Harry R. Warfel, *Noah Webster, Schoolmaster to America* (New York, 1936), pp. 59-60.

this repudiation of the past is a logical extension of Paine's metaphor in *Common Sense* that "youth is the seed time of good habits, as well as in nations as in individuals" and his amazing statement "we have it in our power to begin the world over again."[10]

In addition to abstract notions such as liberty and freedom, the idea of progress incorporated scientific discoveries and the material advances of civilization such as mechanical inventions. The printing press symbolized the combination of enlightenment and technology. As such, it represented one of the milestones in human advancement. The theme was introduced into America thirty years before the Federal period, specifically by James Sterling in a poem dedicated to Samuel Richardson, author of *Pamela*, entitled "On the Invention of Letters and the Art of Printing" (1757). The poem particularly describes the triumph in philosophical thought of the moderns over the ancients as well as the progress in science and technology, symbolized by the printing press. The same theme was developed in 1795 by Robert Treat Paine in a poem with an almost identical title, *The Invention of Letters*. The work, like Sterling's, does not concern polite or belles lettres, but the process of printing, without which, according to Paine, scarcely any scientific discoveries or political reforms would have been possible. That Paine should have written on such a theme is remarkable since he was probably the most dedicated to classical traditions of all American poets of the time. Paine was so gifted that when he was assigned a Greek oration at Harvard, instead of following the general practice of reciting a passage from Demosthenes, Isocrates, or Plutarch, he "chose to write his own in Greek, without first preparing in English."[11]

[10] *Complete Writings of Thomas Paine*, ed. Philip S. Foner, 2 vols. (New York, 1945), 1: 36, 45.

[11] *Works in Verse and Prose of the Late Robert Treat Paine* (Boston, 1812), pp. xix-xx.

Despite his dedication to classical civilization, he clearly espoused in *The Invention of Letters* the side of the moderns in the polemic between the two factions.

> No more presume with bigot zeal to raise,
> O'er modern worth, the palm of ancient days.
> No more let Athens to the world proclaim,
> Her classick phalanx holds the field of fame.
>
> [p. 164]

In subsequent lines, Paine elevated Gutenberg to a position of universal eminence.

> The barbarous Rhine now blends its classick name,
> With Rome's, Phoenicia's, and Achaia's fame.
>
> [p. 165]

The major writers in the French Enlightenment tended to recognize the preeminence of the ancients in the realm of eloquence, but otherwise considered the moderns superior. Following this tradition, David Humphreys in the "Advertisement" to a *Poem on the Death of General Washington* (1800), reflects the tendency to grant to the ancients superiority in the area of rhetoric, even though he leaves the question open without settling it unequivocally. "It is not intended to be decided here," he observes, "that the Greek and Latin poets possess no advantage over the moderns in the copiousness or melody of their languages; or that poesy in those languages does not admit of more boldness in the figures, pomp in the diction, music in the cadences, variety in the numbers, or greater facility for imitative beauty in making the sound an echo to the sense, than in most of the languages." Instead of asserting the supremacy of the moderns in such areas as science or the plastic arts, however, he turns to the examples of illustrious men and finds more inspiring ones in America, the most sublime of whom is, of course, George Washington.

In a shorter poem "On the Love of Country," Humphreys even impugns the patriotism which had throughout the century been accorded to the Romans as one of their outstanding virtues.

> Perish the Roman pride a world that braves,
> To make for one free state all nations slaves;
> Their boasted patriotism at once exprest,
> Love for themselves and hate for all the rest.

Exactly the same disparaging description of classical patriotism appears in Barlow's *Columbiad*.

> Where Grecian states in even balance hung
> And warm'd with jealous fires the patriot's tongue,
> The exclusive ardor cherisht in the breast
> Love to one land and hatred to the rest.
> And where the flames of civil discord rage,
> And Roman arms with Roman arms engage,
> The mime of virtues rises still the same
> To build a Caesar's as a Pompey's name.
>
> [Book X, l. 321-28]

So far as I know, this argument appeared first in Thomas Paine's *American Crisis* no. V (1778). "The Grecians and Romans were strongly possessed of the *spirit* of liberty," Paine remarked, "but *not the principle*, for at the time that they were determined not to be slaves themselves, they employed their power to enslave the rest of mankind."

Madison in *The Federalist* [no. 14] similarly considered it to the glory of the American people that "whilst they have paid a decent regard to the opinions of former times and other nations, they have not suffered a blind veneration for antiquity, for custom, or for names, to overrule the suggestions of their own good sense." Hamilton in the ninth *Federalist* reacted with "horror and disgust" to "the history of the petty republics of Greece and Italy" because of the "distractions with which they were continually agitated" and "the rapid succession of revolutions, by which they were kept perpetually vibrating."

The pattern of superficial obeisance to the classic tradition combined with a rejection of it ideologically is highlighted in an anonymous biblical poem in the *New Haven Gazette* (21 September 1786) entitled "The Trial of Faith." The poem itself does not concern us, but its epigraph from Virgil reveals the paradoxical ambivalence toward the classics which we have been discussing.

Sicelides Musae, paulo majora canamus!

The paraphrase of this line supplied by the author announces that "American Muses aim at higher subjects than those commonly sung in the Eastern continent."

A similar ambivalence is shown by Philip Freneau in regard to the value of studying the classical languages. He was trained at Princeton in both Latin and Greek, filled his poems with classical allusions, wrote an imitation of Horace, and embellished his works with quotations from Virgil, second in number only to those from Shakespeare. At the commencement exercises, 25 September 1771, when Freneau himself was graduated, there was featured on the program "An English forensic dispute on this question, 'Does ancient poetry excel the modern?' " Freneau had been chosen as affirmative "respondent," but was absent from the ceremonies. His remarks were read by another student and answered by a second, who was in turn refuted by a third.

Despite this academic flourish, Freneau later unequivocally disparaged the role of ancient languages in the educational system. In a poem entitled "Expedition of Timothy Taurus, Astrologer" (1775?), he affirms:

This age may decay, and another may rise,
Before it is fully revealed to our eyes,

> That Latin and Hebrew, Chaldaic, and Greek,
> To the shades of oblivion must certainly sneak;
> Too much of our time is employed on such trash
> When we ought to be taught to accumulate cash.

Although these lines are intended to be humorous, they are not meant ironically. Freneau expresses an even stronger antagonism in another of his poems, "Epistle to a Student of Dead Languages."[12]

In France, the relative merits of the classical and modern languages had been treated as part of the battle of ancients and moderns. As early as 1683, for example, François Charpentier published his treatise *On the Excellence of the French Language*, making among other points the practical one that French rather than Latin should be used for inscriptions on public monuments. An essayist in the *New Haven Gazette* (DECIUS, 2 and 16 March 1791) applied the controversy to the subjects of study at Yale University. In his opinion, the traditional curriculum was outmoded in Europe, but still entrenched in America and, therefore, all the more absurd in a new environment. His main point was not that the classical languages were objectionable in themselves, but that the candidate was required to spend two years "in getting a useless smattering of latin and greek" at the end of which he could not even translate a single page of a single book. This author considered Latin and French "desirable, and even necessary," but he felt that knowledge of our own language and literature was indispensable. The worst abuse of the system was the teaching of New Testament Greek by rote. In his

---

[12] See also his prose essay *Pilgrim* no. XII in *The Freeman's Journal*, 13 February 1782, reprinted in *The Prose of Philip Freneau*, ed. Philip M. Marsh (New Brunswick, N.J., 1955), pp. 55-58. Freneau, in politics a radical and in religion a deist, thought that Dwight's epic was ridiculous and superstitious and condemned it for giving the preference of "the dreams and nonsense of antiquity" to "modern rationality" (*Prose*, ed. Marsh, p. 265).

words, "The time for education is short. From twelve years of age to twenty-one, is a period of nine years, and two of these should be employed, by almost every one, in obtaining professional knowledge.—Seven remain. If part of these must be spent in acquiring words, the English and French, are decidedly, the most learned ever spoken by man; nor can I make exception, even of the *Hebrew* or *Mohegan.*"

In treating essays in the *New Haven Gazette*, we have digressed from the poets of the time, but the newspaper background is relevant as exposing the climate of opinion in which these poets developed. The sentiments expressed by the *Gazette* essayist are mild, moreover, compared with those previously set forth in satirical verse by John Trumbull in *The Progress of Dulness* (1772). The latter affirms that half of classical learning merely displays the follies of former days and denies that knowledge must be conveyed to the brain in "ancient strains." At the same time he calls for criticism to accord to "ancient arts" their "real due" and "explain their faults, and beauties too." Another essay in the *New Haven Gazette*, one in the same issue with the criticism of the Yale curriculum, contrasts ancient learning with the doctrine of progress in the precise terms in which the debate had been carried on in Europe [Meddler no. VIII, 16 March 1791]. According to the essayist, "The sophistical reasoning of the ancient schools, served only to lead the minds of men into continued mazes of error and absurdity. . . . The improvements made in the arts and sciences, in the course of the last century, have been more rapid than they ever were at any former period; and if we were to reason from analogy, we should conclude that future improvements will be in an inverse ratio, with the time at which they are distant. . . . The moderns have a manifest superiority over the ancients, in most of the arts and sciences."

The particular American cachet which is placed upon

this essay is a reference to developments in political theory, a consciousness of which grew out of the pamphleteering in the American Revolution. The essayist proceeds imperceptibly from the Baconian theme of the deficiencies of Aristotelian philosophy to the millennial one of international harmony which concludes many of the poems of the Federal period, including Dwight's "America: or, a Poem on the Settlement of the British Colonies" (1780) and Barlow's *The Columbiad*.[13] The essayist concludes, "We are so far enlightened in the present age, as to discard most of the fictions of the ancient schools and render the unknown abstrata [*sic*] by which Aristotle and his followers solved the knotty points of philosophy, into a mere object of ridicule. Should our successors continue to make improvements upon our knowledge, as we have upon that of our *predecessors*, they will become so thoroughly acquainted with the true nature and principles of government, as to form institutions of society, which will promote the internal prosperity of nations, and by shewing the blessings of peace, bring on a universal harmony among the different nations of the earth."

The last sentence could almost serve as a paraphrase of the concluding book of *The Columbiad*, which portrays the future progress of society in all areas including government and reveals, in the words of the "Argument," a "general Congress from all nations assembled to establish the political harmony of mankind." Thomas Paine in *Rights of Man* even used the political argument to support one of the earliest positions of the moderns in the European phase of the ancients-moderns debate, Bacon's paradox

[13] The following couplets illustrate the theme in Dwight:
EUROPE and ASIA with surprize behold
Thy temples starr'd with gems and roof'd with gold.
. . .

No more on earth shall Rage and Discord dwell,
But sink with Envy to their native hell.

Antiquitas saeculi juventus mundi, "ancient times are
the youth of the world." According to Paine, the only
value in studying governments in ancient times is "to
make a proper use of the errors or the improvements which
the history of it presents. Those who lived a hundred or
a thousand years ago, were then moderns as we are now."[14]
Paine in an earlier essay also touches on the millennial
theme and joins it with disparagement of the ancients for
their vanity and ignorance. "Improvement and the world
will expire together," he remarks. "And till that period
arrives, we may plunder the mine, but can never exhaust
it! That '*We have found out everything,*' has been the
motto of every age. Let our ideas travel a little into antiquity, and we shall find larger portions of it than now;
and so unwilling were our ancestors to descend from this
mountain of perfection, that when any new discovery exceeded the common standard, the discoverer was believed
to be in alliance with the devil" [*Writings*, 2: 1111].

One cannot solely on the evidence of the foregoing passages maintain that the European quarrel of the ancients
and the moderns extended itself in a kind of *translatio
studii* to the Western world, but there can be no doubt,
on the other hand, that many of the same principles of
that debate were seriously discussed in the Anglophone
areas of America throughout the second half of the eighteenth century. Certainly the debate reached university
circles in America, for John Witherspoon of Princeton in
an essay "Of Eloquence" summarized the European background of the "controversy . . . upon the preference being
due to ancient or modern writers." Although taking an
eclectic position by recognizing good in both camps, Witherspoon seemed to join Dwight and Barlow in feeling that
Homer had been overpraised. "Now the beauties of Homer
we are easily capable of perceiving," he wrote, "though

---

[14] *Complete Writings*, ed. Foner, 1: 273.

perhaps not his faults. The beauty of a description, the force of a similitude, we can plainly see; but whether he always adhered to truth and nature, we cannot tell, because we have no other way of knowing the manners and customs of his times but from what he has written."

Even though most of the evidence consists of parallel themes, there certainly exists a strong possibility that most of the Americans who expressed themselves in regard to the amount of subservience due to the ancients were fully aware of the ramifications of the ideas they expressed. It is hard to believe, for example, that most of them had not read Swift's *Tale of the Tub* and *Battle of the Books* in which the battle lines were clearly drawn. The poets in question were in a sense products of two cultures—the classical and the modern—and they sought to identify themselves with both.

The painter John Trumbull, who flourished during the period with which we are concerned, recalls in his *Autobiography* a discussion in his youth with his father over his desire to embrace the pictorial arts as his life's work. His father listened gravely to the aspiring painter dwelling rhapsodically upon "the honours paid to artists in the glorious days of Greece and Athens." The senior Trumbull then rejoined, "You appear to forget, sir, that *Connecticut is not Athens*" [New York, 1841, p. 49]. This is a cryptic remark, and, like the young Trumbull, we cannot be sure whether preference was meant to be accorded to ancient Greece or to eighteenth-century America. My discussion of the five major poets of the Federal period in American literature reveals that they shared a similar ambivalence.

By suggesting that American poets were aware of the European quarrel between ancients and moderns and that they consciously espoused the modern side, I am by no means attempting to diminish the stature of the Greek and Latin traditions in early American letters or to portray these poets as unequivocally opposed to classical learning. It could even be maintained that to engage in the debate at all on either side one had to possess both an appreciation and a knowledge of classical culture. Certainly every one of the European critics who espoused the moderns was at the same time skilled in at least the Latin language and possessed more than a rudimentary knowledge of Greek and Latin masterpieces. Boileau, for example, who cherished the ancients with an informed devotion, fought valiantly in their behalf for most of his career until eventually forced to admit with great reluctance that "the Age of Louis XIV is not only comparable but superior to the most famous ages of antiquity, even the Age of Augustus." Voltaire likewise derived more pleasure from being known as the French Sophocles than from any other of his literary distinctions; yet he insisted on the preeminence of the French stage over that of the ancients with the same vigor with which he defended Newton in the realm of science. In England, the best informed classical scholar in the controversy was Richard Bentley, the Royal librarian. It was precisely his classical learning which proved to be most damaging to the position of the British defenders of the ancients.

The classical training of the five American poets with whom I am concerned is impressive to say the least. Dwight, Barlow, and Humphreys were graduates of Yale; Freneau of Princeton, and Paine of Harvard. Even though, according to one of the adverse critics whom I cite, the teaching methods may have depended too greatly on rote learning, graduates of these institutions in the late eighteenth century must inevitably have attained both linguistic and literary competence in both Latin and Greek. Graduates in Barlow's class at Yale, for example, were at the end of their course of studies examined on Cicero and on the Greek Testament.[15] These poets were also living in times of intense nationalism and patriotic fervor, however, times

[15] Theodore Albert Zunder, *The Early Days of Joel Barlow* (New Haven, 1934), p. 54.

in which in any expression of the superiority of former societies would have seemed a betrayal of the ideals of the Revolution. It was acceptable for poets to praise their classical heritage, but they were careful to do so in a manner which made this heritage contributory to American glory and subservient to it. David Humphreys in a poem entitled "On the Happiness of America" written in 1780 during the midst of the Revolutionary War went so far as to portray every society previous to that of America as inferior.

> All former empires rose, the work of guilt,
> On conquest, blood or usupation built:
> But we, taught wisdom by their woes and crimes,
> Fraught with their lore, and born to better times;
> Our constitutions form'd on freedom's base,
> Which all the blessings of all lands embrace;
> Embrace humanity's extended cause,
> A world our empire, for a world our laws.

The strongest evidence of the pervasiveness of classical influences is that found in the poem "Anticipation of the Literary Fame of America," which recasts the appearance of an American masterpiece in many of the classical genres and which describes them in terms of Greek or Latin prototypes.

> Columbian *Livies* throng the historick field,
> A brighter band than ever Greece could yield.
> The morn of eloquence again shall dawn,
> And courtless *Cicero's* our courts adorn.
> Another Plato utter truths divine,
> Another Stagyrite our taste refine.
> Some new Euripides, with tragick art,
> Shall calm the passions, and shall touch the heart,
> Describe with energy *Orestes'* rage,
> And prompt to virtue from the moral stage.

Some future *Virgil* shall our wars rehearse
In all the dignity of epic verse.
Some modern *Ovid* paint his fair one's charms,
Her eyes bright sparkling and her twining arms;
The panting bosom and the ambrosial kiss,
The dying languor and the heavenly bliss.
In ——'s bowers new porticoes shall rise,
And fairer *Lyceums* glad our wondering eyes.
Groves academic grace the sylvan scene,
And Tully's Tusculum again be seen.
The brilliant treasure of the Attick mine,
Shall glow refulgent in our western clime,
Till the Archangel's trump thro' ether ring,
Till earth exulting own the eternal King,
Till ruling planets, from their orbits hurl'd,
Announce the dissolution of the world.[16]

The concluding lines of this poem significantly set forth
the millennial doctrine which exists also in the works of
Dwight, Barlow, and most other poets of the time. Although this work must certainly be considered as important evidence of the vogue of classical models in American
literature, it must not be assumed that the designation of
classical prototypes is peculiarly an American phenomenon or that the practice makes American literature any
more classical than others in Western Europe. Goethe,
who deplored the popularity of poetic imitation in Germany, remarked in his *Autobiography* concerning the
common practice: "We now possessed, if not Homers, yet
Virgils and Miltons; if not a Pindar, yet a Horace; of Theo-
crituses there was no lack."[17] Looking back from the perspective of the nineteenth century, Goethe realized that
the period of neoclassical imitation had passed and that

[16] *Massachusetts Magazine* 1 (1789): 117-18.
[17] Trans. John Oxenford, 2 vols. (Chicago, 1974), 1: 293.

different standards and objectives were necessary for the literature of his age.

The same judgment may, of course, be rendered post facto against the American critics who awaited the appearance of new Virgils or new Ovids. They failed to realize that the time for neoclassical imitation had passed in America also. Not only were Latin and Greek models about to lose their vogue, but the traditional genres were giving way to new ones such as the novel, the romance, the short story, and the personal lyric. Apart from the prose of Franklin and Paine, the first works of American literature to obtain international recognition grew out of the new wave of what is now known as Romanticism. The first of the poets of this school, William Cullen Bryant, took full advantage of the classical tradition—witness, for example, the title of his best-known lyric "Thanatopsis"—but he reacted against the artificial or superficial elements of neoclassical rhetoric. He remarked in 1827, "I am aware that in modern poetry nothing is generally so nauseous and revolting as the introduction of the Pagan deities. Nothing turns us away from the perusal of a copy of verses so soon as any talk about Venus and Cupid, about Bacchus and his bowl, and about Sol and his chariot."[18]

Two of the labels that have been used for the period under discussion—the quarter of a century from the Revolution to the end of the eighteenth century—are paradoxically conflicting, but still relatively accurate. It was a new Age of Augustus in the rhetoric and structure of its literature, based as it was upon arbitrary rules requiring adherence to a single standard of propriety and order. It was the Federal period in ideology, however, allowing for a mixture of intellectual codes in the sense that "in the shallow structures of the mind several cultural codes can

---

[18] R. B. Silber, "William Cullen Bryant's Lectures on Mythology" (Ph.D. diss., State University of Iowa, 1962), p. 123.

operate successfully at the same time."[19] Intellectually, the Federal period was as pluralistic as the political system of the newly organized United States of America.

The history of the debate in eighteenth-century America over the educational value of Latin and Greek has been exhaustively treated by Meyer Reinhold in two articles in the *Proceedings of the American Philosophical Society*: Vol. 112 (1968): 221-34 and Vol. 119 (1975): 108-32. In the later article, Professor Reinhold declares that it is "methodologically wrong" to view the dispute over classical languages in the schools "as a renewal of the debate between the Ancients and the Moderns in the earlier Battle of the Books in Europe, or as a contrast between conservatives and liberals" [p. 116]. My own methodology in the preceding survey has consisted entirely in quoting American authors and suggesting parallels to notions expressed in the European debate. I am inclined to believe, however, that one could legitimately argue that the fundamental issues of the controversy were very much alive in eighteenth-century America and that the debate was continued there rather than merely renewed. The ancient side was favorably presented by John Wesley in his *Survey of the Wisdom of God in the Creation*, which contains long extracts from a work originally printed in French by John Dutens, *An Inquiry into the Origin of the Discoveries attributed to the Moderns: Wherein It is Demonstrated, That our most celebrated Philosophers have, for most part, taken what they advance from the Works of the Ancients*. The Dutens extracts were added to the second edition of Wesley's work (Bristol, 1777) and repeated in subsequent editions. It is impossible to tell how extensively this work circulated in America during the eight-

---

[19] James McLachlan, "Classical Names, American Identities: Some Notes on College Students and the Classical Tradition in the 1770's," in *Classical Traditions in Early America*, ed. James W. Eadie (Ann Arbor, 1976), p. 93.

eenth century, but it appears to be one of those books which people read in their homes, but was not bought for libraries. It is not listed in Evans, *American Bibliography*. The Library of Congress holds the "3d American ed., rev. and enl.; with notes, by B. Mayo. New York, Pub. by N. Bangs and T. Mason, for the Methodist Episcopal Church, 1823." I do not know when the first American edition appeared. The British Museum contains only three editions, the first (Bristol 1763) [which does not have the Dutens extracts], the second (Bristol, 1777) and an un-numbered "new edition . . . adapted to the present state of science by R. Mudie. 3 vol. London, 1836."

As far as political principles are concerned, I am not aware of any serious attempt to join the debates over either classical languages in the curriculum or the preeminence of ancient or modern learning to party or social divisions. Freneau and Barlow conveyed democratic ideals whereas Dwight, Humphreys, and Robert Treat Paine revealed aristocratic sentiments. By and large, however, the democratic writers (those loyal to the administration of Thomas Jefferson in the first decade of the nineteenth century) continued to predict eventual American supremacy in the realm of literature; whereas the opponents of Jefferson (the Federalists) lamented what they considered to be the lack of distinction in American letters.

The opposition to classical languages in the academic curriculum has been partly attributed to the influx of Scottish educators such as William Smith of Pennsylvania and John Witherspoon of Princeton. Perhaps because the speech of their country had been traditionally ridiculed by the English, they placed a premium upon the strength and purity of the English language and maintained that this purity was threatened by the emphasis on Latin and Greek. Even before Smith's appearance in Philadelphia, however, Franklin had proposed that in the institution that eventually became the University of Pennsylvania "all should not be compell'd to learn *Latin*, *Greek*, or the modern foreign languages."[20] He later called Latin and Greek "the quackery of literature."[21] Benjamin Rush, although ambivalent about Scottish educators, expressed grave doubts concerning the value of classical instruction in his *Observations upon the Study of the Latin and Greek Languages* (1789).

Many in the Federal period agreed with Franklin that the classical languages were nothing but elegant and useless ornaments. Thomas Paine not only shared this opinion, but maintained in addition that organized religions had imposed the study of dead languages in order to preserve the system of Christian dogma and to prevent its falsehood from being exposed through scientific discoveries. "It became necessary to their purpose," he charged in *The Age of Reason*, "to cut learning down to a size less dangerous . . . , and this they effected by restricting the idea of learning to the dead study of dead language."[22] This reasoning was duplicated by one of Paine's Latin American disciples, Camilo Henríquez of Chile, in an essay "On the Influence of Enlightenment Writings on the Fate of Humanity" (1812), an essay which is equally as relevant to the final chapter of this book as to the present one. Continuing to teach sciences in Latin, Henríquez affirmed, is the major obstacle which can be offered not only to the diffusion of the Enlightenment, but also to its perfection. "The method of scholasticism, the system of studies of the schools, the obstacles which the popularization of useful books has encountered, have had an enormous influence in the backwardness of letters."[23]

[20] *Papers of Benjamin Franklin*, ed. Leonard W. Labaree et al. (New Haven, 1961), 3: 415.

[21] "Papers of Benjamin Rush," *Pennsylvania Magazine of History and Biography* 29 (1905): 15-30.

[22] *Complete Writings*, ed. Foner, 1: 483.

[23] Quoted in A. O. Aldridge, "Thomas Paine and the Classics," *Eighteenth-Century Studies* 1 (1968): 370-80.

SEVEN

THE APEX OF AMERICAN LITERARY NATIONALISM

URING THE PERIOD of the American Revolution, many writers considered that the level of intellectual achievement in America was high, and they were not reticent about declaring their opinion to the world. John Dickinson in the seventh of his Farmer's *Letters* described the inhabitants of the American colonies as in general "more intelligent than any other people whatever." Paine in the last of his *Crisis* papers maintained that the American Revolution had "contributed more to enlighten the world, and diffuse a spirit of freedom and liberality among mankind, than any human event (if this may be called one) that ever preceded it." And a decade later in his *Rights of Man*, Paine quoted Edmund Burke to the effect "that the people of America are more enlightened than those of Europe, or of any other country in Europe."[1] The euphoria of the Revolution lasted in America until the end of the eighteenth century when it gave way to doubts and fears about the efficacy of the experiment then being carried on in democratic government. This emotional transition coincided roughly with the gradual replacing of the Enlightenment with Romanticism, but no connection other than that of chronology has yet been demonstrated between these shifts in public opinion and literary trends.

[1] *Complete Writings*, ed. Philip S. Foner, 2 vols. (New York, 1945), 1: 366.

European observers remained tolerant of American pride and complacency until early in the nineteenth century. At this time a statement emanating from the Congress of the United States declaring the American nation to be the most enlightened in the world turned the American people into objects of ridicule. In December 1796, the House of Representatives resolved itself into a Committee of the Whole to consider the text of a reply to a state of the union address recently delivered by President George Washington. In this tentative reply to the chief executive appeared an astounding phrase describing the United States literally as "a whole nation, the freest and most enlightened in the world." In the resulting debate over the entire text, one of the more moderate members moved to strike out the boastful phrase. "Although, said he, I wish to believe that we are the freest people, and the most enlightened people in the world, it is enough that we think ourselves so; it is not becoming in us to make the declaration to the world; and if we are not so, it is still worse for us to suppose ourselves what we are not."[2]

The phrase claiming the United States to be the most enlightened nation in the world was never incorporated into an official Congressional document, but it did appear in the printed annals of Congress. Not surprisingly, this pretension to a superior degree of enlightenment provoked varying degrees of critical response from European observers. A contemporary French traveler in America, the Duke de la Rochefoucauld Liancourt, with gentle irony referred to the congressional debate as evidence of the "good opinion" which the people of the United States have of themselves. He cited caustically the labor and long discussion necessary to persuade the House to sacrifice "this superlative, with which the modesty of the

[2] *Debates and Proceedings in the Congress of the United States* (Washington, D.C., 1849), 6: 1614.

majority of the United States had not been embarrassed"
and added seriously that "almost all the books printed in
America, and the individual conversations of the Americans" furnish proof of their inordinate nationalistic pride.[3]

It might be noted in connection with "inordinate nationalistic pride," however, that one of La Rochefoucauld's countrymen, the novelist Balzac, a few years later
described their own nation to be "la plus intelligente du
monde."[4] What might be condoned as natural pride or
even mildly criticized as excessive vanity in a French author, however, would have been harshly condemned in
the early years of the nineteenth century as presumption
and insufferable arrogance in a citizen of the newly formed
United States. It is quite possible, indeed even probable,
that the congressional debate over "the most enlightened
people in the world" led the British critic Sydney Smith
to phrase in the *Edinburgh Review* of 1820 his now-fa-
mous rhetorical question, "In the four quarters of the globe,
who reads an American book? or goes to an American
play? or looks at an American picture or statue?" Reason
for believing that Smith had read the report of the debate
in the House of Representatives is found in a sentence in
his review in which he specifically reprobated the epithets
by which American "orators and newspaper scribblers en-
deavour to persuade their supporters that they are the
greatest, the most refined, the most enlightened, and the
most moral people upon earth."

After Smith's attack, the phrase "most enlightened people of the world" continued to attract attention. In the
middle of the nineteenth century, an even more vicious
denunciation of American arrogance was published by a
conservative German count, Adelbert Heinrich Baudissin,

[3] *Travels through the United States of North America*, 2 vols. (London,
1799), 2: 657.
[4] *La Duchesse de Langeais*, Edition Livre du Poche, Gallimard (Paris,
1958), p. 143.

under the pseudonym of Peter Tütt. His book, entitled *Zustände in Amerika* (1862), is now quite rare, but it had in its own time at least three editions. Baudissin revived the phrase concerning American enlightenment in a colorful passage depicting the state house of Tennessee as an example of the anomalous combination of filth and luxury to be found everywhere in the United States. Although the ceiling of the legislative chamber was adorned with murals and the floor with thick carpets, the legislators sat with their feet on their desks and spat tobacco juice into the air. The German critic wondered how it could be "possible that *the most enlightened people of the world* should leave the weal and woe of the whole nation in the hands of raw and dishonorable men." We are not concerned with this observer's conservative political opinions, but with the persistence of the phrase "the most enlightened people of the world," which Baudissin quoted in English and which he had, therefore, presumably found to be in widespread use. Incidentally, tobacco chewing and spitting without the amenity of a spittoon were among the aspects of American life that the German poet Heinrich Heine, a contemporary of Baudissin, adduced as making him wary of American civilization.[5]

Few European observers at the beginning of the nineteenth century expressed much hope for the imminent development of letters in America. An English gentleman, for example, who had formerly lived in the United States published in the London *Monthly Magazine* for 1802 a survey of what he termed the "disgraceful" and the "wretched state of American literature."[6] He refused to accept as relevant or valid the excuse which many Americans offered "in defence of a literary dearth, that *their's*

---

[5] Benno von Wiese, "Goethe und Heine als Europäer," in *Teilnahme und Spiegelung*, ed. B. Allemann and E. Koppen, (Berlin, 1975), p. 313.
[6] 14 (January, 1803): 624-27.

is a young country, and consequently that science must be in its cradle." This English observer tartly affirmed that "The Americans were the same people as the British, coëval with them; sprung from the same stock; children of one family, inhabiting distant parts, yet speaking the same language, enjoying the very same advantages of preceding authors whereon to form their tastes. Why then should Americans be behind-hand in science with the Britons?" At this period in English journalism the word *science* was loosely used to represent intellectual activity of almost any kind. According to this critic, English books were being constantly sent to the colonies, but little or nothing came back to London in return. It was irrelevant that the Americans paid for their books as a commercial transaction; in his opinion nothing but a cultural exchange could place the two nations on equal terms. "Between nations, genius cannot be bartered but for itself; it is a restless, ever-stirring quality of the human mind, which can only be satisfied with itself, which increases only to be increased; enlightens only to be enlightened the more." This austere English critic would not accept even the works of Franklin as an example of a "literary production to which America hath given birth, stamped with original genius."

These British strictures can be considered as in large measure a reply to an overdrawn appeal for American nationalism that Noah Webster, the pioneer American lexicographer, had issued in his *Dissertations on the English Language* (1789). Webster had proposed therein establishing an independent national language for North America on the grounds that "customs, habits, and *language* as well as government should be national." In his opinion, "to copy foreign manners implicitly is to reverse the order of things, and begin our political existence with the corruption and vices which have marked the declining glories of other republics." It is not strange, therefore, that the writer for the *Monthly Magazine* should have attacked Webster's proposed model for American writing as a "collection of Stuff, having the same affinity to science, which an *Olla podrida*, or hotch-potch, hath to cookery."

A famous French traveler in America during the same period, Brissot de Warville, also believed that the Americans should devise their own language. They should detest the English, he felt, and should carry their hatred so far as to efface all traces of their linguistic origins. In support of this notion, Brissot expressed a principle that would now be considered anathema by French linguists anxious to preserve their heritage from Franglais. According to Brissot, "one is the enemy of the human race and of universal peace by attaching oneself, as do certain writers, to preserving what they call the genius of each language." Brissot advised the Americans to adopt ways of expression peculiar to the French tongue. There would be, he argued, a double advantage in his method of universal naturalization. In his words, "The Americans would draw closer to other peoples and further away from the English; they would manufacture a language that would be appropriate to them; and they would have an American language."[7]

The defensiveness of Webster and many other Americans in regard to their cultural achievements grew out of resentment at a philosophical doctrine originating with Buffon and promulgated by many Europeans throughout the eighteenth century, the doctrine that European biological species of all kinds degenerated when introduced into the Western Hemisphere. Buffon had originally maintained that only plants and animals in the New World were inferior, but in 1768, a French abbé, Cornelius de Pauw, a protégé of Frederick the Great and associate of

---

[7] *Nouveau voyage dans les États-Unis . . . par J. P. Brissot*, 3 vols. (Paris, 1791), 1: 99-100.

Voltaire, published a shocking book, *Recherches philosophiques sur les Américains*, extending the notion of degeneration to the human race.[8] The book had a *succès de scandal*, and for a while almost everyone in Europe, including the abbé Raynal who adopted its doctrine in his own history of the New World, accepted the notion. In 1776, de Pauw applied the concept of inferiority to American letters in an article "Amérique," which appeared in the Pancoucke *Supplément* to the *Encyclopédie*. Here de Pauw remarked that "one does not notice that the professors of the university of Cambridge in New England have formed any young Americans to the point of being able to launch them in the literary world."

Franklin and Jefferson, among major writers, attempted to refute Buffon and de Pauw by pragmatic evidence, and a host of belligerent and satirical squibs against their theory appeared in American newspapers. Thomas Paine in the introductory essay to the *Pennsylvania Magazine*, which he edited before the publication of *Common Sense*, unequivocally affirmed, "degeneracy is here almost a useless word."[9] Foreign vices, he declared, "either expire on their arrival, or linger away in an incurable consumption." Among the category of noxious foreign products, Paine included European wit, which he decried as "one of the worst articles we can import." The *New Haven Gazette* published in 1787 an essay entitled "American Antiquities" devoted to a spurious epic poem, which presumably antedated Homer and predicted the nature of the modern world. The entire essay satirized the doctrine of biological degeneration and its principal exponents Buffon, De Pauw, and Raynal [13 September]. A more sober "Essay on Amer-

---

[8] Full documentation on the history of the theory of biological degeneration may be found in Antonello Gerbi, *The Dispute of the New World*, trans. Jeremy Moyle (Pittsburgh, 1973). This is one of the most important books related to the intellectual background of American literature.

[9] *Complete Writings*, ed. Foner, 2: 1110.

ican Genius," which appeared in the same volume of this newspaper [1 February], both attacked the doctrine of biological degeneration, and celebrated American writers and painters, including Trumbull, Barlow, West, and Copley. A similar essay, praising the literary achievement of Franklin, Edwards, Trumbull, and the memorials of Congress, concluded that "of no other nation can so honourable things be mentioned, at so early a period of their existence" [27 April 1786]. These essays were by no means unusual in their exaggerated view of national esthetic achievement, and contemporary poetry was every bit as extreme. A recent survey has revealed that "during the Revolution and the Period of Confederation [1775-1788], three out of every ten poems which were printed in magazines contained some type of patriotic exploitation; in the 1790 decade the proportion increased."[10]

Long before the doctrine of biological degeneration developed in Europe, the contrary notion of a special pure and salutary environment to be found in America had emerged in the British colonies. This notion has contributed to a type of isolationism or separatism that has existed in North American culture ever since Puritan times. Sometimes known as "exceptionalism" or "historical uniqueness," it has appeared under various guises, including millennialism and Manifest Destiny. One of the most common colonial forms of exceptionalism consisted, as we have already seen, in a variant of the European theme of the westward movement of the arts and sciences from the place of their birth in ancient Greece and Rome. Later writers expatiated on the delights and advantages of America without introducing the *translatio* theme to explain them.

[10] Unpublished dissertation by C. W. Coles quoted by Gordon E. Bigelow, *Rhetoric and American Poetry of the Early National Period*, University of Florida Monographs, Humanities, no. 4 (Gainesville, Fla., 1960), p. 52n.

David Humphreys, who shared with Barlow the distinction of being among the first American poets to attain any degree of international notice, wrote an entire poem on the theme of the salutary environment of his country to which he gave the unequivocal title, "On the Happiness of America" (1780).[11] The following lines are typical:

> All former empires rose, the work of guilt,
> On conquest, blood or usurpation built:
> But we, taught wisdom by their woes and crimes,
> Fraught with their lore, and born to better times;
> Our constitutions form'd on freedom's base,
> Which all the blessings of all lands embrace;
> Embrace humanity's extended cause,
> A world our empire, for a world our laws.

The emergence of a native literature is associated with the author and his fellow poets.

> Thou spirit of the West, assert our fame,
> In other bards awake the dormant flame.

Humphreys also produced a companion piece with the explicit title, "A Poem on the Future Glory of the United States of America" (1800?). Its prose "Advertisement," deliberately seeking to vindicate the theme of aggressive prophecy, makes use of the theological doctrine of the millennium, that divine order has appointed America for the ideal society. In Humphrey's words, "America, after having been concealed for so many ages from the rest of

---

[11] One of Humphrey's Revolutionary poems, "Address to the Armies of the United States of America," was translated by the Marquis de Chastellux, published in Paris, and favorably received in the *Journal de Paris*, 7 May 1786. Since Humphreys served in Madrid as minister plenipotentiary to Spain, it is not surprising that the list of subscribers to his *Miscellaneous Works* (New York, 1804) should include the king and queen of Spain as well as diplomats at Madrid from Denmark, Sweden, Norway, Portugal, Great Britain, Prussia, and France.

the world, was probably discovered, in the maturity of time, to become the theatre for displaying the illustrious designs of Providence, in its dispensations to the human race." Humphreys argues also that the function of the poet is precisely that of looking into the future. "The poet and the prophet have been considered so intimately blended together, that a common name (at least in one language) was expressive of both."

Four years before the Declaration of Independence, Philip Freneau composed for commencement exercises at Princeton University a superpatriotic poem entitled "The Rising Glory of America," in which he established a tradition of pride by anticipation. After consigning to poetic oblivion Memphis, Athens, Rome, and Britain, he affirmed that

> A theme more new, tho' not less noble, claims
> Our ev'ry thought on this auspicious day;
> The rising glory of this western world.

Then celebrating Philadelphia as the "seat of arts, of science, and of fame," the happy city, "where the muses stray," Freneau indicated that fair science "transplanted from the eastern climes, dost bloom / In these fair regions" while "Greece and Rome no more / Detain the muses on Cithaeron's brow."

In a later poem entitled "Literary Importation" (1786, 1788), intended primarily to oppose the bringing over of an English bishop, Freneau suggested that the religious purity of America would lead to intellectual superiority over England.

> Can we never be thought to have learning or grace
> Unless it be brought from that horrible place
> Where tyranny reigns with her impudent face;
> And popes and pretenders
> And sly faith-defenders

> Have ever been hostile to reason and wit,
> Enslaving a world that shall conquer them yet.

In other "Stanzas on the Emigration to America" (1785), Freneau predicted the supremacy of his nation in every possible human activity.

> Far brighter scenes, a future age,
> The muse predicts, these States shall hail,
> Whose genius shall the world engage,
> Whose deeds shall over death prevail,
>   And happier systems bring to view
>   Than all the eastern sages knew.

In a prologue to a French play presented in Philadelphia in 1782, Freneau developed a double contrast, cultural and political.

> Even here where Freedom lately sat distrest,
> See a new Athens rising in the west!

Another prologue, by Robert Treat Paine for the opening of the Federal Street Theatre in Boston in 1794, joined to traditional esthetic excellencies the architecture of the building.

> An Athens, Rome, Augusta, blush to see,
> Their virtue, beauty, grace, all shine—combined in
>   thee.

Crèvecoeur, in his famous *Letters from an American Farmer* (1782) in which he described Americans as "a new race of men," also portrayed his countrymen as perfecting the civilization that had been inadequately developed in Europe. "Americans," he said, "are the western pilgrims, who are carrying along with them that great mass of arts, sciences, vigour, and industry which began long since in the east; they will finish the great circle."[12]

---

[12] Edited by Warren B. Blake (London, 1913), Letter III.

The *translatio* theme, which was obviously exactly the opposite of the notion of biological degeneration, was given a revolutionary twist by Thomas Paine, who defiantly charged in his manifesto of political independence *Common Sense* that "Freedom hath been hunted round the globe" until at last it found a refuge in America. When Paine himself returned to America in 1802 following a disappointing experience with the French Revolution, he told the citizens of the United States that it is "through the New World" that "the Old must be regenerated."[13]

Paine also proclaimed the topographical theme—that the vast and sublime landscape of America together with its salubrious climate will inspire noble and sublime thoughts in its natives and lead to great deeds and artistic triumphs. Although this environmental theme is usually associated with Walt Whitman, who later developed it out of all proportion with the help of his self-recognized bombast, it actually originated in the early years of the republic. According to Paine, the scene that America "presents to the eye of a spectator, has something in it which generates and encourages great ideas. Nature appears to him in magnitude. The mighty objects he beholds, act upon his mind by enlarging it, and he partakes of the greatness he contemplates" [*Rights of Man*, Part Second, Introduction]. The idea was by no means original to Paine. Six years previously the *Columbian Magazine* had associated the esthetic appeal of American sylvan scenes with the production of literature. "The face of nature, throughout the United States, exhibits the *sublime* and *beautiful*. . . . Our mountains, vallies, plains, and rivers, are formed upon a great scale; the extent of the country itself is great; and the whole is rendered magnificiently beautiful." If patriotic deeds are also taken into consideration, "we must

[13] *Complete Writings*, ed. Foner, 2: 912.

allow that nothing can allow more noble themes for our native bards" [October 1786].

In fairness to American authors, one might point out that Goethe makes a similar reference to the influence of the landscape upon mental processes. He remarks in his *Autobiography* that "the undetermined, widely expanding feelings of youth and of uncultivated nations are alone adapted to the sublime, which, if it is to be excited in us through external objects, formless or moulded into incomprehensible forms, must surround us with a greatness to which we are not equal."[14] This is close to, if not identical with, a statement by Thomas Paine, shortly before the publication of *Rights of Man*: "Great scenes inspire great Ideas. The natural Mightiness of America expands the Mind and it partakes of the greatness it contemplates."[15]

The first American author to challenge the topographical argument was the Gothic novelist Charles Brockden Brown. A British traveler who greatly admired Rousseau once asked the Philadelphia author "whether a view of nature would not be more propitious to composition; or whether he should not write with more facility were his window to command the prospect of the Lake of *Geneva*. Sir, said he, good pens, thick paper, and ink well diluted, would facilitate my composition more than the prospect of the broadest expanse of water, or mountains rising above the clouds."[16]

Somewhat later the poet Longfellow expressed the same pragmatic attitude in a novel *Kavanaugh* (1849). By means of one of his characters, the village schoolmaster, Longfellow rejected the call for a "national literature commensurate with our mountains and rivers."

[14] *Autobiography*, Part II, Book VI.

[15] A. O. Aldridge, *Man of Reason, The Life of Thomas Paine* (New York, 1959), p. 109.

[16] John Davis, *Travels of Four Years and a Half in the United States of America* (London, 1803), pp. 149-50.

Great has a very different meaning when applied to a river, and when applied to a literature. . . . A man will not necessarily be a great poet because he lives near a great mountain. Nor being a poet, will he necessarily write better poems than another, because he lives nearer Niagara. . . . Switzerland has produced no extraordinary poet; nor, as far as I know, have the Andes, or the Himalaya mountains, or the Mountains of the Moon in Africa.

[Chapter XX]

One of the paradoxes in American writing at the turn of the century is that glowing predictions of literary glory coexisted with recognition that the social and economic conditions requisite for extensive literary production were almost entirely lacking. A poem by Warren Dutton, *The Present State of Literature*, delivered at the commencement exercises of Yale College in 1800, lamented in allegorical terms the neglect of the muses in "fair freedom's last retreat." Dutton condemned French writers associated with the French Revolution and praised some English writers, but the only American he even mentioned was Royal Tyler because of his having preceded Gifford in satirizing the Della Cruscans.

In the same year, the president of Yale, Timothy Dwight, attempted to explain the dearth of American talent in a discourse on the eighteenth century. "Great literary and scientific attainments," he affirmed, "cannot be made without great leisure, as well as great talents and application. Such leisure is rarely found here. No ample literary foundations are furnished here for the support of ingenious and speculative men, in the pursuits of learning and science."[17]

When British reviewers failed to hail the sporadic productions from western pens as belonging to the category

[17] *A Discourse on Some Events of the Last Century* (New Haven, 1801), p. 16.

of genius, a natural reaction of American writers was to accuse British publishers and reviewers of prejudice. One of the earliest examples of this attitude is a poem by John Trumbull castigating British critics for neglecting American works, allegedly for political motives. His poem, "Lines addressed to Messrs. Dwight and Barlow, on the projected publication of their Poems in London," which was written in December 1775, affirms the existence of bias among British reviewers even though the anticipated publication of the verse of his friends had not taken place.

> And see, where yon proud Isle her shores extends
> The cloud of Critics on your Muse descends!
> From every side, with deadly force, shall steer
> The fierce Review, the censuring Gazeteer.

Not all British journals, however, should be considered hostile or condescending toward polite letters in the United States. An early, perhaps the first, significant Old World recognition of American literature as an independent entity consists of a "Half-Yearly Retrospect of American Literature," a regular feature appearing every six months in the London *Monthly Magazine* beginning in 1809. These regular surveys, parallel to others on domestic English, French, German, and Spanish literatures, sought to attain objectivity and fairness, and in large measure succeeded in doing so.[18]

Even some native Americans expressed adverse opinions about the quality of the literature being produced at the turn of the century, but these were for the most part politically inspired, directed by Federalists against the Democratic-Republican Administration of Jefferson. The

---

[18] A prior publication *Bibliotheca Americana* (London, 1789) is primarily a catalog of books about both North and South America. Its introductory discourse "On the Present State of Literature in those Countries," which will be discussed in Chapter Nine, has an intriguing title, but does not live up to its promise.

Federalists' philosophy was conservative and elitist; the Democratic-Republican, populist and eclectic. The Federalists found one more weapon against the Democrats by citing alleged deficiencies in the cultural milieu. The *Monthly Anthology* affirmed, therefore, in 1805 that "in literature we are yet in our infancy; and to compare our authors, whether in prose or poetry, to those of the old world, can proceed only from the grossest ignorance, or the most insufferable vanity." The *Port Folio*, edited by Joseph Dennie, devoted in 1807 parts of three issues to an "Examination of the causes that have retarded the progress of literature in the United States."[19] Although completely rejecting the doctrine of biological degeneration as a fantasy of discredited French philosophy, the author nevertheless presented the theme of *translatio* in a skeptical light (a rare, almost unique example of such a treatment). Unsympathetic to Puritanism and the egalitarian political notions associated with it, he caustically referred to the early settlers of America "who under we know not what pretext of civil and religious liberty, wandered to the Wilderness of the West." The poor showing of American literature he ascribed to commercialism and avarice, the lack of a national university, the indifference of the federal government, the lack of patronage, and the neglect of classical learning. A hardened Federalist, Fisher Ames, ironically asked in 1809 whether Joel Barlow could be matched with Homer or Hesiod, or Thomas Paine with Plato, but he was not much more flattering to England, which, he affirmed, had not produced a first-rate poet for a long time. In his opinion, if America were to lag behind merely to the same degree as her parent country, "it will not be thought a proof of the deficiency of our genius."[20]

The most extensive analysis of the obstacles to the growth

[19] 3 (1807): 385-89; 4 (1807): 342-46, 356-59.
[20] "American Literature," in *Works* (Boston, 1854), pp. 430-38.

of American letters together with a survey of the contemporary status of American culture came in 1803 in a
two-volume treatise entitled *Brief Retrospect of the Eighteenth Century*, by Samuel Miller, a Presbyterian clergyman from New York. His method of classifying the various literary genres as well as his categories of the major
literatures of Europe probably derived from the twice-yearly
"retrospects" in the London *Monthly Magazine*, previously mentioned. The forthcoming publication of Miller's
own *Brief Retrospect* had been announced therein in flattering terms.[21] Much more moderate than some of his
countrymen concerning the past and future glories of
America, Miller provided the standard explanations to account for the relatively slow rise of literary eminence, but
he made a unique contribution by comparing the status
of America with, in his own words, that of other "nations
lately become literary." After admitting that "the con-
spicuous poets" of the United States were not numerous,
and then naming only a half dozen examples, Miller concluded that "we are by no means to ascribe this circumstance either to the paucity or the barrenness of American
genius." A far more likely cause he considered to be the
lack of "respite from the toils of professional and active
life" among those who have any taste for letters.

According to Miller, the previous century had been notable for "the rise of several nations from obscurity in the
republic of letters, to considerable literary and scientific
eminence." Passing over several nations "of inferior character," he considered "the most important of those which
... have become literary" to be Russia, Germany, and the
United States. At the beginning of the century, he maintained, the whole Russian empire had been "sunk in ignorance and barbarism," and almost nothing was done to
alleviate this condition until Peter the Great came to power.

[21] 11 (July 1801): 614.

Although noting that some progress had been made in printing, the fine arts, the study of languages, and the dissemination of newspapers and literary journals, Miller had little confidence that the fundamental illiteracy of the Russian nation would be unchanged even after another century.

Turning to Germany, Miller admitted that long before the eighteenth century much in the way of science and literature had existed there, but all works of importance were written in the Latin tongue. In Miller's opinion, "the cultivation of the German language; . . . and especially the commencement of a just taste in German literature, may all with truth be ascribed to the eighteenth century." Although citing only Mosheim, Gottsched, and Schlegel among the names that are now considered great, Miller concluded that Germany had produced during the second half of the century "historians, poets and dramatists, whose writings evince that judgment, acuteness, imagination, elegant taste, and every qualification for fine writing." Without mentioning Goethe's *Werther*, which was both admired and condemned in the United States, Miller concluded his survey of Germany with the pronouncement that with the possible exception of France there was no country on earth in which literary enterprise was "made the medium for conveying so much moral and theological poison as in Germany." He may have had in mind the sentimental and sensational plays of Kotzebue without wishing to provide them with additional notoriety by citing them. One would never realize from reading Miller that Kotzebue was the most popular author on the American stage in the last two years of the eighteenth century.[22] The stage provides another interesting example of German-American relations. The setting of a play by Friedrich

[22] Henry A. Pochman, *German Culture in America* (Madison, Wis., 1957), pp. 349-51.

M. Klinger that gave the name to a period of German literary history, *Sturm und Drang* (1776) is America. The action, however, unlike that in the novel *Mis MacRae* by Hilliard d'Auberteuil has no connection with political events on the continent.

Miller prepared his readers for the paucity of materials concerning American literature by affirming that its annals were "short and simple." Even though adding that "the history of poverty is usually neither very various, nor very interesting," he argued that the small amount of literature that did exist in America was better than could have been expected considering the circumstances under which it was produced. During the seventeenth century, he explained, literature was retarded by the general poverty of the colonists, their struggles with a hostile environment, and the rigorous censorship of the press. During the eighteenth century, progress was still being hampered by "defective plans and means of instruction in our Seminaries of learning," the absence of leisure, the lack of encouragement to learning, such as books and libraries, and the dependence upon Great Britain. Americans themselves, he felt, did not sufficiently appreciate their own writers and were "too apt to join with ignorant or fastidious foreigners, in undervaluing and decrying our domestic literature." But Miller closed on an optimistic note: when the time shall arrive when native authors will have equal leisure and equal encouragement with their European counterparts, "it may be confidently predicted, that letters will flourish as much in America as in any part of the world."

Even though it may appear from a twentieth-century perspective that Miller was presumptuous in comparing the United States with Russia and Germany as nations lately become literary, he was by no means overgenerous in assessing the merits of American authors. He was just as aware as the most rigorous British critics of the obstacles to be overcome in the emergence of a national literature. He represents, moreover, indubitable proof that not all Americans were, in the words of Sydney Smith, anxious to persuade the world that they were "the greatest, the most refined, the most enlightened, and the most moral people upon earth." Miller should be credited in addition with preceding Channing by thirty years in exposing the need for a comparatist perspective on American literature and in providing one. Henry Pochman, in praising Miller's coverage of German letters, remarks that his "broad survey was all the more effective because German achievements were set against the background of all other European as well as American accomplishments, thus providing the reader with a perspective which made comparisons inevitable."[23] This comment has equal validity in reference to the other European literatures in Miller's survey.

In the next decade, an article in *Niles' Weekly Register* (28 September 1816) on the "Progress of the United States in Literature" seemed to be a deliberate continuation of Miller's retrospective view. After repeating Miller's application of Thomas Gray's phrase "short and simple annals" to the "depressed literature of our country," the author in a tone of mingled humiliation and hope attributed the neglect of literature in America to the previous subjugation of the people under colonial rule, the low regard for classical learning in public journals, the mercenary nature of the national character, and the influence of religion over the cultivation of intellect.

This common sense attitude would seem to lead to the conclusion that the arrogance and exaggeration of post-Revolutionary years soon gave way to a period of reassessment during which more sober and realistic opinions prevailed. Unfortunately such a conclusion is not sup-

---

[23] Ibid., p. 523.

ported by historical fact. In 1818 a minor poet, Solyman Brown, revitalized the theme of an autonomous national literature in tones as strident and aggressive as any that had been heard at the turn of the century. There followed a steady stream of books and essays vociferously defending the merits of American writing. Because of chronological limits, we shall not go beyond Solyman Brown. In the prose preface to a versified *Essay on American Poetry*, he affirmed that "The proudest freedom to which a nation can aspire, not excepting even political independence, is found in complete emancipation from literary thraldom. Few nations, however, have arrived at this commanding eminence. Greece once possessed it, and she was the glory and wonder of the world." According to Brown, Rome also achieved this enviable position before the coming of the Dark Ages. France was the first in the modern world to recover intellectual eminence and then England attained ascendancy, but used it to smother the rising genius of both Scotland and Ireland. England was now attempting to maintain superiority over America. Brown charged that English writers first portrayed their American brethren as cannibals and savages and when this falsehood was exposed treated them "as a race of intellectual pigmies; bunglers in Art and pedants in Science." Brown specifically accused the British ministry of exporting books to the United States to prevent the growth of an indigenous publishing industry, of filling their books with slanders on American achievements in order to discourage emigration, and of exciting among Americans "a prejudice against the literary work of their compatriots." It had become "the determined resolution of men of letters, in the parent country, not to give the smallest credit to American productions, how meritorious soever." As a result of all these policies, America was left with "native genius without patrons, and the shelves of the bookseller bending beneath a weight of imported volumes." Like Barlow, Brown considered North and South America as a geographical unit and presumably an esthetic one as well, but he mentioned no Hispanic poets. In the verse section of his work, he did not name either Bryant or Ladd, who had already begun to publish. His favorites were Robert Treat Paine, Dwight, and Barlow, and he addressed the last as "Music's heir—Apollo's child."

William Cullen Bryant noticed Brown's work in the *North American Review* (July 1818), but in keeping with the custom of the times had very little to say about the book itself, but presented an independent critical and historical essay of ten pages on American poetry. Without attempting to disparage the poets of his nation, he concluded that "on the whole there seems to be more good taste among those who read, than those who write poetry in our country." Admitting that it is natural that national pride should wish to foster the infant literature, Bryant observed that it is "detrimental to bestow on mediocrity the praise due to excellence. . . . We make but a contemptible figure in the eyes of the world, and set ourselves up as objects of pity to our posterity, when we affect to rank the poets of our own country with those mighty masters of song who have flourished in Greece, Italy and Britain."

Solyman Brown's declaration was published toward the end of the period marking the emergence of the literature of the United States—the period when Philip Freneau, Washington Irving, and William Cullen Bryant were making respectable contributions, but a decade before the appearance of Poe and James Fenimore Cooper. It is somewhat of a paradox that the writers of the Revolutionary period had predicted a resurgence of literature in the classical vein, new Livies, Platos, Ovids, and Virgils; whereas the most significant authors of the nineteenth century chose Romantic themes and developed new forms such as the novel. Brown himself, however, could be cited as a practitioner of the neoclassical version of the Virgilian georgic. In addition to his *Essay on American Poetry*, he published in 1840 *Dentologia: a poem on the diseases of the teeth, and their proper remedies.*

A great contrast exists between Brown's dedication to "complete emancipation from literary thraldom" and William Ellery Channing's advocacy of a more extensive knowledge of "the different modes of viewing and discussing great subjects in different nations." The latter's cosmopolitanism is worthy of comparison to a famous declaration by Goethe in conversation with his friend and secretary Eckermann in 1827. "I like to look at other nations," Goethe said, "and I advise everyone to do the same. National literature has little meaning today; the time has come for the epoch of world literature to begin, and everyone must now do his share to hasten its realization."[24] Even though few voices but Channing's could be found in the United States to echo Goethe's opinion, most critics by the time that American literature had come of age in the 1830s had ceased to make exaggerated claims for the genuine talent that existed and to blame the rest of the world for conditions that had allegedly prevented Americans from producing works of great merit. By that time, there was no longer any need for either diffident apology or chauvinistic puffing.

[24] *Gespräche mit Eckermann.* Quoted by François Jost, *Introduction to Comparative Literature* (New York, 1974), p. 16.

PART III

THE TWO AMERICAS: NORTH AND SOUTH

MANY PARALLELS exist between the literature of Latin America and that of English America before 1830. Both areas went through periods of conquest and exploration, colonial domination, struggle for political independence, and national recogition. Although these stages in development are completely parallel, they were widely separated chronologically on the two continents. Conquest and exploration in South America took place in the sixteenth century, but not until a hundred years later in North America. The relationship is noticed in one of the best New England poems of the seventeenth century, but otherwise almost completely ignored.

> The Spanish project working well, tooke sudden such
>   impression
> In minds of many *Europe* held, who fell to like
>   progression.
> It's strange to see the Spanish fleete so many should
>   provoke,
> In *English* searching for like prize, they are vanisht
>   into smoake.
>
> [Edward Johnson, "Good News from New-England"]

In Spanish America, literature began to flourish almost concurrently with settlement, and it reached a high level of development before the establishment of the first printing press in New England. Highly sophisticated examples of the epic, the satire, and the lyric were produced in Spanish America during the first century of European occupation, but very little of comparable quality can be claimed for the first century of the English colonies, during which nearly all writing was religious or utilitarian. Before 1700, the muses harmonized south of the border, while they remained almost mute in northern climes. In the eighteenth century, however, the situation was reversed. The active struggle for independence began in the English colonies toward the middle of the century and was successfully concluded before its end, decades before the emergence of an independence movement in the Spanish colonies. The Spanish-Americans led in the development of imaginative literature during the era of colonization, but fell behind in literature concerned with independence and political organization.

The two American hemispheres could serve as a useful test case of the theory of literary zones, which has recently been proposed by critics in Eastern Europe. According to this theory, "common characteristics, analogues and parallel features of literatures" belonging to a particular geographical zone may be ascribed to "their common or similar history."[1] To ascertain whether the Western Hemisphere represents a unified literary zone during the period under discussion, that is, in the period before 1830, one should find out the extent of similarities and differences between the northern and southern continents and then to decide whether the similarities derive from a common historical and geographical tradition or from broad literary movements originating in Europe. A major difficulty consists in defining the scope of the zone or zones. Should one conceive of Latin American literature and Anglo-American literature as two separate, more or less homogeneous zones or should an attempt be made to combine the two and consider them together as constituting a single comprehensive zone? Problems arise even with the notion of Latin American or Anglo-American literature. The major countries of the south draw inspiration directly from the various literatures of Europe and North America (not only from the Portuguese and the Spanish), and this connection with Europe and Anglo-America has historically been stronger than any communication with each other. The same principle applies to North America. The literatures of Canada and the United States draw more upon English literature than they do upon each other, and that of French Canada has closer ties with Paris than with New York or Toronto. The concept of literary zones is merely a theory whereas that of independent national literatures represents historical reality, no matter what ties may exist between these independent literatures. Bringing the literatures of the two continents together merely as the products of a geographical-historical zone results in a purely arbitrary classification comparable to other arbitrary units such as separate colonies or *virreinatos*, in-

[1] I am quoting the language of György M. Vajda in his summary of a colloquium concerning the comparative history of literature. "Conclusions," *Neohelicon* 1 (1973): 329. Objections to the theory are presented on pages 149-52 of the same issue of *Neohelicon*.

dependent nations, individual states in the United States, and groups of states (e.g., Southern literature of the United States). While cultural and historical differences may justify such classifications as Canadian literature, the literature of the United States, Mexican or Argentinian literature, the comparatist seeks to transcend these differences. A zone comprising both continents is a more comprehensive unit than that of a state or province, but from the broadest international perspective it has no more logic to recommend it than the smaller divisions. A workable compromise might be to think in terms of universal literature, or of a world system comprising subsystems, as the Mexican poet Octavio Paz has suggested. The two literatures using the Spanish language, Spanish literature and Hispanoamerican literature, would represent subsystems. Similarly individual literatures using the English language, including those of England, the United States, Canada, Australia, and more than a dozen other countries, would also represent subsystems. As far as the literatures of the two American continents are concerned, it is possible to see parallels, analogies, and influences without conceiving of them in terms of a single zone.

One of the irrefutable arguments against treating Anglo-America and Ibero-America as a cohesive unit in the particular period with which we are concerned is that until the nineteenth century the two areas were for the most part unaware of each other's literary production.[2] This situation changed radically, however, after the English colonies became the United States of America. Political leaders in Latin America, in seeking independence from

[2] Interesting material on this point is found in Hans Galinsky, " 'Colonial Baroque': A Concept Illustrating Dependence, Germinal Independence and New World Interdependence of Early American Literature," in *Proceedings of the 7th Congress of the International Comparative Literature Association*, ed. Milan V. Dimic and Eva Kushner (Stuttgart, 1979), 1: 48-49.

Spain, profited from the example of their neighbor to the north and drew upon its political literature. Most important in Latin America were the writings of Thomas Paine. Spanish America did not by any means depend exclusively upon the independence literature of the United States, but drew as well, and perhaps more extensively, upon the advanced political theory of Europe, particularly that of England and France. The social and political writings of Locke, Rousseau, and Montesquieu are part of a broad literary and historical movement known as the Enlightenment, and they circulated in both North and South America.

A distinction should be made between the overlapping movements of classicism and the Enlightenment. The former emphasizes esthetic concepts and the latter, social and political ones, but both rest upon presuppositions of rationalism. Eighteenth-century classicism should be known as neoclassicism, since it consists primarily of the revival and imitation of the ancient writers of Greece and Rome. In a broad sense, the esthetic values of classicism exalt stability over change, norms over individual eccentricities, and the absolute over the relative. The Enlightenment comprises concepts such as deism, religious toleration, human rights, and economic and social reform. Neoclassicism exalts and illustrates reason and order in artistic expression: Enlightenment philosophy seeks to establish principles of reason and order in religion, government, and social relations. Many European figures such as Pope, Swift, Voltaire, and Diderot combine the ideals of neoclassicism and the Enlightenment in their literary work, but many others—in both Europe and America— emphasized one or the other approach, sometimes adhering firmly to one and rejecting the other. Timothy Dwight, for example, followed neoclassical models in poetic style, while vigorously attacking Enlightenment notions of rational religion. Paine, on the other hand, fervently expressed Enlightenment ideals in all areas, but did so in a prose style strongly tinged with elements of Romanticism. His much less successful attempts at poetry, however, do not deviate in their absolute adherence to neoclassical standards. As literary periods, neoclassicism and Romanticism are mutually exclusive, but in both North and South America many writers simultaneously revealed techniques and attitudes reflecting both of these antithetical movements.

The first of the next two chapters will demonstrate the direct influence of Paine's political prose upon various figures in Latin America, and the second will reveal parallel portrayals of various Enlightenment themes and concepts in the literatures of the two continents.

EIGHT

THOMAS PAINE AND LATIN AMERICAN INDEPENDENCE

THE WRITINGS of Thomas Paine provide an outstanding example of literature used for social and political ends. His major works all concern political and social reform, but are not uniform in their purposes and direction. For this reason they met varying fortunes in the several cultures that they penetrated. Paine's two propaganda tracts for the American Revolution, *Common Sense* and *The American Crisis*, attained a phenomenal circulation in North America, where they were first published; achieved moderate success in France and Germany; but were practically ignored in England. In Latin America they were translated only in part, but used as symbols by leaders of the independence movement. Paine's two-volume treatise, *Rights of Man*, an attempt to apply the ideals of the French Revolution to the British Isles, was hotly debated in Great Britain and widely read in the United States, but was known only to small groups of political thinkers in France and Germany and virtually not at all in the Spanish world. His manifesto of deism, *The Age of Reason*, attained an extraordinary circulation in Great Britain and the United States, acquired a certain prestige in Germany, but made very little impression in any other country.

In England and America Paine was a historical figure—a personality almost as well known as Franklin and Washington. The rest of the world, however had virtually no knowledge of his biography and personality. Even in France, where Paine served briefly in the Convention, he did not shine as a public figure. A striking difference may be observed in the reception of his works in North America, where he was a personality, and in South America, where he was merely a name. In both areas he served as a symbol, but in one his behavior was at issue, in the other his political doctrine.

In the Anglo-Saxon world, Paine's opponents attempted to discredit his doctrines by accusing him of drunkenness. Ever since James Cheetham's notorious *Life of Thomas Paine* (1809), the first muckraking biography in American literature, Paine's detractors have pictured him as a disgusting inebriate. The famous phrase of Theodore Roosevelt, "filthy, little atheist," has stuck to him like a burr. Roosevelt used this inaccurate and prejudicial phrase in a biography of Gouverneur Morris, one of Paine's most vindictive ideological enemies. Even Washington Irving in both his *Salmagundi* and his *History of New York* used this simile "red as Thomas Paine's nose."

The contrast with South America is striking. Where nothing was known about Paine as an individual, his name served only as symbol of toleration and individual rights.

As early as 1783, Paine met one of the liberators of South America, Franciso de Miranda, in New York.[1] Ten years later in Paris, where Paine was serving in the Convention and Miranda held the rank of general in the army, the latter was put on trial for treason. Paine, called as a character witness, testified that the success of the French Revolution was intimately linked with the favored object of the general's heart, the deliverance of South America and the opening of its commerce to the rest of the world.[2] Somewhat later Paine grew suspicious that Miranda was

[1] A. O. Aldridge, *Man of Reason, The Life of Thomas Paine* (New York, 1959), p. 111
[2] Ibid., pp. 198-99.

acting as a British agent, but he remained on friendly terms and subsequently tried to obtain Miranda's release from a French prison.[3] There is no reason to believe that Miranda ever exerted any effort to make Paine's writings known in his native Venezuela, even though this was the first place in Spanish America where they were extensively circulated.

A twentieth-century historian, Enrique de Gandía, who has devoted considerable attention to Paine's ideology, has made the paradoxical statement that "the influence of Thomas Paine in the events that led to Hispano-American independence was absolutely nil. It did not exist at any moment or at any time."[4] Time and events are the key concepts in his remarkable statement, which rests upon a distinction between ideology and political action. Gandía gives Paine full credit for providing Hispanic patriots with a clear and logical ideology to justify their efforts to overthrow Spanish rule. He nevertheless argues that by the time Paine's work became known in Spanish America, the independence movement was already in full swing. This historian gives 1810 as the date of the penetration of Paine's thought into the Spanish colonies, the year in which a partial translation of his work was ready for the printer. Before this date, according to Gandía, the number of Hispanics who had even heard of Paine was

---

[3] Ibid., p. 247. Miranda, while visiting the British Parliament in 1791, noted that copies of the second part of Paine's *Rights of Man*, at that time proscribed by the British government, were being sold along with sandwiches in the House of Commons *Archivo del General Miranda* (Caracas, 1930), 4: 309. In the next year, Miranda received a letter from Major A. Jardine with an intriguing passage concerning American men of letters: "We Europeans ought to invite more of these wise Americans among us. You see Franklin, Paine, Barlow, have scattered more truths of importance among us than all Europe could do for themselves." *Archivo* (Caracas, 1930) 6: 218.

[4] *Historia de las ideas políticas en la Argentina*, 6 vols. (Buenos Aires, 1960), 1: 407.

negligible. Gandía admits elsewhere, however, that "ideas run from man to man without the need of being printed,"[5] and it is obvious that Paine's first Spanish translator made his original contact without the aid of a Spanish text. Gandía also maintains that Paine's basic ideas already existed in liberal Hispano-American culture; indeed, that apart from the native Indians "all the inhabitants of Spanish America thought either like Thomas Paine or like his most extreme critics."[6] Liberal political ideology allegedly derived from St. Thomas Aquinas, Francisco de Vitoria, Francisco Suárez, Juan de Mariana, and especially Jean Jacques Rousseau.[7] For illustration, Gandía cites a Hispanic republican, Antonio Picornell, whose thought presumably reveals notable similarities and coincidences with Paine's. In Gandía's opinion, the resemblances derive, not from direct contact, but from "a common ideological substratum: both are established upon Locke, on Rousseau, and, without being aware of it, on St. Thomas." This is probably the only time Thomas Paine has ever been associated with Thomas Aquinas.

The notion of an ideological substratum uniting Paine and liberal Latin American thinkers can be accepted only to the extent that both ultimately depend upon Christian theology. Paine derives, however, from a Protestant tradition and the Latin Americans from a Catholic one. The particular contribution of St. Thomas to political tradition consists in the argument that if the people have the right to elect a king they have a right to dethrone him also.[8] This argument exists in Locke as well, but it is by no means certain that it came to him from St. Thomas. The concept, moreover, is not to be found in Paine's *Common Sense*. Without doubt, Locke, Rousseau, and Paine contributed to an ideological substratum, but this does not

[5] Ibid., 1: 247.
[6] Ibid., 1: 407.
[7] Ibid., 1: 408.
[8] Ibid., 5: 508.

mean that the partisans of one of these thinkers would necessarily be receptive to the arguments of the others or that Paine necessarily depended upon Locke. To this day, scholarship has been unable to discover passages in *Common Sense* that can be conclusively proved to be inspired directly by either Locke or Rousseau. Many of the concepts in Paine that appealed to the Spanish-American liberals, moreover, have nothing in common with either Locke or Rousseau, and still less with St. Thomas or Suárez. Even though a substratum of political thought parallel to Paine's may have existed in the Hispanic tradition, none of Paine's translators or commentators referred to such a substratum nor did they seek to associate his writings with those of any predecessors.

Gandía has two excellent chapters interpreting Paine as "the man who with the exposition of clear and profound ideas that spoke of liberty contributed more than any other ideologue of his time to the triumph of the North American Revolution and of the French Revolution and to the awakening of an infinite number of minds in the civil war for the liberty of the great empire of Hispano-America."[9] Gandía admired Paine greatly despite his paradoxical attempt to minimize Paine's influence. Whether Paine contributed to the birth of the independence movement or served merely to reinspire or invigorate it is relatively unimportant to his fame. What counts for literary history is that he was translated, quoted, and widely respected as a political thinker.

As previously noted, Gandía gives 1810 as the date for the introduction of Paine's ideas into the Hispanic world. He isolates this date because it was in this year that parts of *Common Sense* were first translated into Spanish, but he does not take into account the possibility of the pen-

---

[9] Ibid., 1: 243-44.

etration of French versions. In my opinion, there is absolutely no reason to believe that the French translations
of *Common Sense* which I have mentioned in the fifth
chapter traveled physically across the Atlantic, but Paine's
ideas may have been transmitted by means of a widely
read book of major interest to Spain and her colonies,
Raynal's *Histoire philosophique et politique*, the work
that picked up Franklin's Polly Baker. Raynal did not actually translate Paine in his *Histoire*, but gave a thorough
paraphrase of his main ideas. Raynal's treatise was translated into Spanish, moreover, before the end of the eighteenth century.[10] One cannot, therefore, unequivocally rule
out Paine's influence before 1810.

There exists, moreover, in the work of a writer known
as "the Peruvian Rousseau," convincing evidence that Paine
was known in Hispano-America before the publication of
the first Spanish translation. This writer, Manuel de Vidaurre, had rounded the Horn on a voyage to Spain early
in 1810. On 13 May of that year he wrote the dedication
to a work setting forth a political program for his native
land entitled *Plan del Perú*. In a prologue, he says that he
had composed this remarkable work of over 100 tightly
packed pages in eleven days. Vidaurre recommends Paine
as one of the basic political writers that should be read
in the schools of Peru. In his words, "the first books to
be read should be the histories of Spain and the Americas;
afterwards *Common Sense* by Thomas Paine, the constitution of the Spanish monarchy, and universal morality."
Vidaurre's *Plan del Perú* was not printed until 1823 (in
Philadelphia) at which time he added extensive notes,
including a number of favorable references to Paine's religious ideas. In various other documents, Vidaurre cites

[10] *Historia política de los establecimientos ultramarinos de las naciones europeas*, 5 vols. (Madrid), 1784-1790).

and quotes Paine almost as frequently as he does his other idol, Rousseau.

The most important translations of Paine's works intended for Latin America were originally published in Philadelphia, primarily because of the rigid censorship in the Spanish colonies, and other Spanish translations were published in London. Second editions of two of these translations, however, were printed in the Hispanic world, one in Mexico and the other in Peru. The first translation of any of Paine's work into Spanish was published in Philadelphia under the title *La independencia de la Costa Firme justificada por Thomas Paine treinta años ha*. Although it bears the date 1811 on the title page, the dedication is dated December 1810. In the following year a companion volume appeared, *Historia concisa de los Estados Unidos desde el descubrimiento de la América hasta el año de 1807*, the two works complementing each other and forming "a complete body of doctrine in the service of one idea: the enlightenment of Hispanoamérica."[11] Both volumes were edited by Manuel García de Sena, a native of Venezuela temporarily residing in Philadelphia. The *Historia concisa* consists of a rather rough translation of a utilitarian historical text by a minor writer, John M'Culloch, and *La independencia de la Costa Firme* consists of translations of carefully selected passages from the works of Paine and other North American political authors.

Except for parts of *Common Sense*, the contents of the *Independencia* are dry and prosaic, in large part documentary in nature, and in our day they would seem rather forbidding reading. The prosaic cast of the book makes its vogue in South America seem all the more remarkable. A summary of the contents will indicate why one might not have expected an avid audience for the work. The

[11] Pedro Grases and Albert Harkness, *Manuel García de Sena y la independencia de Hispanoamérica* (Caracas, 1953), p. 31.

selections from Paine consist of the first two parts of *Common Sense;* the *Dissertation on First Principles of Government;* and the *Dissertations on Government; the Affairs of the Bank and Paper Money.* The sections from *Common Sense* include Paine's famous distinction between government and society and his demonstration of the superiority of republican over monarchical government. The *Dissertation on First Principles* further attacks the hereditary principle, repudiates the concept of a property qualification for voting, and defends the principle of majority rule. The work on the bank and paper money explains the concept of public good, distinguishes the law-making function of a state from that of merely carrying on public business, and vindicates a state bank and paper currency.

The other documents in the collection comprise the Declaration of Independence, the Articles of Confederation, the Constitution of the United States, and the state constitutions of Massachusetts, Connecticut, New Jersey, Pennsylvania, and Virginia. Although the extracts from *Common Sense* make up only a small part of García de Sena's book, they received the major attention in the press of Latin America. This is not surprising since *Common Sense* is one of the world's greatest works of forensic literature, whereas the constitutions of the various American states seldom stir the hearts of their readers. But at this period of Latin American history, even the state constitutions were likely to have had some popular appeal: government by constitution was still a novelty since prior to this time the only parallel documents in political science had been charters and royal grants. The edition of García de Sena's translation was a relatively large one for the time and place, for records exist showing that six boxes were consigned to Caracas, each box containing 125 copies of the work.[12] A contemporary observer remarked

---

[12] Ibid., p. 54.

that it circulated from hand to hand in Caracas and became fashionable reading.[13]

García de Sena, in dedicating the *Independencia* to his brother Ramón, took pains to point out that it contained not a single word contrary to their Roman Catholic religion. This caution was necessary, he felt, since the Spanish government had not only sought to conceal the truth that Paine expounded, but had sacrilegiously attempted to make its people believe that monarchical rule had the same divine sanction as their religion, "to turn into an almost divine precept that which was in reality an act of despotism."

García de Sena's anticipation of the charge of irreligion together with his need to defend himself against it underscores a fundamental contrast between the climate of opinion in the Anglo-Saxon world and that in the Spanish. In England at the time of Paine, nobody any longer seriously believed that God had appointed any particular set of temporal rulers, and the arguments for monarchy and hereditary aristocracy which Paine was attacking had nothing to do with theories of divine right.

In the Spanish world, however, the monarchy and the Church were so closely affiliated that the belief was imposed and apparently widely accepted in all sections of society that the monarchy had been constituted by God. The first step for propagandists in Latin America, therefore, was to attack and defeat that concept. Paine, as we all know, made extensive use of Scripture in *Common Sense*, but he did not even bother to notice the concept of divine right; it was monarchy as a mere secular institution that he condemned. It was customary in the North American colonies to appraise any doctrine or mode of behavior by scriptural standards, and Paine merely fell in with this custom. He probably did not have any more belief in divine inspiration at this time than when he

---

[13] Ibid., p. 52.

wrote *The Age of Reason*. Despite the efforts of Paine's translator to remove from his work any suspicion of the taint of irreligion, it was nevertheless condemned by the Inquisition in Mexico in 1815 and placed on the list of forbidden books.[14]

Soon after the publication of *La independencia* in Philadelphia, the section from *Common Sense* on hereditary succession was extracted in two issues of *La Gazeta de Caracas* [14 and 17 January 1812], supplemented by three long footnotes attributed in the text to the editor. The editor was an important revolutionary leader, Francisco Isnardy, but Juan Germán Roscio, another Venezuelan patriot, is thought by some to be the author of the notes. One of them is even more radical than Paine's text in disassociating monarchy from Christianity and suggesting that Scripture had been deliberately misinterpreted by monarchical rulers to mislead their people.

In reference to Paine's affirmation that "all anti-monarchical parts of Scripture have been very smoothly glossed over in monarchical governments, but they undoubtedly merit the attention of countries which have their governments yet to form," the note implies that government should be established with no reference whatsoever to the Christian Scriptures, a position with which Paine would have undoubtedly agreed at the time he wrote *Common Sense*. "If we answer truthfully," ran the note, "perhaps we shall be suspected of heresy in the opinion of those who make use of this scarecrow in order to avoid the reform of certain abuses incompatible with the republican form of government."

Paine had referred to the Book of Samuel, but since his remarks were published in Venezuela on 14 January, shortly after Twelfth Night or the Feast of the Three Kings, the editor made a topical comment on the relationship be-

[14] Ibid., p. 55.

tween religion and government by citing the three Wise Men of Scripture. "We shall not fail to reveal," he affirmed,

> that those wise foreigners, sanctified in the adoration of the newborn God, were imperceptibly converted by vile glossary-makers into crowned Kings. Despots, concerned to make their slaves believe that their authority is all divine and that heaven cares profoundly for their person, were able to impose upon their subjects by having them accept the fiction that the Three Wise Men who came from the orient to Jerusalem were sovereigns, seeking the place where the King of the Jews had been born. Using the same artifice, they had managed to make people believe that comets were destined to announce the death of monarchs. In the Gospel of St. Mark, where this story is narrated, three philosophers and astrologers are found denying the royal character which tyranny combined with religious fanaticism has attributed to them.

In connection with Paine's reference to the eight civil wars and nineteen rebellions which the concept of hereditary monarchy had brought on in England, his commentator affirmed that the record in Spain and France had been equally bloody. "Catalonia and Aragon will never forget the troubled epoch of the introduction of the Bourbon dynasty: and France will always regard with horror the memory of the League, the Barricades, and St. Bartholomew, during which were reciprocally assassinated fathers, brothers, kinsmen, and friends for the rights of a king and a family which afterwards cost France itself all the evils of its last revolution and the foreign despotism to which it was submitted." The Caracas newspaper was thus much bolder than Paine's translator, García de Sena, in condemning the Spanish monarchy per se, not merely as an instrument of colonial exploitation and despotism.

Enrique de Gandía has noticed that Roscio, who may have been Paine's newspaper annotator, uses in one of his own political tracts the argument from *Common Sense* that many verses from the Old Testament demonstrate that the origin of monarchy is not divine.[15] Roscio's work is entitled *El patriotismo de Nirgua y abuso de los reyes* (1811). Gandía does not assert direct influence in this "echo of Thomas Paine," but rather a coincidence of style. In a later work published in Philadelphia in 1817, *El triunfo de la libertad*, Roscio refutes a wider range of arguments in favor of monarchy based on Scripture. An even more significant echo of Paine, moreover, appears in a manifesto of 1811 drawn up by Roscio based on the American Declaration of Independence, *Manifesto que hace al mundo la confederación de Venezuela . . . de las razones en que ha fundado su absoluta independencia de la España*. In reference to "the moral abuse of the maternity of Spain in regard to America," Roscio affirms that "it is widely recognized that in the order of nature it is the father's duty to free his son, so that when leaving his minority he is able to make use of his forces and his reason in order to provide for his subsistence; and that it is the duty of the son to do it [assert his freedom] when the cruelty or dissipation of the father or guardian compromises his destiny or jeopardizes his patrimony."[16] In *Common Sense*, Paine had developed the same metaphor of parental relationship: "But Britain is the parent country say some. Then the more shame upon her conduct. Even brutes do not devour their young, nor savages make war upon their families."[17] In *Crisis* no. VII, Paine returned to the metaphor: "The title she assumed of parent country, led to, and pointed out, the propriety, wisdom and advantage of

[15] *Historia*, 5: 506.

[16] *Obras*, ed. Pedro Grases, 3 vols. (Caracas, 1953), 2: 65.

[17] *Complete Writings of Thomas Paine*, ed. Philip S. Foner, 2 vols. (New York, 1945), 1: 19.

a separation; for as in private life, children grow into men, and by setting up for themselves, extend and secure the interest of the whole family, so in the settlement of colonies large enough to admit of maturity, the same policy should be pursued."[18]

On the day after the Declaration of Independence of the American Confederation of Venezuela, 5 July 1811, Antonio Nicolás Briceño read before the Assembly García de Sena's translation of the American Constitution.[19] One of the fathers of Venezuelan independence, Francisco Javier Yanes, had sought to have independence formally declared on 4 July so that it would coincide with that of the United States. Later, in his respected political treatise, *Manual político del venezolano*, he listed Paine among those who had perfected representative government in the New World and gave him credit for saying that representative government is the invention of the modern world and that its foundation rests upon the equality of rights.[20] Even more important than this explicit recognition of Paine's historical significance is a paragraph from the preface that duplicates the opening lines of *Common Sense*, completely without acknowledgment.

. . . De lo dicho se conoce que la sociedad y el gobierno so diferencian esencialmente en su origen y objeto. La sociedad nació de las necesidades de los hombres; y de los vicios de éstos el gobierno. La sociedad se dirige siempre al bien; y el gobierno debe tirar a reprimir el mal. . . . La sociedad, en fin, es esencialmente buena; el gobierno puede ser, y efectivamente es, malo en muchas partes del globo.

Comparison with Paine's text reveals that Yanes is translating rather than paraphrasing.

[18] Ibid., 1: 154.
[19] Grases and Harkness, *García de Sena*, p. 56.
[20] Ed. Ramón Escovar Salóm (Caracas, 1959), pp. 61, 52.

> Some writers have so confounded society with govern-
> ment, as to leave little or no distinction between them;
> whereas they are not only different, but have different
> origins. Society is produced by our wants, and govern-
> ment by our wickedness; the former promotes our hap-
> piness *positively* by uniting our affections, the latter
> negatively by restraining our vices. . . . Society in every
> state is a blessing, but government even in its best state
> is but a necessary evil.

Indeed Yanes follows Paine more closely than do some
Latin American texts actually described as translations.

In 1811, the same year as García de Sena's *Independencia*, there appeared in London a more extensive translation of *Common Sense* under the title *Reflecciones políticas, escritas baxo el título de "Instinto común,"* published at the expense of the translator, who is described
on the title page as a Peruvian Indian, Anselmo Nateiu.
The latter was a pseudonym based on an anagram for
Manuel José de Arrunátegui.

In his preface Nateiu states that he is translating merely
the sections "applicable to the actual circumstances of
South America." He warns that although Paine's principles are important and incontestable, great prudence must
be exercised in presenting them to the people all at once.
"A violent metamorphosis in their political situation,"
he affirms, could dislodge the people "from the true circle
of liberty and cause them to degenerate into a frenzy de-
grading them into anarchy or despotism." He nevertheless
considers it desirable for the Spanish-Americans to imitate their Anglo-American brothers in forming a patriotic
union and making themselves equally deserving of the
liberty that the latter are enjoying. In one of his footnotes
he follows the *Gazeta de Caracas* in drawing attention
to the passage concerning the large number of civil wars
and rebellions in the history of England. The Spanish peo-

ple have suffered through internal strife, he says, for the famous war of the Spanish succession had no other cause but the personal disputes of the houses of Austria and Bourbon.[21] In another note he displays a remarkable feeling of identity with the North Americans, suggesting not only that the two peoples are alike in their political situations, but that they share a common character. In reference to Paine's praise of American courage and resolution, his translator proudly affirms that recent events in Buenos Aires "are the most authentic testimony of that which the American character is capable of."[22]

A Mexican patriot, Servando Teresa de Mier, made a similar attempt to associate Spanish-American and Anglo-American bravery in reference to Paine. The following significant paragraph appears in his *Historia de la revolución de Nueva España*, written in 1813.

> Enough blood has been shed already to demonstrate that they [the Spanish-Americans] are not cowardly orangutans but very worthy of appearing at the side of the Anglo-Americans. It is impossible that *Common Sense* should not already have said to them as well as to others: "A greater interest has never concerned the nations. It is not the matter of a single town or province, but that of an entire immense continent, or of half of the globe. It is not the interest of a day, but of centuries."

> [Demasiada sangre han derramado ya para evidenciar que no son cobardes uranutanes, sino mui dignos de figurar al lado de los Anglo-americanos. Es imposible ya que su *Sentido común* no les esté diciendo como á los otros: "Jamás un interés más grande ha ocupado a las naciones. No se trata del de una villa ó provincia,

---

[21] *Reflecciones políticas*, p. 18. A second edition was published in Lima, Peru, in 1821.

[22] Ibid., p. 31.

es el de todo un continente inmenso, ó de la mitad del globo. No es el interés de un día, sino el de siglos."][23]

Mier's translation is exceedingly loose. Paine's exact words are:

The sun never shined on a cause of greater worth. 'Tis not the affair of a city, a country, a province, or a kingdom, but of a continent—of at least one eighth part of the habitable globe. 'Tis not the concern of a day, a year, or an age; posterity are virtually involved in the contest, and will be more or less affected, even to the end of time, by the proceedings now.

Mier uses fewer words than Paine, but expands his concepts. Paine has been accused of exaggeration in speaking of one eighth of the globe; Mier inflates the area to one half. He covers fifteen pages of Paine's text in two of his own, not only shortening and paraphrasing, but adding comments and embellishments that are not in Paine at all. When Paine refers to England or Great Britain, Mier substitutes Spain, as in the following passage: "La autoridad de la España sobre América tarde o temprano debe tener un fin. . . . España está demasiado lejos para gobernarnos." ["The authority of Spain over America must sooner or later come to an end. . . . Spain is too far away to govern us."] No better proof could be offered of the relevance of Paine's words to the situation of the Spanish colonies.

Despite the great liberties that Mier took with Paine's text, he took pride in his rendition as a fair translation. In a manuscript not published during his lifetime, he credits Paine for analyzing political principles in the light of the common sense which provided the title of his work. He then adds, "I translated his speech in Book IV of my *History of the Revolution*, accommodating it to our sit-

---

[23] Facsimile ed., 2 vols. (Mexico, 1922), 2: 272. Accentuation is that of the original.

uation, and as despotism has concealed it, I shall reproduce this piece of eloquence."[24] The manuscript does not include Mier's translation, but it may be found in another work of Mier published in Philadelphia in 1821, his *Memoria político-instructiva*, republished in Mexico in the next year.

A separate translation of Paine's *Dissertation on the First Principles of Government* was published anonymously in London in 1819. The translator, who was Gen. José María Vergara according to a handwritten note in the copy at the British Museum, believed that this was the most useful of Paine's works. He devotes most of his prologue, however, to defending Paine for not treating Montesquieu's theories of the influence of climate on human character and social institutions. Vergara replies that Montesquieu's theories have not been generally accepted and as proof quotes an extensive refutation of them by Voltaire. He vehemently rejects the idea that since most of Latin America lies within the torrid zone, its inhabitants are sluggish and unfit for democratic government. Republicanism, he maintains, is the only form of government originating in the nature of man, and climate does not make man lose his rights or change his nature. Paine's principles, therefore, are valid for all people, including the Latin Americans, regardless of the climate or latitude where they live. In his notes, Vergara seems far less liberal than Paine. Although accepting all of Paine's criticisms of hereditary monarchy, he argues that defects of absolutism would be avoided in a constitutional limited monarchy with an elected House of Representatives. He also believes that the rights of man would not be violated in a republic with hereditary succession.[25]

[24] "Nos prometieron constituciones," in *Escritos inéditos de Fray Servando Teresa de Mier*, ed. J. M. Miquel i Vergas and Hugo Díaz-Thomé (Mexico, 1944), p. 359.

[25] *Disertación sobre los primeros principios del gobierno por Tomas Pain* [sic] (London, 1819), pp. 25, 38.

One of the most active political and intellectual figures in the history of Latin American independence, Vicente Rocafuerte, edited sections of *Common Sense* and the entire *Dissertation on the First Principles of Government* in a compilation entitled *Ideas necesarias a todo pueblo americano independiente, que quiera ser libre* (1821) [*Ideas necessary for all the independent people of America who wish to be free*]. A second edition was published in Puebla, Mexico, two years later. Born in Ecuador, Rocafuerte, after studies in France and a political apprenticeship in Spain, came to Philadelphia, where he published *Ideas necesarias* and led a propaganda campaign against the imperialistic aims of Iturbide of Mexico. He later became president of Ecuador (from 1835 to 1839) and fathered a new constitution. The material from Paine in *Ideas necesarias* is essentially a reworking of García de Sena's previous translation with only minor textual changes. In his preface, which is original, Rocafuerte eulogized Paine for doing more than anyone else to tear the reins of government from despotic hands. "The intrepid American," he wrote, destroyed the trappings of monarchy in order that it would never return to establish itself in this precious part of the globe. Rocafuerte also reprinted his adapted translation of *Common Sense* in his defense and interpretation of the United States Constitution entitled *Ensayo político: el sistema colombiano, popular, electivo, y representativo, es el que más conviene á la América independiente* (1823), published not in Philadelphia, but in New York.

Apparently it required almost five years for García de Sena's translation to make its influence felt in the southern part of the continent, for it was not until 6 April 1816 that it was advertised, along with the *Historia concisa*, in *La Gazeta de Buenos Aires*, as being "extremely worthy of the attention of the people during the present crisis." Five days later it was advertised as well in another periodical of Buenos Aires, *El Censor*, with the comment that

"nothing in the present times would better serve to nourish the minds of the young with those ideas which could
strengthen and instruct" them in the cause that was then
being defended. On 16 April 1816, both of García de Sena's
books were advertised in the third newspaper of the city,
La Prensa Argentina, as well as on 15 October 1816, this
time Paine's title being abbreviated to *El sentido de Tomas
Payne*.[26]

During the preceding six years, sentiments of revolution and republicanism had created a climate of opinion
receptive to Paine's forthright mode of expression. According to Bartolomé Mitré, "There was not only the abstract *Contrat social* of Rousseau, the vade mecum of the
revolutionaries; also popular among the youth were the
clear, practical and radical principles of the book of Thomas
Paine on *The Rights of Man*."[27] As we examine the evidence that Paine was well known in Buenos Aires, however, we shall observe that *Common Sense* rather than
Rights of Man represented the source of his fame.

Paine's *Rights of Man* was not translated into Spanish
until 1821, when it was made available under the title *El
derecho del hombre* by an Italian-American language
teacher, Santiago Felipi Puglia, and published in Philadelphia by Matthew Carey. Despite a second edition which
appeared in the following year, no evidence has yet been
uncovered of its being circulated or exerting any influence. Puglia's translation includes both Parts I and II, but
omits all polemics against Burke, all historical descriptions of the French Revolution, all complimentary references to the United States, and all of the famous passage
in which Paine declares "my country is the world." Puglia

[26] In an anonymous *Compendio de la historia de los Estados Unidos*
(Philadelphia, 1825), the title of *Common Sense* was translated as *Luz
de la razón*.

[27] *Historia de Belgrano y de la independencia argentina*, 4 vols., 5th
ed. (Buenos Aires, 1902), 3: 13.

had earlier defended Paine's ideas in a highly original treatise entitled *Desengaño del hombre* (Philadelphia, 1794), and an extract from the manuscript had been published in the form of a prospectus in English in the previous year. Hamilton and Jefferson were among the subscribers to the Spanish edition of 500 copies. In addition to defending Paine's political ideas, the work attacked the abuses of institutionalized Christianity on moral grounds, a rather important development since the work preceded *The Age of Reason*. No evidence of the circulation of *Desengaño del hombre* has yet been discovered other than its being decreed as blasphemous by the Inquisition of Mexico in the year of its publication, a distinction soon to be shared by García de Sena's translation.[28]

The Argentinian periodical that gave greatest space to Paine was *El Censor*, edited at that time by Antonio José Valdés, a Cuban and former deputy to the Cortes. In keeping with its title, *El Censor* exercised a kind of magisterial censorship over the government, and its editors enjoyed a feeling of privileged immunity. The issue of 4 January 1816 devoted its entire eight pages to a single article introduced by the following epigraph in English, "It is not in number, but in unity, that our great strength lies.— T. Paine." The article itself, however, has no reference to *Common Sense*, from which the quotation is taken.

On 20 June 1816 appeared without title but with an anonymous epigraph in French an article on the need for a realistic appraisal of the political situation in Buenos Aires. This article contains a historical anecdote of the North American Revolution attributed to Paine. During a session of Congress, according to this anecdote, a letter from the commander-in-chief to the executive council

[28] All of the material on Puglia is based upon A. O. Aldridge, "A Spanish Precursor of the Age of Reason," in *Papers on French-Spanish, Luso-Brazilian, Spanish-American Literary Relations*, ed. Marie A. Wellington (Elmhurst, Ill., 1969), pp. 1-4.

threw the assembly into consternation by its desperate tone. No one in the assembly uttered a word for some time, until a member known for his readiness to submission said: "If the report in this letter presents the true state of things and we are really in the situation which it represents, it seems to me useless to dispute the affair any longer." Another more courageous spirit dissipated the melancholy atmosphere, however, exclaiming, "It is useless to despair; if events do not go as we should like, we must try to improve them." Thus it was, according to this article, that the members of Congress "preserved their votes, their lives, and their fortunes, and the nation was saved." Neither this narrative nor any other resembling it, however, is to be found in the work of Paine.

On 9 July 1816, the Congress of the United Provinces of Argentina, meeting in the city of Tucumán, issued a Declaration of Independence. *El Censor* on 25 July printed the text of this declaration [pp. 1-3] as well as a political article [pp. 3-12] introduced by the following epigraph in English:

> Notwithstanding our wisdom, there is a visible feebleness in some of our proceedings, which gives encouragement to dissentions. The continental belt is too loosely buckled; and if something is not done in time, it will be too late to do any thing, and we shall fall into a state in which neither RECONCILIATION nor INDEPENDENCE will be practicable.—*T. Paine.*

This is an accurate quotation from *Common Sense.*

On 22 August, Valdés printed a very important quotation in Spanish translation from Paine's *Rights of Man.* This is the first reference I have found to *Rights of Man* anywhere in the Spanish world, and few others followed in the period of the liberation of Spanish America. It preceded by five years Puglia's partial translation in Philadelphia. The quotation does not mention Paine by name, but is preceded by the headline "Rasgo Extractado de los Derechos del Hombre." It corresponds to the following passages in Paine's English text:

> The independence of America, considered merely as a separation from England, would have been a matter but of little importance, had it not been accompanied by a revolution in the principles and practise of governments. She made a stand, not for herself only, but for the world, and looked beyond the advantages herself could receive. . . .
>
> From the rapid progress which America makes in every species of improvement, it is rational to conclude, that if the governments of Asia, Africa, and Europe, had begun on a principle similar to that of America, or had not been very early corrupted therefrom, that those countries must, by this time, have been in a far superior condition to what they are. Age after age has passed away, for no other purpose than to behold their wretchedness. Could we suppose a spectator who knew nothing of the world, and who was put into it merely to make his observations, he would take a great part of the old world to be new, just struggling with the difficulties and hardships of an infant settlement. He could not suppose that the hordes of miserable poor, with which old countries abound, could be any other than those who had not yet had time to provide for themselves.[29]

This passage is extremely important in the history of ideas because it incorporates a unique argument in favor of the Moderns in the controversy over ancient versus modern learning which was not only still going on in the eighteenth century, but which had been carried by Paine

---

[29] *Complete Writings*, ed. Foner, 1: 354-55.

and others from Europe to the New World. Following is the Spanish text, which is not quite a literal translation:

La independencia del Norte de América, considerada solamente como una separación de Inglaterra, sería materia de poca importancia, si no fuese accompañada por una revolución de los principios y práctica de los gobiernos. Ella hizo una parada, no tan sólo notable a la misma América, sino á todo el mundo, y la América logró ventajas muy excedentes á las que se propuso.— Por sus rápidos progresos en todo género se puede concluir racionalmente, que si los gobiernos de Asia, Africa y Europa hubiesen empezado por los mismos principios que esta parte del nuevo mundo, habrían executado adelantos asombrosos, y aquellas naciones se hallarían en estado muy diverso que el que experimentan en el día. No habrían visto sucederse las edades unas á otras sólo para presenciar sus miserias.—Si supusiésemos un espectador, absolutamente ignorante de nuestro globo, en un punto en que le pudiese observar con ojos filosóficos, deduciría ciertamente que la mayor parte del mundo antiguo era nuevo: y la América libre una nación antigua y experimentada. Era imposible que así no lo supusiese al ver los estados de Asia, los del Africa, y gran parte de los de Europa forcejeando con las miserias, ignorancia y dificultades de pueblos nacientes.

After this quotation, Valdés made a pertinent personal comment, applying the experience of the continent of the north to that of the south.

Efectivamente la América del Norte ha dado un paso tan asombroso á la civilización, al comercio y población, que el año de 1807 en que yo la visité, los ministros extrangeros residentes en ella se admiraban de su sistema y progreso singular. Todo esto ha ido en más rápido aumento desde aquel tiempo: la guerra con los ingleses los ha hecho más avisados, y la ruina del imperio francés ha dado un empuje soberbio á su felicidad. Una vecindad tan estimulante coadyuva ventajosamente á la insurrección de Nueva España.

[Indeed North America has given such an astonishing thrust to civilization, to commerce and population, that in 1807, the year in which I visited it, the foreign ministers residing there marvelled at its system and unusual progress. All this has gone on with even more rapid speed since that time; the war with the English (in 1812) has made them more informed, and the ruin of the French Empire has given a superb thrust to their felicity. A neighbor so stimulating aids advantageously in the insurrection of New Spain (Mexico).]

The passages that Valdés extracted from *Rights of Man* are among the most pertinent to Latin America, but there is another passage in this work even more directly concerned with the Southern Hemisphere, which all commentators of the time completely overlooked. In the last section of his work, Paine proposed a kind of North Atlantic Alliance, consisting of a confederation of the fleets of England, France, and Holland together with the dismantling of all the navies in Europe.[30] These confederated powers, he suggested, "together with that of the United States of America, can propose, with effect, to Spain, the independence of South America, and the opening those countries, of immense extent and wealth, to the general commerce of the world, as North America now is." It may be that the patriots of South America would not have been enthusiastic about this method of acquiring their independence, but they would probably have approved of Paine's subsequent remarks concerning trade. "The opening of South America," he affirmed, "would produce an immense field for commerce, and a ready money market for

[30] Ibid., 1: 448.

manufactures, which the Eastern world does not. The East is already a country of manufactures, the importation of which is not only an injury to the manufactures of England, but a drain upon its specie." This remark concerning the economic destiny of Latin America seems to have gone entirely unnoticed to this day. Indeed a scholarly historian of Venezuelan independence affirms "ninguna obra de Paine se refiera específicamente a la Independencia de Hispanoamérica."[31]

Valdés in the month after his reference to *Rights of Man* published in *El Censor* an essay attacking the complete freedom of press in Buenos Aires, using Thomas Paine as a justification for his point of view [26 September 1816]. This is probably the only time in any country when the name of Thomas Paine has been used to oppose the free expression of opinion. The article in *El Censor* belongs to an extended polemical discussion between Valdés and the editor of a rival periodical, Vicente Pazos Silva, a Peruvian of mixed Indian blood, who had come to Buenos Aires early in the Revolution. After taking orders in the Roman Catholic Church, he visited London and returned to Buenos Aires, no longer wearing clerical garb, and bringing with him a wife and a printing press on which he printed a new republican periodical, *La Crónica Argentina*. Silva added to his Spanish names an Indian name Kanki, by which he is now most frequently known.

Kanki in *La Crónica Argentina* began the periodical debate with a magisterial article opposing the scheme of two leaders of the nation to establish an empire in Argentina based on the ancient one of the Incas. Kanki opposed this romantic idea because of its all too apparent monarchical complexion.

Valdés replied in *El Censor* to this criticism of the pro-

---

[31] Pedro Grases, *La conspiración de Gual y España y el ideario de la independencia* (Caracas, 1949), p. 61.

posed empire with a defense of constitutional monarchy as found in England. And since Kanki had handled him rather roughly along with the power-minded politicians behind the scheme, Valdés argued for restraints upon the freedom of press. In order to enlist historical authority on his side, he cited the proscription of the works of Paine by the British government. Somewhat inconsistently, however, he supplied his article with an epigraph in English attributed to Paine: "It is darkness attempting to illuminate light." The essence of Valdés's argument is that Argentina was not yet ready for the complete freedom of the press, a condition that suits only well-established and highly cultured societies. If a free press were to be introduced into a backward country like Turkey, he reasoned, it would lead to disturbances, bloodshed, and ruin. And in a developing country like Argentina, the press would be taken over by impetuous spirits, preaching division and revolution.

> Thomas Paine produced marvelous effects in the United States because he knew the genius of the people, their propensities, and their geographical conditions. Thomas Paine would have written among us in another vein, however, or he would have made a mistake involving us in a thousand evil happenings, as indeed he had contributed to bring them about during the French Revolution. Among us a few superficial geniuses drink his alluring and dangerous doctrine, and without being capable of digesting it, make opportune application and belch pestilences with their proud and insubstantial philosophy. Thus we see all around us in print and in manuscript the principles of Payne, more appropriate to be read than to be adopted in practice.

Dramatically Valdés expressed the hope that his fellow citizens would not weep with tears of blood as a consequence of the enthusiastic extravagancies of Thomas Paine.

In this diatribe against Paine, Kanki was not directly

accused of being the disciple of the author of *Rights of Man*, but since Valdés attempted to discredit his rival by disparaging Paine, Kanki was certainly being condemned by association. He therefore repudiated this method of argument and at the same time rose to the defense of Paine. *"El Censor,"* he wrote, "deceives himself or wishes to deceive the public by indicating Paine as our favorite author."

> Let us grant it, however, for the sake of argument: If the principles of Paine are impracticable how is it that they have been successful in North America? And in what way are our propensities and geographical conditions any different from those of North America? The main consideration is that which has already been accomplished—that is, to have dethroned the king and reassumed our own government. And in what page does Thomas Payne [*sic*] teach that the citizens of a Republic should cut each other's throats, as has taken place in France. This was the effect of other causes and not of his principles. No matter what they were, they are not the basis of the reasoning which we used to discredit in a convincing manner, and not by the use of proscription, the projected Inca monarchy.

Kanki observed that Valdés was in effect opposing not only the freedom of press but also the freedom to read. This would be the logical outcome of the argument that Paine should be prohibited in Argentina since he had been prohibited in England. Drawing on recollections of his sojourn in London, Kanki explained the paradox of the British government prosecuting Paine's works under a system of a free press. The British people, Kanki affirmed, are allowed to condemn the institution of kings and monarchs or to revile ministers as assassins, as they do every day, but they must not speak against their actual king or reigning house. And this is the reason why the reprinting of Paine's works was prohibited. Kanki went on to describe a recent incident involving a London printer who had been condemned to stand in the pillory for the offense of publishing Paine. The enlightened English public, however, instead of abusing or insulting the printer, as was expected, paid tribute to him with flowers and music, thereby turning the event into a triumph over the sentence of the judges. Kanki was indeed very generous toward the British nation in his description of how it maintained a free press, but unfortunately his explanation is not very accurate. *Rights of Man* was actually prosecuted as a seditious publication, not because it condemned George III as an individual, and the story of the printer's triumph in the pillory is, as far as I have been able to determine, purely imaginary.

Valdés in the following number of *El Censor* completely passed over the question of freedom of the press and concentrated his continuing criticism of Paine on the subject of monarchy. Paine's strongest argument, he believed, is that the present generation has no right to establish a monarchy since it would thereby be enslaving all future generations to the monarch and his successor. To Valdés, this reasoning was superficial and sophistical. By failing to make provision for the stability of future generations, he countered, the present one would be enslaving itself to these later generations, since it would be obliged to live in continuous disorder merely to keep from limiting future generations. The latter, he argued, would be much more grateful to have as their heritage, instead of a turbulent and ruinous republic, a constitutional monarchy in which the ruler protects order as prescribed by the constitution and guarantees to each citizen the free and certain possession of his rights. Paine, according to Valdés, had used his natural genius to expose the defects of monarchy, but in so doing had confounded the constitutional type of monarchy with the absolute. His magnification of democracy had nevertheless acquired for him an infinity of unsophisticated proselytes.

As an example of Paine's subtlety, Valdés cited his interpretation of the Book of Samuel, in which he had depicted the Hebrew people as constituting a republic and bringing down the anger of God upon them by asking for a monarch. In refutation, Valdés argued that the Hebrews had never had a republican form of government, but had been a patriarchy until the time of Moses, and subsequently they had been ruled by judges and tyrants, the latter designed by God as a punishment for the crimes of the Chosen People. The rule of the judges, Valdés maintained, represented a theocracy mixed with aristocracy. When the Hebrews called for a king, they were, therefore, rejecting their God in favor of a despot, not a constitutional king. This interpretation, Valdés considered, was corroborated by the words of God to Samuel: "they have not rejected thee, but they have rejected me" [I Samuel 8:7]. Finally, Valdés observed, as many others have done, an apparent inconsistency in Paine's attitude toward the Scriptures, that in *Common Sense* he regarded the Old and New Testaments as an authority to persuade his readers; whereas in *The Age of Reason* he labeled them apocryphal. This is the first time that Paine's work on religion is known to have been mentioned in Latin America.

Kanki in replying (30 November) made no effort to carry on the debate over Scripture, but returned to the concept of a free press. The very prohibition of Paine's works in England, Kanki affirmed, "is the best recommendation they contain, for the English are too enlightened and too liberal to fear incendiary writers merely because they are heated." Paine had not been proscribed because he spoke in general terms against the ruling house, but because "disseminating principles opposed to the constitution of the state with the aid of his vivid imagination, he had forced the common sense of his readers to an irresistible conviction, and this is what they have reason to fear and have feared."

Since Valdés had leveled the charge of inconsistency against Paine, Kanki turned it against Valdés. He cited the previous numbers of *El Censor* in which Paine had been warmly praised, specifically the issue in which the García de Sena translation had been recommended for its ability "to nourish the minds of the young with those ideas which could strengthen and instruct them in the cause that we defend" (11 April) and the issue containing the Argentinian declaration of independence (25 July), in which an epigraph from Paine had introduced the lead article. Kanki reminded his opponent that he had "publicly praised Thomas Paine, proposed him as a model for the enlightenment of youth, and pointed to him as a teacher to form their minds."

After this controversy, Paine disappeared from Argentinian periodicals until 23 December 1825, when an intriguing item appeared in the *Mensajero Argentino* reporting the circulation of a Portuguese translation of *Common Sense*.[32] The report does not indicate where the translation was published or what title it bore, but since it is based upon a letter from Liverpool, presumably the translation itself also originated in England. According to the Liverpool letter, five thousand translated copies of *Common Sense* were introduced clandestinely into Brazil. The size of this edition is enormous compared to the press run of 750 copies of García de Sena's *Independencia* and 500 of Puglia's *Desengaño*. What is more surprising, however, is that no other trace of this Portuguese edition has ever been uncovered; there is not a single copy known to exist today. According to the *Mensajero Argentino*, the successful introduction of Paine's work into Brazil should

---

[32] Merle E. Simmons, *U.S. Political Ideas in Spanish America before 1830: A Bibliographical Study* (Bloomington, Ind., 1977), p. 55.

be considered as "very favorable to inflame the fire, which aggravated by the attempted crimes of despotism, appears from time to time in all parts of the empire" ["muy propio a encender el fuego, que a pesar de los conatos del despotismo, aparece de cuando en cuando en todos los lugares del imperio"].

The direct influence of Paine in the southern part of the hemisphere was by no means limited to discussions in the periodical press of Buenos Aires. Evidence indicates that a number of important political personalities drew inspiration from Paine's works as presented in the García de Sena translation. At the opening of the Biblioteca Pública in Montevideo in January 1816, the inaugural discourse given by an ecclesiastic listed Paine's works among "the classic texts that speak of our rights." That this speaker attributed great significance to Paine's ideas is revealed by the complete list of his classic texts: these comprised "the wisest constitutions, including among others the Britannic, with its commentator Blackstone; that of North America with the acts of its Congress up to the present, the state constitutions, and principles of government by Paine; that of the Peninsula, with the journals of the Cortes; that of the Italian Republic by Napoleon and his famous Code of the French People."[33]

José Artigas, the chief of the Uruguayan Orientals, wrote to the Cabildo of Montevideo on 17 March 1816, describing the two translations of García de Sena as "the two volumes which you promised me concerning the discovery of North America, its revolution, the various contrasts, and its progress up to the year 1807." Artigas added that he would rejoice if each one of the eastern states could have this very interesting history. Two months later he wrote to the Cabildo of Corrientes, transmitting "the

[33] Hugo D. Barbagelata, *Artigas y la revolución americana* (Paris, 1930), pp. 118-19.

compendium of the history of North America, anxious
that its light be sufficient to clarify the ideas of the Magistrates and everything contribute to bring about our progress."[34]

One of the greatest of the liberators, José de San Martín,
the George Washington of Argentina and Chile, also knew
the work of Paine and proposed to circulate it through his
own efforts. On 15 December 1816, he wrote to the local
leaders of Buenos Aires, "We are in need of a number of
copies of the work of Thomas Paine, *Historia de la revolución de Estados Unidos e Independencia de la Costa
firme* in order to distribute them in Chile. I hope your
excellencies will bring this to the attention of the supreme
government."[35]

In the following year, when a diplomat from the United
States, Henry Marie Brackenridge, visited Artigas near
Montevideo, he reported the leader of the Orientals to be
"under the guidance of an apostate priest, of the name
Monterosa," who professed "to be in the literal sense, a
follower of the political doctrines of Paine."[36] In Montevideo itself, Brackenridge engaged in conversation with a
merchant's clerk, who "thought Rousseau's Social Con-
tract a visionary theory, but Paine's Common Sense and
Rights of Man, sober and rational productions."[37]

The various Latin American translators of Paine or pop-
ularizers of his work considered up to this point were not
literary figures, as opposed to statesmen or politicians
(with the exception of Puglia, who perhaps should be best
labeled as a pioneer in adult education or bilingual edu-

---

[34] These extracts are printed by Pedro Grases and Albert Harkness in
their introduction to *Manuel García de Sena y la independencia de
América.*

[35] Ricardo Levene, "El constitucionalismo de Mariano Moreno," *Historia* 3 (1958): 53-71.

[36] *Voyage to South America,* 2 vols. (London, 1820), 1: 209.

[37] Ibid., 1: 235.

cation). In Chile, however, Paine's works did attract the
attention of a professional man of letters, Camilo Henríquez, the pioneer dramatist of his country and, like Paine,
a journalist and zealous partisan of Enlightenment thought.
Although a Roman Catholic clergyman, at one stage in
his career called "el fraile de la Buena Muerte," Henríquez
held religious ideas bordering on the deism of Paine. He
was scarcely more orthodox than the French abbés Raynal
or Morellet, notorious in the eighteenth century for their
independent thinking. One of his contemporary clerical
opponents even accused him of holding that philosophy
had been neglected for a period of eighteen centuries, but
the dawn of its triumph was impending and beginning to
raise its luminous countenance, which meant, according
to Henríquez's attacker, that impiety and error would prevail over the religion of Jesus Christ. Not only did Henríquez embrace with Paine the ideals of tolerance, free
inquiry, and universal education associated with the Enlightenment, but he was the first to call for an independent Chile.

Before discussing in detail the impact that Paine made
upon Henríquez and as a consequence upon the people of
Chile, it is necessary to make a few preliminary observations upon the various types and degrees of literary influence. Ordinarily one considers the translator of the works
of another writer as a disciple or a follower of the original
writer if the translation has been performed as a labor of
love and is not mercenary hackwork. A writer may also
be considered a disciple if he directly acknowledges an
indebtedness or does so indirectly by frequently quoting
or imitating his author. A writer may draw upon a preceding author, however, without his becoming in either
of these senses a disciple: the influence may either be
only moderate in itself or combined with the influences
of so many other authors that its single force is greatly
outweighed by the others. Although major writers are

sometimes so greatly dominated by a single author that they may properly be classified as his disciples, they are more likely to come under the spell of so many and so diverse predecessors that no real discipleship exists to any single one of them. In literary history, this kind of moderate influence upon a major author is sometimes more significant than an extensive influence upon a minor one.

As we have seen, Paine had some translators in Latin America, who may justly be called his disciples, but Henríquez hardly belongs to their number. He never translated more than a few lines of Paine's works, and he derived his liberal political philosophy from a multitude of sources besides Paine. Yet because of his eminent position as a man of letters and his key role in the history of Chilean independence, his achievement in circulating the ideas of Paine below the equator is certainly as notable as that of Paine's Spanish-American translators. As a journalist, Henríquez was gifted with the same powers as Paine to prevail upon his fellow citizens through a lucid, penetrating, and persuasive style to adopt enlightened principles of government. Paine's Hispanic translators, on the other hand, were not literary men at all, and their translations have absolutely no pretense to stylistic excellence.

We shall see that although Paine's influence upon Henríquez's intellectual development was extensive, the latter referred to Paine only once in *La Aurora de Chile* (1812), the first periodical and first publication of any kind to be produced in Chile, and twice in the succeeding *El Monitor Araucano* (1813), the second periodical published in Chile. In the *Aurora*, Henríquez included a brief translation of one paragraph from Paine's *Common Sense*. In the *Monitor* he based one feature article upon an English sentence from Paine's *American Crisis* and concluded his article with a translation of merely ninety-three words from the same source. In a later number he made a further complimentary reference to the *Crisis*. The most remarkable link between the patriot of North America and the patriot of Chile is poetical. In a third periodical, Henríquez translated one of Paine's complete poems under the strange illusion that it was the national anthem of the United States.

Henríquez probably gained his first knowledge of Paine from three citizens of the United States who went to Chile expressly to operate the printing press that produced *La Aurora*, the first and only printing press then in the country. It had been imported as a commercial venture by a naturalized North American of Swedish descent, Hoevel, who wrote his given names in the Spanish style, Mateo Arnaldo. The press had been accompanied on its voyage from the United States by the three printers, Samuel Burr Johnston, William H. Burbidge, and Simon D. Garrison. The government bought the press from Hoevel, hired the three Americans as printers, and engaged Henríquez as editor to publish an official periodical "para unificar la opinión pública a los principios del Gobierno." Probably Hoevel or one of the three printers had a copy of Paine among his possessions, which he showed to Henríquez.[38]

He learned English thanks in great measure to Hoevel. This genial man of the world received a number of periodicals from the United States from which he made translations for Henríquez, and later he gave English lessons to the dedicated editor. If we are to believe Henríquez's statement in *La Aurora* (9 April 1812), two months after the founding of the journal, he learned this difficult language in record-breaking time: The editor, he wrote, animated by a fervent desire to please the public and to earn the confidence of his country, took upon himself the study of the English language, and in the space of less than a

[38] Biographical material concerning Henríquez is documented by A. O. Aldridge, "Camilo Henríquez and the Fame of Thomas Paine and Benjamin Franklin in Chile," *Inter-American Review of Bibliography* 17 (1967): 51-67.

month qualified himself to translate English newspapers without help. Only the people who know this language, Henríquez added, would be able to appreciate the greatness of this work or the extent of the fatigue involved. According to Henríquez's biographer, this is not vainglory, but merely a means of giving readers confidence in the editor's veracity. It also seems to indicate that methods of modern language teaching have not actually made much progress since the early nineteenth century.

The American diplomat, Brackenridge, who met Henríquez in Beunos Aires five years later, had the following comment on his literary and linguistic attainments:

> ... Henríques, [sic] is a Chilean of considerable literary acquirements, of a philanthropic turn of mind, and an enthusiastic admirer of our institutions, which he has endeavoured to explain to his fellow citizens. He understands the English language extremely well, and translates from our newspapers such articles as are likely to be useful.[39]

Brackenridge's further testimony concerning the journalism of this period is invaluable in giving us some idea of circulation figures. Information of this kind is extremely difficult to obtain, and for most early periodicals in both North and South America is virtually nonexistent. Brackenridge tells us that the journals of Buenos Aires in 1817 circulated to the rate of about two thousand weekly. Also in reference to the translation of García de Sena, he remarked: "I believe these have been read by nearly all who can read, and have produced a most extravagant admiration of the United States, at the same time accompanied with something like despair."

Less than two months after Henríquez made his statement in *La Aurora* concerning his mastery of English, he

---

[39] *Voyage to South America*, 2: 138.

introduced Paine's *Common Sense* to the Chilean public in a lead article (4 June 1812) bearing the title "Exemplo Memorable." Here he sketched the plight of Boston in the early days of the Revolution, while it was suffering the hardships of the blockade and other British efforts to bring it to submission. The great need of the English colonies at this time, Henríquez explained, was that of forming a constitution—to prove that the conflict was not brought on by private individuals seeking to gratify personal ambition, but that it was a struggle between the Parliament of England and the Congress of America, that is, a war between two nations. At this point Henríquez turned to his printed authority:

Ayudó á determinarlos á tomar esta resolucion una obra que se publicó en aquellos dias intitulada el *Sentido Comun*: decia entre otras cosas,—"Sea nuestro primer paso una constitucion que nos una. Este es el momento de formarla. Mas tarde se expondria á un porvenir incierto, y á los caprichos del acaso. Será mas dificil mientras mas nos aumentemos y seamos mas ricos. ¿Como conciliar entonces tantos intereses, y tantas provincias? Los hombres se unen por grandes desgracias, y grandes temores: entonces nacen esas amistades fuertes y profundas, que asocian entre si las almas y los intereses. Entonces el genio de los estados se forma por el espiritu errante del pueblo, y las fuerzas esparcidas forman un cuerpo único y formidable. Pocas naciones se aprovecharon del momento oportuno para formarse un gobierno. Este momento no vuelve por muchos siglos, y el descuido es castigado por la anarquia ó la esclavitud. Aprovechemonos de este instante único. Podemos organizar la constitucion mas bella que ha conocido el mundo. Habeis leido en los libros santos la historia de la especie humana abismada en la inundación general del globo. Una sola familia escapó, y fué

encargada por el Ser Supremo de renovar la tierra. Esta
familia somos nosotros. El despotismo lo ha inundado
todo, y nosotros podemos renovar otra véz el mundo.
Vamos en este momento á decidir de la suerte de una
raza de hombres mas numerosa tal véz que todos los
pueblos de la Europa reunidos. Esperaremos ser presa
de un conquistador, y que se destruya la esperanza del
universo? Sobre nosotros estan fixos los ojos de todas
las generaciones futuras, y nos piden la libertad. Nosotros vamos á fixar su destino. Si defraudamos sus es-
peranzas, si les hacemos trahision, ellas algun dia
arrastrarán sus cadenas sobre nuestros sepulcros, y nos
cargarán de inprecaciones."

[*Common Sense,* a work published in those days,
helped them to make up their minds to undertake the
revolution. Among other things, it said: "Let our first
step be a constitution which will unite us. This is the
moment to form it. At a later time the project would
be exposed to an uncertain future and to the caprices
of chance. The task will be more difficult after our population grows and we become richer. How would it be
possible then to reconcile so many interests and so many
provinces? Men unite themselves through great trage-
dies and great fears. It is then that those great and profound friendships are born which bring people and their
interests together. The genius of the state is formed by
the wandering spirit of the people, and the extended
forces form one whole and formidable body. Few nations have taken advantage of the opportune moment
to form a government for themselves. This moment
may not return for many centuries, and failure to act
is punished by anarchy or slavery. Let us take advantage
of our unique moment. We are able to create the most
perfect constitution that the world has ever known. You
have all read in the Holy Books the history of the human

species engulfed by the general inundation of the globe, allowing only one family to escape. It was sent by the Supreme Being to restore the earth. We are this family, despotism has flooded everything, and we are able to renovate the world. Let us in this moment decide the future of a race of men more numerous perhaps than that of all the peoples of Europe together. Are we waiting to be victims of a conqueror? Is the hope of a Union to be destroyed? Upon us are fixed the eyes of all future generations, asking us for freedom. It is up to us to decide their destiny. If we disappoint their hopes, if we commit treason against them, they will some day drag their chains over our tombs and curse us."]

Immediately after these words, Henríquez added his own equally stirring appeal: "Comencemos declarando nuestra independencia" ["Let us start to declare our independence"].

One would look in vain for this long passage in *Common Sense*, for, despite Henríquez's statement, it is not there. Indeed only part of the passage has any resemblance to Paine's original. Henríquez's first three sentences in the Spanish text may be based upon the following from *Common Sense*: "Should an independency be brought about by the first of those means [the voice of Congress], we have every opportunity and every encouragement before us, to form the noblest, purest constitution on the face of the earth." Henríquez's ninth sentence resembles the following in *Common Sense*: "Should we neglect the present favorable and inviting period, and an Independance be hereafter effected by any other means, we must charge the consequence to ourselves." Henríquez's twelfth to fifteenth sentences were probably suggested by the following in *Common Sense*: "A situation similar to the present, hath not happened since the days of Noah until now. The birthday of a new world is at hand, and a race of men, perhaps as numerous as all Europe contains, are to receive their portion of freedom from the event of a few months."[40] The rest of the alleged transcription of Paine's thought is not even a paraphrase, but an elaboration of sentiments previously sketched.

A similar mystery exists in regard to Henríquez's use of *The American Crisis*. Henríquez began the sixty-third number of his *Monitor Araucano* with the following epigraph:

> There [sic] are the times that try men's souls. Paine. American crisis n. 2.
>
> [September 2, 1813]

Apart from the substitution of "There" for "These," which is probably a typographical error, the great puzzle in this epigraph is why the quotation should be attributed to *Crisis* no. 2, when it is universally recognized by all who have read Paine as the opening sentence of *Crisis* no. 1. The mystery may be cleared up by reference to the publishing history of Paine's works. The first London printer of the *Crisis*, Daniel Isaac Eaton, was not certain of exactly which writings of Paine were originally issued under this title, and in his edition published in 1796 he included as no. 1 an essay from an earlier "Crisis" series published in London by another author. In a later issue of his edition, also in 1796, Eaton included a note acknowledging that no. 1 of his collection was not by Paine.

This bibliographical circumstance shows that the *Crisis* did not make its way into Henríquez's hands directly from Philadelphia, but that he used a copy published in England. This suggests that his copy of *Common Sense* may also have come from England and that other Latin Amer-

---

[40] All three sentences from *Common Sense* are to be found on the same page in *Complete Writings*, ed. Foner, 1: 45.

icans may likewise have read London imprints as well as Philadelphia ones or the García de Sena translation.

In a sense, Henríquez's entire essay is an elaboration of Paine, for he begins with the opening sentences of Crisis no. 1 and concludes with its final sentences. Paine is used as a means of introducing the theme of revolutionary struggle:

> El célebre Paine en las vicisitudes de la fortuna de la revolución de Norte América decía: *estos son los tiempos que prueban las almas.* En verdad en las revoluciones todo se descubre a nuestra vista: los talentos, las virtudes, la incapacidad, los visios, los caracteres nobles y sublimes, y los seres pequeños y ridículos que suspiran por la opresión y la infamia de la servidumbre.

Henríquez's last paragraph, as we have already indicated, consists of his translation of the conclusion of the first Crisis:

> Tal es nuestra situación, y todos la conocen. Por la perseverancia y fortaleza tenemos el prospecto de un éxito dichoso; por la cobardía la perspectiva de los males más terribles; la devastación del país; la despoblación de las ciudades; la deshonra de las familias; las habitaciones sin seguridad; una esclavitud sin esperanza; una posteridad infame; la patria cubierta de cadalsos; miseria, desesperación: ¡Oh! Contemplad esta pintura, y penetraos de ella: si hay alguna tan insensible que no se horrorice, o que no lo crea, sufra estos males, y no haya quien lo lamente.

This translation is relatively close to its original, except for the softening beyond all recognition of one of Paine's forthright and original thrusts—the dire prediction that, unless the Americans were victorious in battle, they would have their "homes turned into barracks and bawdy-houses for Hessians, and a future race to provide for, whose fa-

thers we shall doubt of." Henríquez's "una posteridad in-
fame" hardly conveys the same idea. Probably the traditional Spanish reticence toward treating sexual matters
in print rather than failure to understand Paine's English
explains the discrepancy.

One month later in an article on the need for joint action
of all the American peoples against the European powers,
Henríquez again paraphrased Paine in calling for the organization of constitutional government in all the American countries:

> Estos cuerpos soberanos y legislativos son los únicos
> que pueden autorizar a los Plenipotenciarios y para ello
> es indispensable que conste a todo el mundo que están
> en libertad y constituidos legítimamente. Da mucha
> fuerza a lo expuesto el siguiente artículo de la preciosa
> obra de Tomás Paine, titulada *The American Crisis*. El
> Continente corre riesgo de ser arruinado si pronto no
> se organiza y constituye en independencia.
>
> [October 2, 1813]

The importance of this article is not in a particular quotation or translation, but in the implication that Paine's
ideas had stimulated Henríquez's own thinking.

Almost concurrently with the appearance of *El Monitor*,
a young native of Guatemala, Antonio José de Irisarri, was
editing in Santiago a weekly political organ, *El Semanario
Republicano*, which ran from 7 August 1813 until 19 February 1814. Henríquez succeeded the younger man as editor on 23 October 1813.

Following the example of Henríquez, Irisarri drew upon
Paine's *Common Sense* to inculcate liberal political principles. As a matter of fact, he was more democratic than
Henríquez; Irisarri wanted a republican form of government, whereas Henríquez preferred a limited monarchy. In 1817 Henríquez even translated Robert Bisset's
Sketch of Democracy, an attack upon popular government

in favor of monarchy, in which Paine is compared to Wat
Tyler and Jack Straw.

In his article "Sobre el origen y la naturaleza de las
monarquías," a determined attack, Irisarri cites one of the
fundamental principles of *Common Sense*: "El Gobierno,
dice Paine, es un mal necesario para los Pueblos." In the
same article, Irisarri adopts Paine's scriptural argument
to refute the doctrine of divine right: "Dicen algunos que
las Monarquías son instituídas por Dios, y para esto se
valen de una aplicacíon violenta de los textos de la sagrada
escritura. El autor del Sentido Común, rebate poderosa-
mente este error con una convicción, que me ha, parecido
digna de imitarse." After a close paraphrase of Paine's
reasoning, Irisarri follows him in quoting a long passage
from 1 Kings, and then comments:

> En vista de estas palabras de Samuel, dice Paine, es
> preciso convenir en una de dos cosas, o en que Dios es
> enemigo de los Reyes, o en que es falsa la escritura. Si
> creer lo último es una impiedad, debemos aceptar lo
> primero como uno de los misterios de nuestra santa
> religión. ¿Cómo, pues, los Católicos hemos sido tan
> ignorantes que creyésemos a los Reyes establecidos por
> la voluntad de Dios?

Henríquez certainly had a valuable ally in his campaign
to promote both political and theological liberalism.

When Henríquez succeeded Irisarri as editor of *El Semanario*, the only Paine material he then published was
his translation of Paine's poem already mentioned, in a
sense the most important of all his writings inspired by
Paine.

Not even Paine's warmest admirers consider his poetry
much better than mediocre: it is labored, conventional,
and amateurish. Here again the parallel with Henríquez
stands firm. The text of the poem that Henríquez chose
for translation, "Hail Great Republic of the World," exists

in two widely different versions, one that now appears in collected editions of Paine's works and another, presumably earlier, that was printed in *Tom Paine's Jests* (Philadelphia, 1796) and not reprinted.[41] The second version is the basis of Henríquez's translation, but he presumably used an anonymous copy. Otherwise, he would probably have given the author's name and he would also have been spared from describing the work as the national anthem of the United States. He included it in *El Semanario Republicano*, "Extraordinario—Miércoles 10 de Noviembre de 1813."

Following is the text from *Tom Paine's Jests* together with the text as translated by Henríquez:

HAIL GREAT REPUBLIC OF THE WORLD

Hail great Republic of the world,
    Which rear'd her empire in the West,
Where fam'd Columbus' flag unfurl'd,
    Gave tortured Europe scenes of rest;
      Be thou forever great and free,
      The land of Love and Liberty!

Beneath thy spreading, mantling vine,
    Beside each flowery grove and spring,
And where thy lofty mountains shine,
    May all thy sons and fair ones sing,
      Be thou forever, etc.

From thee may rudest nations learn,
    To prize the cause thy sons began;
From thee may future, may future tyrants know,
    That sacred are the Rights of Man.
      Be thou forever, etc.

From thee may hated discord fly,
    With all her dark, her gloomy train;
And o'er thy fertile, thy fertile wide domain,

---

[41] A. O. Aldridge, "The Poetry of Thomas Paine," *Pennsylvania Magazine of History and Biography* 79 (1955): 94-95.

May everlasting friendship reign.
Be thou forever, etc.

Of thee may lisping infancy,
The pleasing wond'rous story tell;
And patriot sages in venerable mood,
Instruct the world to govern well.
Be thou forever, etc.

Ye guardian Angels watch around,
From harms protect the new born State;
And all ye friendly, ye friendly nations join,
And thus salute the Child of Fate.
Be thou forever, etc.

VERSIÓN LIBRE DEL CÁNTICO NACIONAL DE ESTADOS UNIDOS "HAIL GREAT REPUBLIC OF THE WORLD"

AL PUEBLO DE BUENOS AIRES

¡Salve, gloria del mundo, República naciente
Vuela a ser el imperio más grande de occidente,
¡Oh Patria de hombres libres, suelo de libertad!

Que tus hijos entonen de vides a la sombra,
O entre risueñas fuentes sobre florida alfombra:
¡Oh Patria de hombres libres . . . !

Que a estimar la gran causa aprendan los
    humanos,
Y a hacer que sus derechos veneren los tiranos.
¡Oh Patria . . . !

Que canten tus jijuelos con balbucientes labios,
Y enseñando a los pueblos en la vejez tus sabios.
¡Oh Patria . . . !

Tus ángeles custodios te cubran con sus alas;
Y unidas las naciones en fe y amistad pura,
Te saluden con lágrimas, lágrimas de ternura.
¡Oh Patria . . . !

It will be noticed that Henríquez omitted Paine's fourth stanza, possibly because it did not appear in the copy from which he worked. As far as I know, this is the only poem by Paine ever translated into any language. And, as we have seen, Henríquez himself probably did not know that Paine was the original author. Yet it cannot be denied that Paine made a significant impression upon Henríquez.

If, as Enrique de Gandía maintains, Paine did not influence the events leading up to the Latin American independence movement, he certainly made a significant contribution to the development and final success of that movement. Before 1825, there were three separate translations of *Common Sense*, two of a *Dissertation on the First Principles of Government*, and one of *Rights of Man*. Paine's doctrines were discussed in seven different newspapers in Venezuela, Argentina, and Chile; sections of *Common Sense* were paraphrased in the *Manual politico* of Francisco Yanes and in the *Memoria* of Servando Teresa de Mier; Paine's reasoning was echoed in the *Manifesto* concerning Venezuelan independence by Germán Roscio; and his *Crisis* no. 1 was paraphrased by Camilo Henríquez. As Paine had argued in Philadelphia that the struggle against England was the affair of a whole continent, not of individual cities or colonies; so his disciples in Spanish-America used his words to preach the doctrine of unity in the Hispanic world. His concepts were not confined to merely one or two parts of the Spanish colonies, but were promulgated by at least a dozen translators or commentators in the major population centers from Mexico to Chile.

NINE

THE ENLIGHTENMENT IN THE AMERICAS

ONLY WITHIN recent years has the term Enlightenment been generally applied to the literature of
either North or South America. The traditional
term has been that of "colonial" in both areas for most
of the eighteenth century and that of "revolutionary" for
North America after 1776 and for South America after
1810. At the present time historians of Latin American
literature speak freely of *las luces* or *la ilustración;* whereas
critics of North American literature still seem hesitant
to utilize the term Enlightenment, confining themselves
to the more traditional expressions "rationalism" or "Age
of Reason." This is paradoxical since the Anglo-Saxon
tradition in general was rich in the philosophical thought
associated with the Enlightenment; whereas the Hispanic
world, suffering during this period under the influence of
a despotic monarchy and a stifling religious Inquisition,
could make little claim to an atmosphere of free inquiry
or political reform.

The degree to which either culture can be said to have
participated in the Enlightenment depends primarily on
the way this movement of ideas is defined. If it is considered primarily from the epistemological and scientific
perspectives, that is, considering reason as the basis of all
knowledge, recognizing experimental science as the road
to progress in human development, and favoring secular-
ization of social relations, the Hispanic world may indeed

be said to have participated in the movement. But if it is considered in addition—as it is in France, Germany, and England—as open opposition to every form of superstition and fanaticism; as toleration of a wide diversity in religious opinions and practices; and as reform of political, economic, and social abuses of the state, the Spanish mainland was hardly touched at all by this powerful current of ideas, and Spanish America was little affected until the period of independence early in the nineteenth century.

The pioneers in drawing attention to the Enlightenment as a unified movement in the Americas have been historians rather than literary critics. For more than thirty years intellectual historians have been associating the Enlightenment with Latin America,[1] but the term "American Enlightenment" in reference to North America had no currency, if indeed it was used at all, until the publication in 1965 of an anthology with that title edited by Adrienne Koch. This significant collection of documents is based entirely on the writings of five major "philosopher-statesmen," namely, Benjamin Franklin, John Adams, Thomas Jefferson, James Monroe, and Alexander Hamilton, and the emphasis is understandably not on literature. The only one of these five who knew Spanish was Thomas Jefferson. For this and other reasons he enjoyed considerable renown in Latin America, comparable to that which Franklin gained in France.

In the Bicentennial year another historian, Henry F. May, published an excellent work entitled *The Enlightenment in America*, but its focus is on politics and religion, specifically the balance between deism and Christianity, and it considers literary matters only incidentally. The brief definition of Enlightenment which the author

---

[1] See, for example, Arthur P. Whitaker, ed., *Latin America and the Enlightenment* (Ithaca, N.Y., 1942, rev. ed., 1961).

provides, moreover, is unfortunately inadequate. This intellectual attitude, which dominated much of the eighteenth century, according to May, consisted merely in the belief in two propositions, "first, that the present age is more enlightened than the past; and second, that we understand nature and man best through the use of our natural faculties."[2] This definition is at once too comprehensive and too limited. Not all Enlightenment thinkers believed in the doctrine of progress, and the exceptions included many of the defenders of the ancients whom we have previously treated as well as the advocates of primitivism. The second proposition would cover almost everyone in the entire century except religious enthusiasts. It would certainly comprise stalwart anti-Enlightenment figures such as Jonathan Edwards and Edmund Burke. In addition to sense perception, both reason and instinct were regarded as natural faculties, and except for divine revelation no other sources of knowledge were considered possible. It has also been convincingly argued that social action among the major Enlightenment thinkers counted for much more than reasoning, ideas, or acquiring knowledge. It is a mistake to overlook the great emphasis on scientific research and social reform, which were almost the lifeblood of the Enlightenment.

The best definition of the Enlightenment spirit that I have ever encountered comes from a contemporary French disciple of Voltaire, abbé André Morellet, who played a major role in French-American literary relations. This emancipated ecclesiastic was a close friend and correspondent of Benjamin Franklin; he translated Jefferson's *Notes on Virginia*, and he served as intermediary between Thomas Paine and the Archbishop of Toulouse in an exchange of letters involving Edmund Burke, which Paine described in his *Rights of Man*. Referring to the intellec-

[2] (New York, 1976), p. xiv.

tual activity of the *philosophes* involved with the *Ency-clopédie*, Morellet wrote: "All of these men had an identical philosophy; it is this desire to know, this mental activity which refuses to leave an effect without seeking its cause, a phenomenon without an explanation, an assertion without proof, an objection without a reply, an error without combatting it, an evil without seeking the remedy, a possible good without trying to attain it; it is this general movement of minds which characterized the eighteenth century and which will be its glory forever."[3]

One of the major types of evidence used to prove the existence of an Enlightenment spirit in Spain and Latin America consists of lists of books by enlightened authors of other countries available in libraries or private collections during that chronological period. The assumption is that if the works of such luminaries as Voltaire, Montesquieu, and Rousseau were on the shelves of libraries in any part of the world, they must have contributed to the dissemination or indigenous development of Enlightenment ideology in that area. Daniel J. Boorstin, however, has denied that library holdings in themselves prove strong evidence of intellectual influence.[4] Books in a library may not be read or they may be read to be refuted. According to Boorstin's skeptical view, even though the works of Voltaire and Montesquieu circulated in the Americas, they may not have contributed to fostering a spirit of toleration or other ideals of the *philosophes*. Most scholars, however, continue to regard library holdings as realistic evidence of the spread of ideas, particularly since the recent vogue

---

[3] This definition was originally published by Morellet in his "Eloge de Marmontel." I have previously used it in a collection of essays by various scholars concerning North America, South America, and the Iberian Peninsula under the title of *The Ibero-American Enlightenment* (Urbana, Ill., 1971), p. 5.

[4] "The Myth of an American Enlightenment," in *America and the Image of Europe* (New York, 1960), pp. 65-78.

of quantitative methodology in historical studies. Certainly, from the literary perspective, bibliography is an indispensable part of research—all aspects of bibliography, including that which takes account of actual copies as well as titles. It is relevant to add, moreover, that even though library holdings do not offer absolute proof that works were being read with approval in a particular milieu, the lack of evidence of physical presence and circulation does not prove, on the other hand, that books were not being read. Sometimes the most popular and widely circulated books at a specific time leave almost no trace in libraries. An example is John Wesley's *Survey of the Wisdom of God*, which was discussed in the sixth chapter.

Ideas were successfully disseminated, moreover, by means of monthly journals published in England and on the continent, the prototype of which was the *Journal des Sçavans*, which began publication in 1665. Others from the seventeenth century included *Acta Eruditorum, Nouvelles de la République des Lettres, Bibliothèque Universelle et Historique*, and the first in English, *Universal Historical Bibliothèque*. Norman Fiering has provided an absorbing account of these journals and traced the circulation of several later ones in America, including *History of the Works of the Learned* (established 1699), *Memoirs of Literature* (established 1710), and *The Present State of the Republick of Letters* (established 1728). According to Fiering, the first book written by an American to be noticed by a learned journal on the continent was by a Harvard professor, Charles Morton. His *Enquiry into the Physical and Literal Sense of that Scripture Jerem. VIII, 7. "The Stork in the Heaven knoweth her appointed Times"* was announced in the January 1687 issue of the *Bibliothèque Universelle*. Concerning the scientific problem of the migration of birds, Morton argued that they migrated back and forth from the moon. The first essay by an American in a learned journal was Samuel Johnson's "Introduction to the Study of Philosophy," which, according to Fiering, appeared in the May 1731 *Present State of the Republick of Letters.*

In a further article, Fiering maintains that "the very first American enlightenment was French, if the advent of Cartesianism may be thought of as at least a pre-enlightenment." This qualification extends the definition of Enlightenment so broadly, however, that it would also include most of Hispanic America as well as the New England colonies. We must remember that Voltaire and others insisted that the system of Descartes in contrast to that of Newton was almost as obsolete as that of the Church fathers. The early contribution of French thought to the American colonies consisted in the dissemination of notions of free inquiry by means of learned journals, but the concept of Enlightenment as knowledge in action in the sense in which we have defined it earlier in this chapter came originally to America through the writings of the English deists.[5]

Henry F. May and David Lundberg in a quantitative survey of major European writers in American libraries and bookstores in North America from 1700 to 1813 have compiled impressive evidence of the availability of the works of the dominant Enlightenment figures.[6] Another

[5] "The Transatlantic Republic of Letters: A Note on the Circulation of Learned Periodicals to Early Eighteenth-Century America," *William and Mary Quarterly*, 3rd ser., 33 (1976): 642-60; "The First American Enlightenment: Tillotson, Leverett, and Philosophical Anglicanism," *New England Quarterly* 54 (1981): 307-44. I have quoted from p. 322. This second article won the Walter Muir Whitehall Prize in Colonial History in 1981.

[6] "The Enlightened Reader in America," *American Quarterly* 28 (1976): 262-301. An exhaustive account of books in North American libraries about Latin America is provided by Harry Bernstein, "Las primeras relaciones intelectuales entre New England y el mundo hispánico (1700-1815)," *Revista Hispánica Moderna* 5 (1938): 1-17. See also Harry Bern-

scholar, on the basis of personal sampling in libraries in the Philadelphia area, moreover, has concluded that May and Lundberg have considerably undercounted the actual numbers.[7] One of the most significant findings of May and Lundberg is that the various printings of some works actually exceeded the number of individual copies recorded. During this period, for example, there were forty-seven different issues or editions of Pope's *Essay on Man*, but the compilers were able to locate only thirty-three single copies.

In the British colonies of North America, neoclassical trends in style virtually coincided with Enlightenment subject matter. Neoclassicism could be discerned early in the eighteenth century; signs of the Enlightenment were apparent soon after; and the movement reached its apex in the period between 1765 and 1815, "an age of revolutions and constitutions," as John Adams remarked. Adrienne Koch has even suggested "the continuing hold" of Enlightenment ideals not only throughout the half century before the Civil War but even beyond.[8]

In peninsular Spain, neoclassicism did not flourish until the middle of the eighteenth century, far later than in England or France; and in the Spanish colonies the lag was even greater. Scant evidence of its existence can be found in Latin America before the last two decades of the eighteenth century, and the period of its highest development was the first half of the nineteenth century. In-

stein, *Making of an Inter-American Mind* (Gainesville, Fla., 1961); A. Owen Aldridge, "An Early Cuban Exponent of Inter-American Cultural Relations: Domingo del Monte," *Hispania* 54 (1971): 348-53; José de Onís, *The United States as Seen by Spanish American Writers, 1776-1890* (New York, 1952); Estuardo Nuñez, *Autores ingleses y norteamericanos en el Perú* (Lima, 1956).

[7] Arthur H. Scouten, "The Paradox of Deism in Colonial America," *Lex et Scientia* 14 (1978): 222-25.

[8] "Aftermath of the American Enlightenment," *Studies in Voltaire and the Eighteenth Century* 56 (1967): 762.

deed, neoclassicism and Romanticism arrived in Hispanic America almost simultaneously. Historians of the comparative development of literature should be aware of this phenomenon, not only of the existence of neoclassicism and Romanticism side by side in the same chronological period but also of the merging of characteristics of the two movements in particular literary artifacts. Examples are so numerous as to be superfluous, but the poetry of José de Olmedo could be considered a *locus classicus*. Even in North America the same blending of neoclassicism and Romanticism may be seen in many of the poems of Philip Freneau.

In studying the Enlightenment, one must be on guard against the process that Daniel Boorstin has described as homogenizing; that is, of assuming the presence of a complex of ideas or climate of opinion in a particular culture merely because these intellectual currents existed somewhere else in the same chronological span. A type of distortion just as serious as homogenizing, however, is that of provincializing; that is, of attributing a special or unique character to the people or way of life of a certain region while ignoring international currents.

The first step in studying the Enlightenment in North and South America is to seek evidence as to whether this complex of ideas and ideals actually existed. If the evidence is affirmative, one may next try to determine whether it was primarily a native growth in each area or whether it was part of the spirit of the times. In the scope of a single chapter, I cannot hope to provide definitive conclusions, but I shall attempt to introduce some relevant parallels and relations. I shall not deal with political prose, however, which has generally been considered as the chief claim of the Americas to the Enlightenment, but shall concentrate instead on belletristic works. Nor shall I treat a significant document on Enlightenment ideas in the tradition of the picaresque novel, *El Periquillo Sarniento*

(1816), by Fernández de Lizardi. It was preceded in North America by Hugh Henry Brackenridge's *Modern Chivalry* (1792-1797), which also uses the picaresque genre with emphasis on humor. In this work, however, it is ideals of the Enlightenment that are frequently satirized.

One of the most important Latin American poets of the period of independence is José Joaquín de Olmedo of Ecuador. His best poem is generally recognized to be "La Victoria de Junín: Canto a Bolívar" ["The Victory of Junín: Song to Bolívar"], a tribute to the revolutionary general Bolívar for a decisive military victory, published in 1825 and written with the advice and consultation of the general himself. Olmedo also published a translation of the first three epistles of Alexander Pope's *Essay on Man*. From an international perspective this translation represents prima facie evidence of the Enlightenment spirit. From an indigenous point of view, however, Olmedo's tribute to Bolívar is equally a document of the Enlightenment. This poem not only celebrates two famous battles in the struggle for independence, but also reincarnates, in the spirit of the traditional epic, the ghost of the Inca emperor Manco-Capac who prophesies the future glorious destiny of America. In passing, Olmedo celebrates Las Casas, the protector of the Indians, as a national hero, and eulogizes the people of the United States as "primogénito dichoso de libertad." The dedication of the author to political liberty and social equality is obvious, but the poem also contains cosmological overtones typical of the Enlightenment. In the introductory lines, for example, Olmedo describes the enormous extent of the Andes mountains and suggests in a note that their size is intended to help compensate for the difference in land mass between the Northern and Southern Hemispheres.

Since Pope's *Essay on Man* is one of the most significant deistic documents in world literature, the connection of Olmedo's translation with the metaphysics of the Enlightenment can be assumed without commentary. Olmedo himself, however, points out an ethical relationship which otherwise would have gone unperceived. In the notes of the first epistle published in 1823, Olmedo affirmed that he conceived of his translation of Pope as a means of giving the people of his country a sound moral system to compensate for their lack of a comprehensive code of laws, the Spanish statutes having been rendered obsolete by the independence of the former American colonies.[9]

A remarkable parallel to this political intrepretation of the *Essay on Man* exists in a North American poem, almost a century earlier, which provides hitherto unsuspected political applications of precepts in Pope's *An Essay on Criticism*. A satirical poem published in the *Pennsylvania Gazette* in 1733 entitled "Against Party-Malice and Levity, usual at and near the time of Electing Assembly-Men" [no. 252, 28 September 1733] is interlarded with quotations from the English neoclassicist. In the following example, the first four lines are by the Pennsylvania author, the last two by Pope:

> For little Faults great Merit should not fall;
> First find th' applauded Man with none at all.
> In brave old Patriots, when small Faults are seen,
> Think of the Weight they've borne and check your
> Spleeen!
> "Of Old, those met Rewards who cou'd excel,"
> "And such were prais'd as but endeavour'd well."

Olmedo also translated a "Fragmento del Anti-Lucrecio," which is published in his *Poesías completas* directly after his translation of *An Essay on Man*. There is a good reason for this placement. The section from the famous

---

[9] *Ensayo sobre el hombre. De M. Pope. Versión del inglés* (Lima, 1823), p. 9. This note is not reprinted in *Poesías completas*, ed. A. E. Pólet (Quito, 1945).

Latin poem of Cardinal de Polignac [Book IX] is filled with concepts of natural religion comparable to those in Pope. Olmedo's "Canto a Bolívar" provides an excellent illustration of the high regard in which many Latin American authors held the Indian races native to their land. By and large South American authors identified with the Indians and considered the natives as part of their own race and tradition, although some Argentinian authors represent an exception to this characteristic. Esteban Echeverría in a narrative poem, *La Cautiva*, portrays Indians as debauched, and Sarmiento in prose considers the race as inferior. Yet, as we have seen in the preceding chapter, a political group in Argentina in the second decade of the nineteenth century had actually proposed the creation of an empire based on the past glories of the Incas. North American authors, on the other hand, at best patronized the Indian in the manner of the European Noble Savage tradition, considering him as physically powerful, but intellectually primitive and naive. Perhaps the most significant early portrayal of the Indian in favorable terms was that of William Penn in a letter to the Free Society of Traders in August 1683, in which he maintains that Europeans, despite their superior knowledge, have not been able to surpass the Indians in a wholesome way of life. This letter was immediately printed in London and has been reprinted many times. It was incorporated into a travel book by Richard Brome, which was translated into French as *L'Amérique angloise* (Amsterdam, 1688) and may have been partly responsible for the glowing portrayals of the American Indian in the works of Diderot and Montesquieu. The most sympathetic North American portrayal appeared in the verse of Philip Freneau, who preceded Chateaubriand in delineating the Indians as a noble race predestined to extinction through the predatory advance of the white man. Even Freneau, however, kept the red man on an inferior intellectual and spiritual level.[10] Many North Americans, moreover, even poets, were bitterly hostile toward the Indians and openly paraded their animosity in literary works. A forthright example is a poem published in 1764 entitled "A New and mild Method totally to extirpate the Indians out of No. America." The method advocated was to encourage drunkenness.[11]

Joseph Dennie, who disliked Indians about as heartily as he detested Jeffersonian Democrats, published an essay in the *Port Folio* entitled "An Indian Plagiary," which supported two of his favorite themes, that close imitation of European models contributed to the wretched condition of the literature of the United States and that the Indian should not be portrayed as a noble sage, but as a "natural brute beast."[12] The essayist reprints from a Ver-

[10] See, for example, Freneau's "The Indian Burying Ground" and William Cullen Bryant's "An Indian at the Burying-Place of His Fathers." In a sprightly narrative with the misleading title, *God's Protecting Providence Man's Surest Help and Defence* (Philadelphia, 1699), Jonathan Dickinson provided a realistic portrayal of encounters with Indians. Dickinson, who was shipwrecked off the coast of Florida, described his trip by land and canoe northward to Philadelphia during the course of which he was humanely received by the Spanish governor of St. Augustine, a rare example of early contact between the two cultures. His book, which despite the pietistic title consists of a day-by-day account of his experiences, belongs to the related literary genres of shipwreck and Indian captivity and is one of the first American best sellers. In addition to the first printing, there were fourteen others between 1700 and 1826 together with a Dutch translation published in Leyden, a German translation published in Germantown, Pennsylvania (1756), and a further German translation published in Frankfort (1774). The Dutch translation contains an appended sixty-line poem of commentary. See *Jonathan Dickinson's Journal*, ed. E. W. Andrews and C. M. Andrews (New Haven, 1945).

[11] J. A. Leo Lemay, *A Calendar of American Poetry in the Colonial Newspapers and Magazines and in the Major English Magazines through 1765* (Worcester, Mass., 1972), p. 271.

[12] 5 December 1807. The essay is presented as a contributed piece, but it could be by Dennie himself.

mont journal an anecdote which had "run its merry round through most of the newspapers as a proof of Indian genius." An Indian, discovering that some venison which he had hung up in his hut to dry had been stolen, set out in search of "a *little old white man* with a *short gun* and accompanied by a *small dog* with a *bobtail.*" When asked how he knew all these details, the Indian replied that the thief was little because he had made a pile of stones to stand on when stealing the venison, he was old because of his short steps, and he was white because his tracks showed a turning out of his toes, which Indian tracks never do. His gun, moreover, was little because of the mark it made on the bark of a tree on which it was leaning, and the dog was small and bobtailed because of its tracks and the mark it made in the dust when sitting down while his master engaged in thievery. The essayist considered this journalistic composition to be as "rude as the rocks of Scandinavia" even though he proceeded to expose it as a plagiary from a passage in Voltaire's *Zadig*, which by contrast he held to be "full of the glory of Invention, and the brightness of Genius; . . . embellished by Taste, and consummated by Art, . . . the style of Refinement and Civility." The essayist thereupon reproduced the third chapter of *Zadig* in the original and in translation even though Smollett's translation of the entire work had already been reprinted in two issues (one separately under the title *The Princess of Babylon* and once in Voltaire's *Miscellanies*) in Philadelphia in 1778. In the relevant chapter, Zadig recognizes by deductions similar to those of the Vermont Indian that the king's horse was five feet high with small hoofs and a tail three and a half feet in length, that the studs on his bit were twenty-three carat gold, and the silver of his shoes was almost pure. What the American essayist did not know is that the story was no more original with Voltaire than it was with the Vermont scribe who adapted it. Voltaire's source is a story

in the *Bibliothèque orientale* of Barthélemy d'Herbelot
(1697) about three Arab brothers who deduce the major
physical features of a lost camel. The anecdote in its Ara-
bian, French, and Vermont versions obviously provides a
splendid example of Early American letters in contact
with universal literature. A parallel to the charge of pla-
giarism in the *Port Folio* exists, moreover, in a French
periodical *L'Année littéraire*, edited by one of Voltaire's
most persistent enemies, Elie Fréron. In 1767, Fréron accused Voltaire of plagiarizing another episode of *Zadig*
(Chapter XVIII) from the English poet Parnell.[13]

A theme more closely linked to Enlightenment thought
than the relative intelligence of the natives of America is
that of the dissemination of knowledge. It is indicated in
an ode "Sobre la invención y libertad de la imprenta"
published by an Argentinian Juan Cruz Varela in 1822. It
is strongly indebted to a very similar ode "A la libertad

[13] *L'Année littéraire* (Amsterdam, 1767), Vol. 1, Letter 3. The *Port
Folio* also introduced to America an original translation of another of
Voltaire's *contes*, "The World as it Goes, or the Vision of Babouc." It
was not identified as Voltaire's, however, but merely as "from the French"
[20, 27 April and 4 May 1805]. This was apparently the second translation
in the English-speaking world, the only previous one consisting of a
pamphlet, *Babouc, or the World as it Goes* (London, 1754, and Dublin,
1754). None of the foregoing material appears in the excellent study by
M. M. Barr, *Voltaire in America, 1744-1800* (Baltimore, 1941). Barr indicates, however [p. 45], that the second chapter of *Zadig* was translated
in the *New York Weekly Museum*, 20 August 1796, under the title "The
Nose." Voltaire's contribution to the Enlightenment in America has
never been thoroughly treated as such although the basic materials are
available in Barr's study. His poem "Temple du gout" was actually noted
as early as 9 August 1733 in Franklin's *Pennsylvania Gazette*. Voltaire's
Treatise on Toleration especially was widely known and respected. As
could be expected, he was regarded by the anti-Enlightenment forces as
the epitome of evil. The outstanding example of this attitude is the
ironic dedication to Voltaire of Timothy Dwight's poem *The Triumph
of Infidelity* (Hartford, 1788) in which Voltaire is portrayed as teaching
"that the chief end of man was to slander his God, and abuse him
forever."

de imprenta," by an exponent of liberal ideas in Spain, Manuel José Quintana. Praise of the printing press for making possible the efficient diffusion of ideas was widespread in most western European literatures of the eighteenth century. As we have already seen, it was expressed in 1728 by James Sterling and in 1795 by Robert Treat Paine.

Even more important, one of the pioneer printing craftsmen of America, Isaiah Thomas, published in 1810 an encyclopedic *History of Printing in America* in two volumes, which was printed on his son's press at Worcester, Massachusetts. The work also contains a "Concise View of the Discovery and Progress of the [Printing] Art in Other Parts of the World." For his discussion of Spanish America, Thomas was forced to rely exclusively on secondary sources, including two famous histories of the Conquest, one by the Scotsman William Robertson and the other by the Mexican Francisco Javier Clavigero. Thomas also provided a rather extensive bibliography, drawn entirely from Robertson, of books printed in Mexico and Lima on the history of America, together with a comparison of book production in both western continents, a perspective remarkably free from chauvinism or religious intolerance. Within seven years of its publication Thomas's book was known in Chile, where it was cited by the leading journalist of Santiago, Camilo Henríquez, as the source of a statement concerning the large number of periodicals being published in North America.[14]

The only neoclassical poem of the English colonies to obtain any kind of renown in England was a topographical piece based on Virgil's *Georgics* entitled "A Journey from Patapsco to Annapolis, April 4, 1730." It was reprinted in Britain at least five times. Implying the deistic belief that the beauty and order of the universe reveal the existence

[14] *El Censor*, no. 88 (22 May 1817).

of a benevolent deity, the author, Richard Lewis, describes a typical farmer, the fruit trees of his orchard and those of the forest, together with thoughts on life and immortality in a day's journey through the country. Many parallels are to be found in a Spanish georgic written almost one hundred years later, "To the Agriculture of the Torrid Zone" ["A la agricultura de la zona tórrida"] (1826), by Andrés Bello. It features such commonplaces on the Enlightenment as social peace and order, the dignity of labor, and the benevolence of the Creator, but dwells upon the organizing of nature through agriculture rather than on the landscape in general. Except for their relative brevity, these two poems resemble James Thomson's *The Seasons* and Saint-Lambert's *Les Saisons* as closely as the English and the French georgics resemble each other. A poem in the Virgilian tradition preceding Bello's was *Rusticatio Mexicana*, by Rafael Landívar, published in Latin in 1781. This description of rural life in Mexico is clearly neoclassical, but its being composed in Latin partially disqualifies it as an Enlightenment document since progressive thought of the movement exalted the vernacular over the ancient languages. Landívar's inclusion of a good deal of natural science, however, certainly represents an Enlightenment tendency.[15] The only complete translations of the poem into Spanish belong to the twentieth century, although the Cuban poet José María Heredia in 1836 translated a lengthy section concerning cockfighting.[16]

Bello, in another poem of the same decade as his panegyric to agriculture, "Alocución a la poesía," called upon the genius of poetry to leave Europe and to take up her abode among the burgeoning nations of America. Since

[15] Graciela P. Nemes, "Rafael Landívar and Poetic Echoes of the Enlightenment," in *The Ibero-American Enlightenment*, ed. Aldridge, pp. 299-301.

[16] Heredia, "Pelea de gallos," in *Poesías líricas*, ed. Elías Zerolo (Paris, n.d.), pp. 91-94.

we have already given several examples of *translatio studii* in North American literature, we shall provide only one more at this time, an anonymous poem of 1729 attributed to Richard Lewis.

> E'er Time has Measured out an hundred Years
> Westward from *Britain*, shall an *Athens* rise,
> Which soon shall bear away the learned Prize;
> Hence Europe's Sons assistance shall implore,
> And learn from her, as she from them before.[17]

Both in Europe and America, the theme of westward movement was applied to liberty as well as to learning and the arts. One example is "El regreso" (1830), by Esteban Echeverría.

> La libertad de Europa fugitiva,
> Un asilo buscando,
> Ha passado el Oceano,
> Su dignisimo trono levantando
> Do se agitan los pechos a su nombre,
> Y do con dignidad respira el hombre;
> En el hermoso suelo americano.

> [The fugitive liberty of Europe,
> Seeking an asylum,
> Has traversed the ocean,
> Raising its sublime theme
> On the fair American soil,
> Where hearts exalt its name
> And where men breathe with dignity.]

A more interesting example is "En el aniversario del 4 de julio de 1776" (1825) by José María Heredia, which associates liberty with both North and South America. The poet addresses "sacred liberty," which, enlightened by

---

[17] J. A. Leo Lemay, *Men of Letters in Colonial Maryland* (Knoxville, Tenn., 1972), p. 132.

Athens and Rome, has left the tyranny of Europe and braved the horrors of the ocean waves to find a refuge in America.

After the American Revolution the theme of the westward movement of the arts merged into a more strident nationalistic affirmation of the superiority of the western world in physical nature and in human virtue. Patriotic fervor expressed itself through pride in geographic location, military exploits, and national identity however, rather than common awareness of an intellectual heritage.[18] In Latin America as well the wars of independence inspired scores of patriotic odes and verse discourses comparing the New and the Old Worlds to the disadvantage of the latter, but the cultural heritage of Spain and Portugal was nearly always recognized, even though sometimes rejected.

So far we have seen several parallel themes that have united the Enlightenment in North and South America, but very little in the way of direct influence of one area upon the other. Before the beginning of the nineteenth century, practically none existed. The first and major impact of the United States upon the land to the south was political. The writings of Paine, Jefferson, Hamilton, and Monroe were quoted, reprinted, and discussed during the struggle for independence from Spain and the succeeding period of quest for sound government. Washington, moreover, became a symbol in Latin American poetry of military hero, patriot, and father of his country much as he was in the literature of the United States and many European countries. Heredia, for example, in 1824 addressed a poem "A Washington escrita en Monte Vernón," and wrote an essay in prose entitled "Washington," in which he both expressed reverence for the "sublime character"

---

[18] An excellent study of this phenomenon is Merle Curti, *The Roots of American Loyalty* (New York, 1946).

of the North American hero and affirmed, contrary to many contemporary and later historians that "the war of 1776 was strictly a war of principles."[19] Heredia also translated the first act of Voltaire's drama against the use of religion as a political weapon, *Mahomet*. Heredia's translation, under the title "El fanatismo," is in verse and closely follows the original text.[20] The Cuban author also conceived the project of an *Ensayo filosófico sobre la historia universal*, on the scale of Voltaire, from earliest times to the present, but the idea was never executed.[21]

At this period the North American public was still for the most part totally unaware of the intellectual life in Hispanic America. Jared Sparks, influential New England scholar and editor, wrote in September 1825, "The difference of language, and the infrequence of communication, have sent out as many errors as truths. Hardly an editor in this country knows the Spanish language, and there is not to this day taken in Boston a single regular file of a newspaper from the whole South American continent, or Mexico."[22]

[19] *Poesías líricas*, ed. Zerolo, p. lxix.

[20] It was completed in 1821. Pedro J. Guiteras, "José María Heredia," *La Revista de Cuba* 9 (1881): 25.

[21] Ibid., p. 24.

[22] E. F. Helman, "Early Interest in Spanish in New England (1815-1835)," *Hispania* 29 (1946): 344-45. One of the few echoes of peninsular Spanish letters in an English colony consists of an essay by Dr. Alexander Hamilton in the *Maryland Gazette*, 29 June 1748, signed Quevedo and loosely following the structure of the *Sueños* of the luminary of the Golden Age as paraphrased in English by Sir Roger L'Estrange. Lemay, *Men of Letters*, p. 233. A reference to Portugal occurs in a remarkable short story by Charles Brockden Brown in which he treats a mythical biography of the absolutist ruler Pombal, who is usually considered an exponent of enlightened despotism. Brown's work is remarkable, however, not because of its reference to Pombal or even an ingenious parallelism between Pombal and Cicero, but because of the literary genre to which it belongs. Entitled "Walstein's School of History," it purports to be an essay on a German historian, but the historian and his books

Two reasons may be advanced to account for North American ignorance or indifference. One is the generally recognized principle that intellectual relationships usually follow political and economic ones, and the language of the dominant race or nation invariably takes precedence over the less developed one. Another is the Anglo-

---

are purely imaginary. To be sure, there is nothing unusual about inventing nonexistent professors and writers. Swift and Voltaire did it brilliantly before Brown. What is remarkable about Brown is that his invented works are not instruments of satire, but fictional materials devoted to a serious portrayal of life and art. His work, which I have called a short story, has amazing resemblances to the style and method of Jorge Luis Borges, and it deserves to be treated as a valuable precursor of the fiction of the Argentinian master, particularly "El acercamiento a Almotásim" ["The Approach to Al-mu'tasim"]. "Walstein's School of History" appeared originally in the *Monthly Magazine and American Review* (August-September 1799), and has been reprinted in *The Rhapsodist and Other Collected Writings by Charles Brockden Brown*, ed. Harry R. Warfel (New York, 1943), pp. 145-56.

Borges himself deserves special mention as perhaps the only major creative writer outside of the United States possessing an extensive knowledge of early North American literature. In his autobiography he ranked Jonathan Edwards as author of one of the world's masterpieces, a view rarely expressed elsewhere. Borges wrote, moreover, an *Introducción a la literatura norteamericana* (Buenos Aires, 1967), a book of less than 100 pages which contains, nevertheless, some interesting insights and novel perspectives. It has been translated under the somewhat inaccurate title *An Introduction to American Literature* [ed. L. Clark Keating and Robert O. Evans (Lexington, Ky., 1971)]. In his first chapter entitled "Origins," Borges treats John Winthrop, William Bradford, Cotton Mather, Jonathan Edwards, and a single poet, Philip Freneau. He recognizes "The Indian Burying Ground" as the best-known of Freneau's poems and "The hunter and the deer, a shade" as its most famous line, reminding him of a hexameter in the eleventh book of the *Odyssey*. Borges shows particular interest in the narrative poem "The Indian Student," about a gifted native who abandons Harvard College for his natural haunts, which Borges calls "at once a poem and a short story." He treats Franklin in his second chapter along with Cooper, Irving, Prescott, and Parkman. Like Balzac, he draws attention to Franklin's enjoyment of mystifications (a major characteristic of Borges as well) and compares him in this regard to Poe.

Saxon distrust of the Spanish character prevailing in the eighteenth and early nineteenth century, which was based on Protestant suspicion of the Catholic religion, particularly the notorious Spanish Inquisition, together with horror of the alleged mistreatment of the Indians during the period of the Conquest, the equally notorious Black Legend.

The well-known author of *Letters from an American Farmer* (1782), the French-American St. Jean de Crèvecoeur, also wrote a "Sketch of the Contrast between the Spanish and the English Colonies," which even today is almost unknown.[23] In the spirit of Voltaire and the *philosophes*, Crèvecoeur tore into the religious ostentation and "multiplicity of priests" in Lima. The Spanish in America, he charged, had kept their country so closely shut against foreigners that it was virtually impossible to know anything about it. Crèvecoeur, nevertheless, contrasted the ostentation, superficial observances, and ceremonies of religion in South America with the simplicity, sincerity, and social benevolence of that in North America; the oppressive government of the one with the toleration of the other.

The conclusion of Crèvecoeur's essay even more starkly reveals the depth of his distrust of the Spanish colonies and his admiration of the United States.

An incomprehensible Gov't [in South America] permits but few branches of Industry to flourish—How can the Earth be tilled? How can manufactories araise [*sic*]? how can trade improve? how can population increase? how can a people become opulent & strong where so many

[23] Ed. H. L. Bourdin and S. T. Williams, *University of California Chronicle* 28 (1926): 152-63. The editors indicate that a free translation appears in Crèvecoeur's *Lettres d'un cultivateur américain*, 2 vols. (Paris, 1784), but I have found that the only resemblances are remote and superficial. See, for example, 2: 361.

canker worms gnaw the great vital Root of the National tree, suck & exhaust the Sap which was Intended to Vivify its numerous Branches. . . .

. . . .

Happy provinces *these* [in North America] on the contrary now become the azilum [*sic*] of all the unfortunate from the old world, which can boast of the happiest Gov't, the Mildest Laws, the Simplest Relligion. How happy for Mankind that the Era of their different Foundations was that of Knowledge & science by which they were taught to divert themselves of those antient civil errors to which many had fell victims. Happy Regeneration for Mankind! Human Nature everywhere Insulted & oppressed, here can breathe the Purest air & boast of that which I believe no society ever cou'd before, of the full enjoyment of every Natural & necessary Right, consistent with a State of Society. I sincerely wish that the Spanish Colonies may one day become partakers of some of those great blessings by being placed so contiguous to these Provinces, that from the large & copious Source of Freedom which they contain some happy Sparks of it may be disseminated to all the world.

Crèvecoeur's very unflattering view of South America can be contrasted not only with the favorable view of North America in his sketch, but also with his even more rhapsodic picture of the Northern Hemisphere in his widely read "What Is an American?"[24]

A similar denigratory portrayal of eighteenth-century

[24] *Letters from an American Farmer* (London, 1782). In the first quarter of the nineteenth century, a debate took place in Chile concerning the character of a North American—one author accused the citizens of the United States of materialism and greed; another attributed to them virtually all the same qualities claimed by Crèvecoeur. A. O. Aldridge, "The Character of a North American as Drawn in Chile, 1818," in *Hispania* 49 (1966), 489-94.

Latin America appeared in *Bibliotheca Americana; or, a Chronological Catalogue of the most Curious and Interesting Papers, &c. upon the Subject of North and South America*, which was published in London in 1789.[25] Its "Introductory Discourse on the Present State of Literature in those Countries" charges that South America is in a state of bondage and consequently produces "nothing conducive to the good or happiness of mankind." Personified as the elder sister, South America is portrayed as "decorated with gold; but that gold, fabricated into chains, and as is too commonly the fate of wealth, serving only to exclude, what is conducive to happiness, and to confine what is essential to misery." The twin forces which oppose all "scientific," that is, intellectual progress, are the Inquisition and censorship of the press. Despite this disparaging portrayal of South American letters, *Bibliotheca Americana* includes a seven-page catalog of European and Creole authors who have written on Christianity and moral subjects in the indigenous languages of New Spain, transcribed completely from "that curious, entertaining, and valuable Work, entitled The History of Mexico," by Francisco Javier Clavigero, which had already acquired an international reputation.

Although the literature of North America is said to be in much better condition than that of the Latin countries, the author of the "Discourse" is unable to provide a much more impressive catalog. In his words: "At the head of their philosophers and politicians, stands the venerable Franklin. In the first class, the ingenious Lorimer must not be forgotten.—In mathematics, the self-taught Rittenhouse.—In divinity, Weatherspoone.—In history, criticisms, and policy, the modern Tacitus (Payne).—In poetry, Barlow, Smith, and Ray.—In painting, West" [pp.

---

[25] Several names have been proposed as the compiler of the work, including Lehman Thomas Rede.

10-11]. We are presented here with two major authors, Franklin and Paine, and two minor ones, Barlow and Witherspoon, but the only poets named, Smith and Ray, are so obscure that it is doubtful that anyone in London had ever read their works.[26] And the philosopher Lorimer seems to be as legendary as the continent of Atlantis. The remainder of the discourse is primarily concerned with the printing, distribution, and sale of books in North America. We are told that the "demand for foreign literature is inconsiderable, . . . very little for French books, and still less for Italian, Spanish and Portuguese." German works sell relatively well in districts inhabited by the Germans, but these are principally school and devotional texts. "When a Dutchman is not at prayers, he is either at work or asleep." Finally, the French have tried to introduce their language and literature, but "without success."

The first Latin American work to influence a major North American author was a lyric "En una tempestad" ["In a Tempest"] by Heredia published in New York in 1825. During this period of Cuban history, many advocates of independence or at least reform of the Spanish administration were living, like Heredia, in voluntary or forced exile in the United States. "En una tempestad" is a typically neoclassic statement of the relationship of a particular aspect of nature to the cosmic order, a theme that belongs to the Enlightenment as well as to neoclassicism. The poem served as the basis of a free rendering in English by William Cullen Bryant under the title "The Hurricane" written in 1827 and published five years later.[27] Bryant also published in 1832 an original poem on the same theme, "After a Tempest." Thirty-five years before

[26] Presumably these are Charlotte Smith, *Elegiac Sonnets* 1787; and William Ray, *Poem on Visiting the Academy of Philadelphia*, 1753; *Ode on the New Year*, 1753.

[27] *Poems by William Cullen Bryant, An American*, ed. Washington Irving (London, 1832).

Heredia's poem, moreover, Philip Freneau had published another verse description of a storm with the identical title, "The Hurricane." With no reference to the Creator, or to the ordered universe, but with a statement of personal fear and loneliness, Freneau's eighteenth-century poem paradoxically has more of the Romantic spirit than either Heredia's or Bryant's in the nineteenth century.

Bryant also had a hand in an English translation of the poem regarded by some critics as Heredia's best, an ode, "Niágara," which records his feelings on visiting the famous waterfall. The translation by Thatcher Taylor Payne was revised and corrected by Bryant and published in January 1827 in the *United States Review and Literary Gazette*, of which Bryant was one of the editors.[28] Probably the earliest verses on Niagara Falls in any language were those contained in a descriptive poem "Night," published in 1728 by a Pennsylvanian James Ralph, a friend of Benjamin Franklin, whose name was appropriated by Voltaire as the purported author of *Candide*.[29]

Bryant was not only a major poet, but also a literary critic of extraordinary range and acuteness. In addition to his extensive criticism of European and North American literature, he also published the first essay to be written in any language on a Latin American historical novel, *Jicoténcal*. This work on the conquest of Mexico by Cortez has the distinction of being the first historical novel ever written in the Spanish language. It was published

[28] Héctor H. Orjuela, "Revaloración de una vieja polémica literaria: William Cullen Bryant y la oda 'Niágara' de José María Heredia," *Thesaurus. Boletín del Instituto Caro y Cuervo* 19 (1964): 248-73.

[29] James Ralph, *Night: A Poem. In Four Books* (London, 1728). Pope parodied the poem in his *Dunciad* probably because Ralph in his preface quoted a passage from Pope's *Homer* but suggested that it contained various infelicities which could have been avoided had he used blank verse instead of rhyme. Charles M. Dow's *Anthology and Bibliography of Niagara Falls* (Albany, 1921) lacks these details and includes practically no eighteenth-century poetry.

anonymously in Philadelphia in 1826, and to this day its author can still not be definitely ascribed, although there are good reasons for believing that it was Félix Varela (a Cuban, not the Argentinian Varela, author of the poem on printing).[30] Bryant published his analysis of the novel in February 1827 in the *United States Review and Literary Gazette* [1, 336-46]. Although not enthusiastic about *Jicoténcal* as a work of fiction, Bryant praised its "just and enlightened notions on political government and other important subjects." He also contrasted the progressive spirit of Latin America with the backwardness of Spain. "It might almost seem," he wrote, "as if a nobler race of men had grown up in those countries."

> In the midst of their political storms, they have taken care to found institutions for the purpose of forming the minds of those, who are soon, under better auspices, to take the place of the men who threw off the Spanish yoke. In the mean time, more enlightened notions of government are diffusing and perfecting themselves, and a tolerant spirit is fast displacing the old bigotry.

It is a coincidence worthy of notice that the first novel written in English with a Mexican setting was *Francis Berrian, or, The Mexican Patriot* by Timothy Flint, published in the same year as *Jicoténcal*. Another novel concerning Mexico, *Calavar, or, the Knight of the Conquest* (1834) by Robert Montgomery Bird, was translated into German and published in St. Louis in 1848. It was followed in the next year (1835) by another romance concerning the Conquest, *The Infidel; or The Fall of Mexico*.

The illustrations of Enlightenment themes and tendencies presented so far show for the most part that English America was at least a half century in advance of Spanish America. This is not the result of arbitrary selection of

---

[30] Luis Leal, "*Jicoténcal*, Primera novela histórica en castellano" *Revista Iberoamericana* 25 (1960): 9-31.

texts. It would be impossible to find illustrations proving the reverse situation. Priority in developing Enlightenment themes in North America, however, does not necessarily mean artistic superiority. As a matter of fact, the quality of Spanish-American literature in the first forty years of the nineteenth century was much better than that in English America before the Revolution.

During the eighteenth century, moreover, no work of formal history written in the English part of North America attained the European reputation of the work of the Mexican historian, Francisco Javier Clavigero, *Historia antigua de México*, to which we have already alluded. Since the author was a Jesuit and like many of his order lived in Italy after the disbanding of the Jesuits, the first edition of 1780 was published in Italian. The first Spanish edition was a posthumous translation in 1826.[31] Two editions in English appeared in North America before the Spanish edition, one in Philadelphia in 1806, the other in Richmond in 1817.[32] Clavigero made several animadversions on William Robertson's *History of America* to which Robertson responded in later editions.[33] More important, Clavigero was the first author in either North or South America to undertake a formal refutation of the notorious thesis of Buffon and de Pauw which held that biological species degenerated when transplanted to the western world.[34]

Another historical work from Latin America promptly

[31] 4 vols. Colección de Escritores Mexicanos (Mexico, 1945), 1: 13.

[32] Bernstein, *Making of an Inter-American Mind*, p. 34; neither of these editions is mentioned in the Mexico, 1945, edition.

[33] (London, 1817), 8: 382, 9: 320.

[34] Antonello Gerbi, *The Dispute of the New World: The History of a Polemic 1750-1900*, trans. Jeremy Moyle (Pittsburgh, 1973), pp. 196-211. Clavigero also enjoyed extensive relations and exchange of compliments with Gian Rinaldo Carli, author of *Delle lettere americane* (1780), [Gerbi, p. 239]. Jefferson's *Notes on Virginia* is in part a rebuttal of Buffon. In Argentina, Felix de Azara published a parallel *Memorial concerning the rural conditions of the Rio de la Plata in 1801*.

taken up in the United States was a treatise on Chile published originally in Italian by Juan Ignacio Molina, which was translated from French and Spanish versions in 1808 by Richard Alsop as *The Geographical, Natural and Civil History of Chile*. The appendix, bearing a separate title page, consisted of a "Sketch of the Araucana with Copious Translations from that Poem." The sketch was taken from William Hayley's notes to an essay on the epic and the translations, all of the third and fourth cantos, were taken from another English author, the Reverend H. Boyd, who had also translated Dante. The prose summary to a harangue delivered by an ancient warrior is prefaced by the remark that it was preferred by Voltaire to the speech of Nestor on a similar occasion in the *Iliad*.

One would assume that *La Araucana*, published originally in the sixteenth century (1569 and 1578), well before the birth of Anne Bradstreet, would, because of its subject matter, have been of interest to colonial British America, especially to authors dealing with the subjugation of the Indians there. No evidence of any awareness whatsoever of this work in the British area of North America, however, can be found until the Revolution, when as we have seen Joel Barlow adopted some of its themes and structural features for his epic in English, *The Vision of Columbus*. In 1805, when Barlow returned to the United States from a long sojourn in Europe, Voltaire's chapter on Ercilla was extracted from his essay on epic poetry and published in the *Port Folio*.[35] A contributor who had never seen a copy of *La Araucana* and who believed that it was difficult for the "jaundiced eye of the philosopher of Ferney, to discover any beauties, in another author," nevertheless translated Voltaire's remarks because the poem was "little known" and because he believed Ercilla to be "the only epic poet, that Spain can boast." Thanks to Voltaire and the *Port Folio*, therefore, the attention of

[35] 12 January 1805.

many North Americans was drawn to the existence of a major epic concerning the foundations of the civilization of South America which antedated by two centuries the efforts of Dwight and Barlow in the genre.[36]

The objection might perhaps be raised that apart from the connection with Voltaire, the topic of epic poetry has little or nothing to do with the Enlightenment. To the contrary, the portrayal of South American Indians in Barlow's *Vision of Columbus* is intimately involved with concepts of rational government and rational religion. Between the second and third books of his epic, Barlow inserted a prose "Dissertation on the Genius and Institutions of Manco Capac," the legendary leader and lawgiver of the pre-Columbian Indians in Peru. In his portrayal, Barlow treats Manco Capac as superior to parallel figures in Jewish, Mahometan, and, by suggestion, Christian societies. His system of government, according to Barlow, was "the most simple and energetic conceivable, and capable of reducing the greatest number of men under one jurisdiction." In treating the religion of Manco Capac as pure deism, Barlow completely ignores the Christian tradition.

Perhaps no single criterion can be given, which will determine more accurately the state of society in any age or nation, than their general ideas concerning the nature and attributes of the Deity. In the most enlightened periods of antiquity, only a very few of their wisest

---

[36] Another resident of Connecticut, Richard Alsop, to whom the translation of Molina's history has been attributed, tried his hand in the epic style with an international theme in *The Conquest of Scandinavia*. Only an excerpt from this work has ever been published, the introduction to the fourth book, in Elihu Hubbard Smith, ed., *American Poems* (Litchfield, Conn., 1793). Alsop, the first literary millionaire in America, also translated from the Greek, Latin, Italian, and Spanish. Another of his historically significant translations is one of the earliest in America from Dante. Joseph G. Fucilla, "An Early American Translation of the Count Ugolino Episode," *Modern Language Quarterly* 11 (1950): 480-85.

Philosophers, a Socrates, a Tully, or a Confucius, ever formed a just idea on the subject, or described the Deity as a God of purity, justice and benevolence. Can anything then be more astonishing than to view a savage native of the southern wilds of America, rising in an age, void of every trace of learning or refinement, and acquiring by the mere efforts of reason, a sublime and rational idea of the Parent of the universe!

We have seen that both North and South Americans made a conscious effort to separate the Old World from the New, to create a New World personality or climate of opinion based on political independence. We may wonder whether there also existed a consciousness of an Enlightenment spirit—an awareness of an intellectual movement transcending political relationships. In France, for example, the writers associated with the *Encyclopédie* were known as the *philosophes* and they considered themselves as part of a common effort to reform their society in nearly every aspect.

In Hispanic America one likewise encounters a specific awareness of the Enlightenment as a philosophical movement vitally affecting the political and social institutions of the times. One example is a poem of Heredia celebrating (1826) the opening of the Institute of Mexico ["En la apertura del Instituto mejicano" (1826)].

> Es la alma libertad madre fecunda
> De las artes y ciencias; ella rompe
> La atroz cadena que al ingenio humano
> Los déspotas cargaron, y á la sombra
> De su manto benéfico y su oliva
> Crece la ilustración.

The application to contemporary life is made even more specific by Varela in his poem of 1822 on the invention of printing.

Por esta noble libertad se llama
el siglo en que vivimos
el siglo de las luces.

[For this noble liberty is called
The century in which we live
The century of enlightenment.]

These references to a period of enlightenement are completely different in character and spirit from the assertions of Paine, Dickinson, and the House of Representatives that the United States as a political entity was the most enlightened in the world. Thomas Paine's title *The Age of Reason* is hardly relevant to our subject since his book has no special reference to America, and it was both written and published in Europe. A tentative approach to recognition of the years immediately following the American Revolution as a period of enlightenment, however, may be found in a circular letter of June 1783 from George Washington to the governors of the thirteen states. According to Washington, "The foundation of our Empire was not laid in the gloomy age of ignorance and superstition, but at an Epoch when the rights of mankind were better understood and more clearly defined, than at any former period; the researches of the human mind after social happiness, have been carried to a great extent, the treasures of knowledge, acquired by the labours of Philosophers, Sages and Legislators, through a long succession of years, are laid open for our use, and their collected wisdom may be happily applied in the establishment of our forms of government."[37]

A similar tentative statement in more traditional literature may be found in Enos Hitchcock's *Memoirs of the Bloomsgrove Family*, a treatise on education in the form of an epistolary novel, based on Rousseau, which was

[37] Adrienne Koch, ed., *The American Enlightenment* (New York, 1965), p. 24.

published in Boston in 1790. According to this enterprising author, "The present may with propriety be styled the age of philosophy; and America, the empire of reason. The agitations which usually follow such convulsions are rapidly subsiding, and she is fast rising into superior consequence. America now promises fair to be the asylum of genius and liberty, the seat of arts and learning, and the universal emporium of wealth and commerce."[38] In kindred vein, Samuel Miller, in his *Brief Retrospect*, sketched the achievement of French and English authors usually associated with the Enlightenment and came to the moderate conclusion "that the century of which we have just taken leave has produced an unusual number of revolutions, and at least some improvements."[39] Although Miller devoted a long chapter to Oriental literatures, including Hebrew, Persian, Hindu, and Chinese, he had absolutely nothing to say about Spanish literature or Spanish culture. His only references to Spanish America were geographical, apart from an admission that printing existed in Mexico not long after the middle of the sixteenth century.[40] In Miller's mind and in his literary achievement, incredible narrowness and provinciality coexisted with a spirit of free inquiry.

There may be some connection between the near-contemporary references to the Enlightenment as a movement in Latin American letters and the frequent usage of the term in twentieth-century scholarship in the same area. We have already indicated that the Spanish equivalent for "Enlightenment" has been used in Latin American intellectual history much earlier than in that of the United States. Since the cultural traditions of Hispanic America go back to the early sixteenth century, literature there has commonly been viewed in parallel terms with

[38] 2: 10-11.
[39] 2 vols. (New York, 1803), 1: 7.
[40] Ibid., 2: 332.

that of the Peninsula, comprising Renaissance, Golden Age, the baroque [since the use of this term], neoclassicism, and the Enlightenment. The early literature of North America, on the other hand, has conventionally been divided into strictly national segments, Colonial, Revolutionary, and Federal, and even in the nineteenth century Romanticism is ordinarily not used as a period designation. Once more the paradox may be noted that scholars have talked extensively about the Enlightenment in Latin America, but that the movement existed to a much greater degree in English America.

Also to be noted is that writers in the former Spanish colonies of South America bitterly denounced Spain for its failure to reflect the ideals and principles of the Enlightenment which were widespread in France and England. From the perspective of the New World, Spain was an intellectually backward nation, and in its colonies it deliberately opposed the dissemination of learning and toleration as part of a conscious policy of oppression. A Colombian critic, Camilo Torres, for example, accused the Spanish government of completely prohibiting the study of natural rights. The barbarous cruelty of Spanish despotism, he charged, made that nation "the enemy of God and men."[41] Even the most determined opponents of British rule in the American colonies such as Thomas Paine, however, respected the intellectual achievements of England and never suggested that the British government sought to keep the colonies in a condition of philosophical ignorance. To the contrary, the colonists separated British culture from British rule, remaining loyal to the first and declaring independence of the second. To be sure, there

---

[41] *Memorial de agravios* (1809; reprinted, Bogota, Colombia, 1960), p. 388. I am unable to develop this concept further in this book, but I have dealt with it at length in a previous article, "Las ideas en la América del sur sobre la ilustración española," *Revista Iberoamericana* 24 (1968): 282-97.

were some priests and royalists in South America who defended the Spanish monarchy against "los afrancesados y los liberales" just as there were a number of ministers and Federalists in the United States who denounced the French Revolution. But the French Revolution was by no means identical with the Enlightenment.

The Enlightenment was primarily a period of philosophies and ideas and one cannot say that it existed in any particular area merely because a group of authors claimed that it did so. In both North and South America, the major manifestations of the Enlightenment were in the political realm, but political aspirations and achievements were also reflected in literary works. Direct literary relations between North and South America seem to have been extremely limited during this period, but many resemblances in theme and subject matter may be discovered, resemblances that may reasonably be attributed to the combination of ideas and attitudes known as the Enlightenment.

TEN

CONCLUSION

SINCE the foregoing chapters do not pretend to give a comprehensive or synoptic view of early American literature, but present instead a number of selective illustrations of relations with other literatures, a great deal in the way of broad conclusions can hardly be expected. It is clear, however, that the major literary movements of Europe between the beginning of the sixteenth century and the end of the eighteenth, that is, Renaissance, baroque, neoclassicism, Enlightenment, and Romanticism, had repercussions of one kind or another in Anglo-America. Anne Bradstreet was strongly affected by one particular continental author, and Edward Taylor, without attaching himself to any single British or continental predecessor, developed a close and pervasive affinity to the baroque style. These two representatives of New England Puritanism have been treated in the foregoing pages, not because their resemblances to writers in other cultures stand out in particular, but rather because Bradstreet is indelibly registered in literary history because of her early chronological position and Taylor is highly regarded by many contemporary critics for his poetic achievement. Even Jonathan Edwards, one of the least cosmopolitan of authors, could (and should) be treated from the comparatist perspective. Without venturing in quest of philosophical parallels into the nebulous territory of Spinoza, one could uncover analogies with various European necessitarians, particularly atheists such as Frederick the Great, as well as with introspective metaphysicians such as Pascal.

The most innovative literary work produced in Anglo-America before the nineteenth century is also the most universally famous—Franklin's autobiography, which has been accorded merely cursory mention in this book. Today this work is as well known in some remote parts of the world as it is throughout the United States. In Taiwan and Japan, for example, it is part of the curriculum of many secondary schools. Franklin's "Speech of Polly Baker" gained almost immediate attention in France, but it does not seem to have made any impression whatsoever upon the Hispanic world. To this day, no Spanish translation exists. In the Anglo-Saxon world the speech has been treated as either a factual account or as an amusing hoax, but in France its ideological overtones have been seriously heeded.

Many of the intellectual themes associated with the Enlightenment and eighteenth-century Europe have been vigorously discussed in America. These include the Golden Age, the quarrel of ancients and moderns, biological degeneration in the New World, *translatio studii*, deism, and natural rights. Other major units in the history of ideas not treated at length in this book but equally important in early American literature are the state of nature, primitivism, and determinism. The major contribution of American letters to the rest of the world was in the area of political thought. In the words of the English observer quoted in the eighth chapter, "Franklin, Paine, Barlow, have scattered more truths of importance among us than all Europe could do for themselves."

Although many parallels exist in the historical development of Anglo-American literature in the North and Ibero-American in the South, few direct contacts between the two existed until the very end of the eighteenth century. But both literatures maintained close connections with the mainstreams of Europe, not only with the national tradition from which they developed, English, Spanish, or Portuguese. The literature of the British colonies of North America and of the first decades of the United States with which we have been primarily concerned is not a product of men and women writing in isolation. It is not as individual as it is sometimes portrayed (whether exceptional, exclusive, original, on one hand, or confined, insular, provincial, on the other), and for good or for bad it has more in common than appears on the surface with the writing of other nations. It is, in other words, a small, but respectable, part of universal literature.

BIBLIOGRAPHY

BIBLIOGRAPHIES, COLLECTED WORKS, AND EDITIONS

Amacher, Richard E. *Franklin's Wit and Folly. The Bagatelles.* New Brunswick, N.J., 1953.

Balzac, Honoré de. *Oeuvres complètes.* Edited by Jean-A. Ducourneau. 26 vols. Paris, 1965-1976.

Bibliotheca Americana: or a Chronological Catalogue of the Most Curious and Interesting Papers, &c. upon the Subject of North and South America. [Edited by Lehman Thomas Rede?]. London, 1789.

Borges, Jorge Luis. *An Introduction to American Literature.* Edited by L. Clark Keating and Robert O. Evans. Lexington, Ky. 1971.

Bowe, Forrest, and Mary Daniels, eds. *French Literature in Early American Translation. A Bibliographical Survey of Books and Pamphlets Printed in the United States from 1668 through 1820.* New York, 1977.

Bradstreet, Anne. *Works.* Edited by Jeannine Hensley. Cambridge, Mass., 1967.

Brown, Charles Brockden. *The Rhapsodist and Other Collected Writings.* Edited by Harry R. Warfel. New York, 1943.

Bryant, William Cullen. *Poems.* Edited by Washington Irving. London, 1832.

Butcher, Philip, ed. *The Minority Presence in American Literature.* 2 vols. Washington, D.C., 1977.

Camoëns, Luiz de. *Os Lusiadas.* Edited by Theophilo Braga. Lisbon, 1898.

Clavijero, Francisco Javier. *Historia antigua de México.* 4 vols. Colección de Escritores Mexicanos. Mexico, 1945.

Condorcet, M.J.A.N.C. de. *Oeuvres.* Edited by A. O'Connor and F. Arago. 12 vols. Paris, 1847-1849.

Crashaw, Richard. *Poems.* Edited by L. C. Martin. Oxford, 1927.

BIBLIOGRAPHY

Crèvecoeur, Michel Guillaume St. Jean de. *Letters from an American Farmer*. Edited by Warren B. Blake. London, 1913.
———. "Sketch of a Contrast between the Spanish and the English Colonies." Edited by H. L. Bourdin and S. T. Williams. *University of California Chronicle* 28 (1926): 152-63.
Cruz, Sor Juana Inés de la. *Obras escogidas*. Edited by Juan Carlos Merlo. Barcelona, 1968.
Debates and Proceedings in the Congress of the United States. Printed and Published by Gales and Seaton. 42 vols. Washington, D.C., 1834-1856.
Dickinson, John. *Letters from a Farmer in Pennsylvania*. Edited by R.T.H. Halsey. New York, 1903.
Dickinson, Jonathan. *Journal*. Edited by E. W. Andrews and C. M. Andrews. New Haven, 1945.
Diderot, Denis. *Oeuvres complètes*. Edition Club français du livre. 15 vols. Paris, 1969-1973.
Dow, Charles M. *Anthology and Bibliography of Niagara Falls*. Albany, 1921.
Du Bartas, Guillaume de Salluste. *Bartas His Devine Weekes and Workes (1605)*. Translated by Joshua Sylvester. Facsimile ed. Gainesville, Fla., 1965.
———. *Works*. Edited by Urban Tigner Holmes Jr. et al. 3 vols. Chapel Hill, N.C., 1935-1940.
Ercilla y Zúñiga, Alonso de. *La Araucana*. Edited by José Toribio Medina. 5 vols. Santiago de Chile, 1910-1918.
Franklin, Benjamin. *Papers*. Edited by Leonard W. Labaree et al. New Haven, 1959-
Freneau, Philip. *Poems*. Edited by Harry Hayden Clark. New York, 1929.
———. *Prose*. Edited by Philip M. Marsh. New Brunswick, N.J., 1955.
Goethe, Johann Wolfgang. *Autobiography*. Translated by John Oxenford. 2 vols. Chicago, 1974.
Grimm, Melchior. *Correspondance littéraire*. Edited by Maurice Tourneux. 16 vols. Paris, 1877-1882.
Henríquez, Camilo. *Escritos políticos*. Edited by Raúl Silva Castro. Santiago de Chile, 1960.
Heredia, José María. *Poesías líricas*. Edited by Elías Zerolo. Paris, n.d.

Madison, James et al. *The Federalist.* Edited by Max Beloff. New York, 1948.

Mier, Servando Teresa de. *Escritos inéditos.* Edited by J. M. Miquel i Vergas and Hugo Díaz-Thomé. Mexico, 1944.

Miranda, Francisco de. *Archivo.* 24 vols. Caracas, 1929-1950.

Monaghan, Frank. *French Travellers in the United States, 1765-1932: A Bibliography.* New York, 1933.

Olmedo, José Joaquín de. *Poesías completas.* Edited by A. E. Pólet. Quito, 1945.

Paine, Robert Treat. *Works in Verse and Prose.* Boston, 1812.

Paine, Thomas. *Complete Writings.* Edited by Philip S. Foner. 2 vols. New York, 1945.

Rush, Benjamin. *Letters.* Edited by L. H. Butterfield. 2 vols. Princeton, 1951.

————. "Papers." *Pennsylvania Magazine of History and Biography* 29 (1905):15-30.

Smith, Elihu Hubbard, ed., *American Poems.* Litchfield, Conn., 1793.

Smith, Sydney. *Works.* Boston, 1874.

Taylor, Edward. *Poems.* Edited by Donald E. Stanford. New Haven, 1960.

Trumbull, John. *Poetical Works.* Hartford, 1820.

Varela, Juan de la Cruz. *Poesías.* Edited by Vicente D. Sierra. Buenos Aires. 1916.

Voltaire, François-Marie Arouet de. *Complete Works.* Edited by Theodore Besterman et al. Geneva, Banbury, and Toronto. 1968-

————. *Oeuvres complètes.* Edited by Louis Moland. 52 vols. Paris, 1877-1885.

Yanes, Francisco Javier. *Manual político del venezolano.* Edited by Ramón Escovar Salóm. Caracas, 1959.

BACKGROUND, GENERAL WORKS, AND SPECIFIC STUDIES

Aldridge, A. Owen. *Benjamin Franklin et ses contemporaines français.* Paris, 1963. [An expanded version of *Franklin and His French Contemporaries.*]

————. *Benjamin Franklin Philosopher and Man.* New York, 1965.

Aldridge, A. Owen. "The Character of a North American as Drawn in Chile, 1818." *Hispania* 49 (1966):489-94.

———. "An Early Cuban Exponent of Inter-American Cultural Relations: Domingo del Monte." *Hispania* 54 (1971):348-53.

———. *Franklin and His French Contemporaries*. New York, 1957.

———. "Las ideas en la América del sur sobre la ilustración española." *Revista Iberoamericana* 24 (1968):282-97.

———. "The Influence of Thomas Paine in the United States, England, France, Germany and South America." In *Proceedings of the Second Congress of the International Comparative Literature Association*, edited by W. P. Friederich, 2:369-83. Chapel Hill, N.C., 1959.

———. "Jacques Barbeu-Dubourg, a French Disciple of Benjamin Franklin." *Proceedings of the American Philosophical Society* 95 (1951):331-92.

———. *Man of Reason, The Life of Thomas Paine*. New York, 1959.

———. "The Poetry of Thomas Paine." *Pennsylvania Magazine of History and Biography* 79 (1955):81-99.

———. "A Religious Hoax by Benjamin Franklin." *American Literature* 36 (1964):204-9.

———. "Thomas Paine and the Classics." *Eighteenth Century Studies* 1 (1968):370-80.

———. "Thomas Paine and the idéologues." *Studies in Voltaire and the Eighteenth Century* 152 (1976):109-17.

———, ed. *The Ibero-American Enlightenment*. Urbana, Ill., 1971.

Arner, Robert D. "The Connecticut Wits." In *American Literature, 1764-1789*, edited by Everett Emerson. Madison, Wis., 1977.

———. "The Structure of Anne Bradstreet's *Tenth Muse*." In *Discoveries & Considerations*, edited by Calvin Israel. Albany, 1976.

Arnold, Hans. "Die Aufnahme von Thomas Paines Schriften in Deutschland." *Publications of the Modern Language Association* 74 (1959):365-86.

Arrunategui, Manuel José de [Anselmo Nateiu]. *Reflecciones políticas, escritas baxo el titulo de "Instinto común."* London, 1811.

Azara, Félix de. *Memorias sobre el estado rural del Rio de Plata en 1801*. Madrid, 1847.

Baker, Ray Palmer. *A History of English-Canadian Literature to the Confederation: Its Relation to the Literature of Great Britain and the United States*. Cambridge, Mass., 1920.

Barbagelata, Hugo D. *Artigas y la revolución americana*. Paris, 1930.

Barlow, Joel. *The Columbiad*. Baltimore, 1807.

———. *Vision of Columbus*. Hartford, 1787.

Barr, Mary Margaret. *Voltaire in America, 1744-1800*. Baltimore, 1941.

Baudissin, Adelbert Heinrich [Peter Tütt]. *Zustande in Amerika*. Altona, 1862.

Beck, Thor J. *Northern Antiquities in French Learning and Literature (1755-1855)*. 2 vols. New York, 1934-1935.

Bernstein, Harry. *Making of an Inter-American Mind*. Gainesville, Fla., 1961.

———. "Las primeras relaciones intelectuales entre New England y el mundo hispánico (1700-1815)." *Revista Hispánica Moderna* 5 (1938):1-17.

Bigelow, Gordon E. *Rhetoric and American Poetry of the Early National Period*. University of Florida Monographs, Humanities, No. 4. Gainesville, Fla., 1960.

Boccaccio, Giovanni. *The Decameron . . . Translated into English Anno 1620 with an Introduction by Edward Hutton*. London, 1909.

Boerner, Peter. "The Images of America in Eighteenth-Century Europe." *Studies in Voltaire and the Eighteenth Century* 99 (1976):323-32.

Boorstin, Daniel J. "The Myth of an American Enlightenment." In *America and the Image of Europe*. New York, 1960.

Brackenridge, Henry Marie. *Voyage to South America*. 2 vols. London, 1820.

Brissot de Warville, Jacques Pierre. *Nouveau voyage dans les États-Unis*. 3 vols. Paris, 1791.

Brome, Richard. *L'Amérique angloise*. Amsterdam, 1688.

Brown, Ruth Wentworth. "Classical Echoes in the Poetry of Philip Freneau." *Classical Journal* 45 (1949):29-34.

Brown, Solyman. *Essay on American Poetry*. New Haven, 1818.

BIBLIOGRAPHY

Brumm, Ursula. *American Thought and Religious Typology.* New Brunswick, N.J., 1970.

Burrus, E. J. "The First Literary Production of the New World." *Classical Journal* 43 (1947):31-33. [Three Latin dialogues published in Mexico City, 1554.]

Cazden, Robert E. "The Provision of German Books in America during the Eighteenth Century." *Libri* 23 (1973):81-108.

Channing, William Ellery. "On National Literature." *Christian Examiner* 36 (1830):269-95.

Charpentier, François. *De l'excellence de la langue françoise.* Paris, 1683.

Cheetham, James. *Life of Thomas Paine.* New York, 1809.

Chinard, Gilbert. *L'Amérique et le rêve exotique dans la littérature française au XVIIᵉ et au XVIIIᵉ siècle.* Paris, 1933.

————. *Volney et l'Amérique d'après des documents inédits et sa correspondance.* Baltimore, 1923.

Compendio de la historia de los Estados Unidos. Philadelphia, 1825.

Condorcet, M.J.A.N.C. de, marquis de, ed. *Bibliothèque de l'homme publique* 9 (1791).

Curti, Merle. *The Roots of American Loyalty.* New York, 1946.

Dabezies, André. "The First American Faust (1720)." *Comparative Literature Studies* 8 (1971):303-9.

Davies, Thomas M. and Arthur Forslater. "Edward Taylor's 'A Fig for Thee Oh! Death.' " In *Discoveries & Considerations,* edited by Calvin Israel. Albany, 1976.

Davis, John. *Travels of Four Years and a Half in the United States of America.* London, 1803.

Del Monte, Domingo. "Bosquejo intelectual de las Estados Unidos." In *Escritos,* edited by José A. Fernández de Castro. Havana, 1929.

De Onis, José. *The United States as Seen by Spanish American Writers, 1776-1890.* New York, 1952.

Desmarets de Saint-Sorlin. *Discours pour prouver que les sujets chrétiens sont seuls propres à la poésie heroïque.* Paris, 1673.

Dutens, Jean. *An Inquiry into the Origin of the Discoveries attributed to the Moderns.* London, 1769.

Dutton, Warren. *The Present State of Literature.* New Haven, 1800.

Dwight, Timothy. *A Discourse on Some Events of the Last Century.* New Haven, 1801.

———. *Dissertation on the History, Eloquence, and Poetry of the Bible.* New Haven, 1772.

———. *The Triumph of Infidelity.* Hartford, 1788.

Echeverría, Durand. *Mirage in the West. A History of the French Image of American Society to 1815.* Princeton, 1957.

Emerson, Everett. "The Cultural Context of the American Revolution." In *American Literature, 1764-1789,* edited by Everett Emerson. Madison, Wis., 1977.

Englekirk, J. E. "Franklin en el mundo hispano." *Revista Iberoamericana* 21 (1956):319-71.

Fess, Gilbert M. *The American Revolution in Creative French Literature (1775-1937).* Columbia, Mo., 1941.

Fiering, Norman. "The First American Enlightenment: Tillotson, Leverett, and Philosophical Anglicanism." *New England Quarterly* 54 (1981):307-44.

———. "The Transatlantic Republic of Letters: A Note on the Circulation of Learned Periodicals to Early Eighteenth-Century America." *William and Mary Quarterly,* 3rd ser., 33 (1976):642-60.

Flanagan, John T. "An Early Novel of the American Revolution." [*Mis Mac Rae* by Hilliard d'Auberteuil]. *New York History* 32 (1951):316-22.

Fridlender, G. M. " 'Voskresenie' L'va Tolstogo i 'Reč' Polli Beker' B. Franklina," in E. A. Smirnova, ed., *Sravnitel'noe izučenie literatur [The Comparative Study of Literatures]* Leningrad, 1976.

Fucilla, Joseph G. "An Early American Translation of the Count Ugolino Episode." *Modern Language Quarterly* 11 (1950): 480-85.

Galinsky, Hans. "Anne Bradstreet, Du Bartas and Shakespeare in Zusammenhang kolonialer Verpflanzung und Umformung europäischer Literatur." In *Festschrift für Walther Fischer,* 1:43-51. Heidelberg, 1959.

———. " 'Colonial Baroque': A Concept Illustrating Dependence, Germinal Independence and New World Interdependence of Early American Literatures." In *Proceedings of the 7th Congress of the International Comparative Literature*

Association, edited by Milan V. Dimíc and Eva Kushner, 1: 43-51. Stuttgart, 1979.

——. "Exploring the 'Exploration Report' and Its Image of the Overseas World: Spanish, French, and English Variants of a Common Form Type in Early American Literature." *Early American Literature* 12 (1978):5-24.

——. "Frühkoloniales Amerika in dreifacher europäischen Sicht: Pedro de Castañeda, Samuel de Champlain, Thomas Hariot." In *Beiträge zur vergleichenden Literaturgeschichte: Festschrift für Kurt Wais*, edited by Johannes Häsle and Wolfgang Eitel. Tubingen, 1972.

——. "Kolonialer Literaturbarock in Virginia: eine Interpretation von *Bacons Epitaph* auf der Grundlage eines Forschungsberichtes." In *Amerika und Europa. Sprachliche und Sprachkünstlerische Wechselbeziehungen in amerikanistischer Sicht*. Berlin, 1968.

Gandía, Enrique de. *Historia de las ideas políticas en la Argentina*. 6 vols. Buenos Aires, 1960.

Gerbi, Antonello. *The Dispute of the New World: The History of a Polemic 1750-1900*. Translated by Jeremy Moyle. Pittsburgh, 1973.

Góngora, Luis de. *Obras en verso del Homero español, 1627*. Facsimile edition. Madrid, 1963.

Grant, Loomis C. "An Unnoted German Reference to Increase Mather." *New England Quarterly* 14 (1941):374-75 [in W. E. Tentzel's *Unterredungen*, September 1694, on converting Indians. See L. Országh below].

Grases, Pedro. *La conspiración de Gual y España y el ideario de la independencia*. Caracas, 1949.

——, and Albert Harkness. *Manuel García de Sena y la independencia de Hispanoamérica*. Caracas, 1953.

Grégoire, Henri. *De la littérature des Nègres*. Paris, 1808.

——. *Critical Observations on the Poem of Mr. Joel Barlow*. Washington, D.C., 1809.

Grueningen, John Paul von, ed. *The Swiss in the United States*. Madison, Wis., 1940.

Guiteras, Pedro J. "José María Heredia." *La Revista de Cuba* 9 (1881):20-30.

Gummere, Richard M. "The Heritage of the Classics in Colonial North America: An Essay on the Greco-Roman Tradition." *Proceedings of the American Philosophical Society* 99 (1955): 68-78.

———. *Seven Wise Men of Colonial America.* Cambridge, Mass., 1967.

Hall, Max. *Benjamin Franklin and Polly Baker.* Chapel Hill, N.C., 1960.

Haus, Rudolph. "Some American Contributions to World Literature." *Yearbook of Comparative and General Literature* 26 (1977):17-23.

Hedges, William L. "Toward a Theory of American Literature, 1765-1800." *Early American Literature* 4 (1969):5-14.

Helman, Edith F. "Early Interest in Spanish in New England (1815-1835)." *Hispania* 29 (1946):339-351.

Hennings, August. *Olavides.* Copenhagen, 1799.

———. *Philosophische Versuche.* 2 vols. Copenhagen, 1779.

Hilliard d'Auberteuil, Michel René. *Mis MacRae Roman historique.* Philadelphia [Paris?], 1784.

Hitchcock, Enos. *Memoirs of the Bloomsgrove Family.* 2 vols. Boston, 1790.

Humphreys, David. *Miscellaneous Works.* New York, 1804.

Ilie, Paul. "Franklin and Villarroel: Social Consciousness in Two Autobiographies." *Eighteenth-Century Studies* 7 (1974):321-42.

Isari, Mukhtar Ali. "Edward Taylor and Ovid's *Art of Love*: The Text of a Newly-Discovered Manuscript." *Early American Literature* 10 (1975):67-74.

Jacobson, David L. *John Dickinson and the Revolution in Pennsylvania 1764-1776.* University of California Publications in History. Berkeley and Los Angeles, 1965.

Jaffe, Adrian H. "French Literature in American Periodicals of the Eighteenth Century." *Revue de littérature comparée* 38 (1964):51-60.

Jantz, Harold. "American Baroque." In *Discoveries & Considerations,* edited by Calvin Israel. Albany, 1976.

Johnson, James William. "The Meaning of 'Augustan.'" *Journal of the History of Ideas* 19 (1958):507-22.

Jones, Howard Mumford. *America and French Culture, 1750-1848*. Chapel Hill, N.C., 1927.

————. *Revolution & Romanticism*, Cambridge, Mass., 1974.

Jost, François. "German and French Themes in Early American Drama." *Journal of General Education* 28 (1976):190-222.

————. *Introduction to Comparative Literature*. New York, 1974.

Kaestle, Carl F. "The Public Reaction to John Dickinson's Farmer's Letters." *Proceedings of the American Antiquarian Society* 78 (1968):322-59.

Kane, Elisha Kent. *Gongorism and the Golden Age*. Chapel Hill, N.C., 1928.

Keller, Karl. *The Example of Edward Taylor*. Amherst, Mass., 1975.

Koch, Adrienne. "Aftermath of the American Enlightenment." *Studies in Voltaire and the Eighteenth Century* 56 (1967): 735-63.

————, ed. *The American Enlightenment*. New York, 1965.

La Motte, Antoine H. de. *Discours sur Homère*. Paris, 1714.

La Rochefoucauld Liancourt, François A. F. duc de. *Travels through the United States of North America*. 2 vols. London, 1799.

Leal, Luis. "*Jicoténcal*, Primera novela histórica en castellano." *Revista Iberoamericana* 25 (1960):9-31.

Lebano, Edoardo A. "Vittorio Alfieri and the United States of America." *Comparative Literature Studies* 8 (1971):310-16.

Le Breton, Maurice. *The French in Boston in the Eighteenth Century*. Bordeaux, 1929.

Lemay, J. A. Leo. *A Calendar of American Poetry in the Colonial Newspapers and Magazines and in the Major English Magazines through 1765*. Worcester, Mass., 1972.

————. "Franklin and the Autobiography. An Essay on Recent Scholarship." *Eighteenth Century Studies* 1 (1968):185-211.

————. *Men of Letters in Colonial Maryland*. Knoxville, Tenn., 1972.

————. "The Text, Rhetorical Strategies, and Themes of 'The Speech of Miss Polly Baker.' " In *The Oldest Revolutionary. Essays on Benjamin Franklin*. Philadelphia, 1976.

Levene, Ricardo. "El constitucionalismo de Mariano Moreno." *Historia* 3 (1958):53-71.

Lind, Sidney E. "Edward Taylor: A Reevaluation." *New England Quarterly* 21 (1948):519-30.

Longfellow, Samuel Wadsworth. *Kavanagh.* Boston, 1849.

Lopez, Claude-Anne. *Mon Cher Papa.* New Haven, 1966.

Marino, Adrian. "Benjamin Franklin in Rumanian Literature." *Comparative Literature Studies* 13 (1976):132-42.

Marraro, Howard R. "Views on America and the American Revolution in Contemporary Italian Reviews." *Forum Italicum* 5 (1971):67-81.

May, Henry F. *The Enlightenment in America.* New York, 1976.

—————. "The Problem of the American Enlightenment." *New Literary History* 1 (1969):201-14.

—————; and Lundberg, David. "The Enlightened Reader in America." *American Quarterly* 28 (1976):262-301.

McKee, Kenneth N. "The Popularity of the 'American' on the French Stage during the Revolution." *Proceedings of the American Philosophical Society* 83 (1940):479-91.

McLachlan, James. "Classical Names, American Identities: Some Notes on College Students and the Classical Tradition in the 1770's." in *Classical Traditions in Early America,* edited by John W. Eadie, pp. 81-98. Ann Arbor, 1976.

McMahon, Helen. "Anne Bradstreet, Jean Bertault, and Dr. Crooke." *Early American Literature* 3 (1968):118-23.

Medlin, Dorothy. "Thomas Jefferson, André Morellet, and the French Version of *Notes on the State of Virginia.*" *William and Mary Quarterly* 35 (1978):85-99.

Mier, Servando Teresa de. *Historia de la revolución de Nueva España.* Facsimile ed. 2 vols. Mexico, 1922.

—————. *Memoria político-instructiva.* Philadelphia, 1821.

Miller, Samuel. *Brief Retrospect of the Eighteenth Century.* 2 vols. New York, 1803.

Mirollo, James. *The Poet of the Marvelous, Giambattista Marino.* New York, 1963.

Mitré, Bartolomé. *Historia de Belgrano y de la independencia argentina.* 4 vols. 5th ed. Buenos Aires, 1902.

Molina, Ignacio. *The Geographical, Natural and Civil History of Chile.* Translated by Richard Alsop. Middletown, Conn., 1808.

Morellet, André. *Eloge de Marmontel.* Paris, 1805.

BIBLIOGRAPHY

Morse, Jedediah. *American Universal Geography*. Worcester, Mass., 1796.

Murphy, Francis. "Edward Taylor's Attitude toward Publication: A Question concerning Authority." *American Literature* 34 (1962):393-94.

Nelson, Lowry. *Baroque Lyric Poetry*. New Haven, 1963.

Nemes, Graciela P. "Rafael Landívar and Poetic Echoes of the Enlightenment." In *The Ibero-American Enlightenment*, edited by A. O. Aldridge. Urbana, Ill., 1971.

Newcomb, Robert. "Benjamin Franklin and Montaigne." *Modern Language Notes* 72 (1957):489-91.

Nuñez, Estuardo. *Autores ingleses y norteamericanos en el Perú*. Lima, 1956.

———. *El nuevo Olavide*. Lima, 1970.

Olmedo, José Joaquín de, trans. *Ensayo sobre el hombre. De M. Pope. Versión del inglés*. Lima, 1823.

Orjuela, Héctor H. "Revaloración de una vieja polémica literaria: William Cullen Bryant y la oda 'Niágara' de José María Heredia." *Thesaurus. Boletín del Instituto Caro y Cuervo* 19 (1964):248-73.

Országh, Ladislas. "A Seventeenth-Century Hungarian Translation of a Work by Increase Mather." *American Literature* 34 (1962):94-96. [A Latin letter in 1688 on converting Indians. See L. C. Grant above.]

Pablón y Suárez de Urbina, Jesús. *Franklin y Europa 1776-1785*. [Included primarily for the title.] Madrid, 1957.

Pace, Antonio. *Benjamin Franklin and Italy*. Philadelphia, 1958.

———. "The Fortunes of Luigi Castiglioni, Traveler in Colonial America, with an Extract from a Recently Discovered Manuscript of *Viaggio nell'America Settentrionale* (1785-1787)." *Italian Americana* 1 (1974):247-64.

Pauw, Cornelius de, abbé. *Recherches philosophiques sur les Américains*. 2 vols. Berlin, 1768-1769.

Penn, William. *Some Account of the Province of Pennsylvania*. London, 1681.

Picón-Salas, Mariano. *De la conquista a la independencia*. México, 1944.

Pochman, Henry A. *German Culture in America*. Madison, Wis., 1957.

Pocock, J.G.A. *The Ancient Constitution and the Feudal Law.* New York, 1967.

Poggioli, Renato. *The Oaten Flute.* Cambridge, Mass., 1975.

Puglia, Santiago Felipi. *El derecho del hombre* [translation of Paine's *Rights of Man*]. Philadelphia, 1821.

———. *Desengaño del hombre.* Philadelphia, 1794.

Quillen, Elisabeth M. "Relations américaines d'André Chénier." *Revue de littérature comparée* 47 (1973):556-75.

Raymond, Agnes G. "Figaro, fils naturel de Polly Baker? ou la Réhabilitation de Marceline." *Comparative Literature Studies* 12 (1975):34-43.

Raynal, Guillaume Thomas François. *Histoire philosophique et politique des deux Indes.* 6 vols. Amsterdam, 1770.

———. *Historia política de los establecimientos ultramarinos de las naciones europeas.* 5 vols. Madrid, 1784-1790.

Reinhold, Meyer. "Opponents of Classical Learning in America during the Revolutionary Period." *Proceedings of the American Philosophical Society* 112 (1968):221-34.

———. "The Quest for 'Useful Knowledge' in Eighteenth Century America." *Proceedings of the American Philosophical Society* 119 (1975):108-32.

Reish, Joseph G. "Mme de Genlis and the Early American Stage." *Proceedings of the Pacific Northwest Conference on Foreign Languages* 28 (1977):22-25.

Rice, Howard C. "Cotton Mather Speaks to France: American Propaganda in the Age of Louis XIV." *New England Quarterly* 16 (1943):198-233.

Robertson, William. *History of America.* 4 vols. 13th ed. London, 1817.

Rocafuerte, Vicente. *Ensayo político: el sistema colombiano, popular, electivo, es el que más conviene a la América independiente.* New York, 1823.

———. *Ideas necesarias a todo pueblo americano independiente, que quiera ser libre.* Philadelphia, 1821.

Roscio, Juan Germán. *El triunfo de la libertad.* Philadelphia, 1817.

Rousset, Jean. *La Littérature de l'âge baroque en France. Circé et le paon.* Paris, 1954.

Rush, Benjamin. "An enquiry into the Utility of a knowledge of the Latin and Greek languages as a branch of liberal studies." *American Museum* 5 (1789):525-35. Reprinted as "Observations upon the Study of the Latin and Greek languages." In *Essays, Literary, Moral, and Philosophical*, pp. 21-56. Philadelphia, 1798.

Scheick, William J. *The Will and the Word*. Athens, Ga., 1974.

Scouten, Arthur H. "The Paradox of Deism in Colonial America." *Lex et Scientia* 14 (1978):215-28.

Seeber, Edward D. "The French Theatre in Charleston in the Eighteenth Century." *South Carolina Historical and Genealogical Magazine* 42 (1941):1-7.

Sharma, Mohan Lai. "Of Spinning, Weaving and Mystical Poetry: The Fine Yarn of Taylor, Indian Yogis, and Persian Sufis." *Mahfil* 6 (1970):51-61.

Silber, R. B. "William Cullen Bryant's Lectures on Mythology." Ph.D. dissertation, State University of Iowa, 1962.

Simmons, Merle E. *U.S. Political Ideas in Spanish America before 1830: A Bibliographical Study*. Bloomington, Ind., 1977.

Smith, John. *Generall Historie of Virginia, New England and the Summer Isles*. London, 1624.

Spell, J. R. "An Illustrious Spaniard in Philadelphia: Valentín de Faronda." *Hispanic Review* 4 (1936):136-40.

Spurlin, Paul M. *Montesquieu in America, 1760-1801*. Baton Rouge, La., 1940.

——. *Rousseau in America, 1760-1809*. University, Ala., 1969.

Stanford, Ann. *Anne Bradstreet: The Worldly Puritan*. New York, 1974.

Stillé, Charles J. *The Life and Times of John Dickinson*. Philadelphia, 1891.

Sullerot, Evelyne. *Histoire de la presse féminine en France, des origines à 1848*. Paris, 1966.

Thomas, Isaiah. *History of Printing in America*. 2 vols. Worcester, Mass., 1810.

Tichi, Cecelia. "Charles Brockden Brown, Translator." *American Literature* 44 (1972):1-12.

Tilton, Elizabeth M. "Vashington: A Revolutionary Tragedy." *French Review* 49 (1976):975-84.

Tourtellot, Arthur Bernon. *Benjamin Franklin The Shaping of Genius*. Garden City, N.Y., 1977.

Trumbull, John [painter]. *Autobiography*. New York, 1841.

Tyler, Moses Coit. *A History of American Literature during the Colonial Period, 1607-1765*. 2 vols. New York, 1898.

———. *The Literary History of the American Revolution, 1763-1783*. New York, 1897.

Vajda, György M. "Conclusion [regarding a comparatist history of literature]." *Neohelicon* 1 (1973):326-35.

Van Doren, Carl. *Benjamin Franklin*. New York, 1938.

Vergara, José María. *Disertación sobre las primeros principios del gobierno por Tomas Pain* [sic]. London, 1819.

Victory, Beatrice M. *Franklin and Germany*. Philadelphia, 1915.

Vidaurre, Manuel de. *Plan del Perú*. Philadelphia, 1823.

Wade, Ira O. *The Clandestine Organization and Diffusion of Philosophic Ideas in France from 1700 to 1750*. Princeton, 1938.

Wadepuhl, Walter. *Goethe's Interest in the New World*. Jena, 1934.

Waggoner, H. H. *American Poets: From the Puritans to the Present*. Boston, 1968.

Waldo, Lewis P. *The French Drama in America in the Eighteenth Century*. Baltimore, 1942.

Walsh, Henry Hill. "On the Putative Influence of Benjamin Franklin on Tolstoi." *Canadian-American Slavic Studies* 13 (1979):306-9.

Walz, John A. "Increase Mather and Dr. Faust." *Germanic Review* 15 (1940):20-31.

Warfel, Harry R. *Noah Webster, Schoolmaster to America*. New York, 1936.

Warnke, Frank J. *European Metaphysical Poetry*. New Haven, 1974.

Warren, Austin. *Rage for Order. Essays in Criticism*. Chicago, 1948.

Watanabe, Toshio. "Benjamin Franklin and the Younger Generation of Japan." *American Studies International* 18 (1980): 34-49.

Watts, George B. "Thomas Jefferson, the *Encyclopédie*, and the *Encyclopédie méthodique*." *French Review* 38 (1965):318-25.

BIBLIOGRAPHY

Webster, Noah. *Dissertations on the English Language*. Boston, 1789.

Wellek, René. *Concepts of Criticism*. New Haven, 1963.

Wesley, John. *Survey of the Wisdom of God in the Creation*. 2nd ed. Bristol, 1777.

Whitaker, Arthur P., ed. *Latin America and the Enlightenment*. Ithaca, N.Y., 1942.

White, Elizabeth Wade. *Anne Bradstreet, "The Tenth Muse."* New York, 1971.

Wiese, Benno von. "Goethe und Heine als Europäer." In *Teilnahme und Spiegelung*, edited by B. Allemann and E. Koppen, pp. 295-315. Berlin, 1975.

Wilhite, John. "The Inter-American Enlightenment." *Revista Interamericana de Bibliografía* 30 (1980):254-61.

Wolf, Edwin L. "The Classical Languages in Colonial Philadelphia." In *Classical Traditions in Early America*, edited by John W. Eadie. Ann Arbor, 1976.

Woods, M. J. *The Poet and the Natural World in the Age of Góngora*. Oxford, 1978.

Zunder, Theodore Albert. *The Early Days of Joel Barlow*. New Haven, 1934.

INDEX

Library of Congress Cataloging in Publication Data

Aldridge, Alfred Owen, 1915-
  Early American literature.

  Bibliography: p.
  Includes index.
  1. American literature—Colonial period, ca. 1600-1775
—History and criticism.   2. American literature—
Revolutionary period, 1775-1783—History and criticism.
  3. American literature—1783-1850—History and criticism.
  4. Literature, Comparative.   I. Title.
PS185.A38   1982   810'.9'001   82-47580
ISBN 0-691-06517-9

A. Owen Aldridge is Professor of Comparative Literature at the University of Illinois. Currently president of the American Comparative Literature Association, he is founder and editor of *Comparative Literature Studies* and the author of many books, including biographies of Franklin, Paine, and Voltaire.